PRAISE FOR *THE GIRL...*

It was my privilege to have known Maria. Her kindness and generosity touched everyone around her. Her indomitable spirit carried her from the horrors of World War II in Croatia to a new life in tropical Queensland. The girl who left tells the tale of a young woman whose faith and courage enabled her to thrive through the challenges of war in Europe and immigration to Australia. A wonderful story of hope and love from a time not so long ago.

—Prof. James Scott, QIMR Berghofer
Medical Research Institute

The girl who left is a timeless story of familial love, and the horrors of war. This beautifully captured story of survival of Maria, a young girl living through the horrors of WW2 in Yugoslavia, who makes a brave decision to leave her homeland, culture, family and friends behind in search of a better life as a proxy-bride in Australia, demonstrates the importance for Australians to appreciate and continue the conversation about our kaleidoscope of stories from our post-World War II immigration history. Debra Gavranich has delivered her mother's lullaby as a lesson in gratitude and humility.

—Cheryl Koenig OAM, Author & Motivational Speaker

This is a beautiful family story of one woman's courageous journey to a new and foreign country on the other side of the world, richly woven with touching detail of her life—from war-torn Yugoslavia, to finding her place in the rugged and remote landscape of North Queensland... A quintessential Australian immigration story, showcasing our diverse cultural heritage, our multicultural identity and what it means to be Australian.

—Tania Blanchard, best-selling author

Debra Gavranich's recreation of her mother's life story is a timely reminder of the resilience and hope of Australia's post-World War II immigrants. Gavranich also provides a glimpse into the complexity of Croatia's recent past. The book is a fitting tribute to a courageous woman, one of many.

—Vesna Drapac, Assoc. Prof in History, University of Adelaide

The girl who left

From Croatia to the canefields

DEBRA GAVRANICH

WILD
DINGO
PRESS

Published by Wild Dingo Press
Melbourne, Australia
books@wilddingopress.com.au
www.wilddingopress.com.au

First published by Wild Dingo Press 2021

Cover designer: Janine Nicklin
Editors: Bernadette Foley & Melanie Myers
Maps supplied by Shutterstock
Printed in Australia.

Gavranich, Debra 1960- author.
The girl who left: Croatia to the canefields/Debra Gavranich

 A catalogue record for this
book is available from the
National Library of Australia

ISBN: 9780645140521 (paperback)
ISBN: 9780645140538 (ebook:pdf)
ISBN: 9780645140545 (ebook)

Author's Note

My mother was a constant in my life, a rock, my best friend. Losing her when I was thirty-five years of age, with three young children under five, was unbearably painful. The first few years were so difficult. Even now, years later, I cry when I speak of her. I listen to my friends with envy when they talk about the close connection their children have with their grandparents. I feel the hole in my life and sad that my children never knew her. This story is for them.

From the first time I visited Blato as a twenty-two-year-old, I felt the connection to the village, to the country my parents came from. Like a boomerang I keep returning, loving it more with each visit. Maybe, in my heart, Croatia makes me feel closer to my parents. I am lucky that my parents were good people. Life was not always easy but they worked hard, had kind hearts and they loved each other. For this I am grateful.

This book is an historical account of my mother's life and told through her eyes. She was born in Blato on the island of Korčula, in Croatia. At the time, Croatia was a part of a union or federation of states called Yugoslavia, so there will be references to the former Yugoslavia throughout the story when that political entity was still in existence. While I have endeavoured to keep it factual, some names have been changed, and certain events and scenes have been compressed, expanded or changed to fulfil the needs of the story. Some of the conversations and encounters have been approximated and some are correct according to the people who kindly shared their memories with me.

GAVRANICH FAMILY TREE

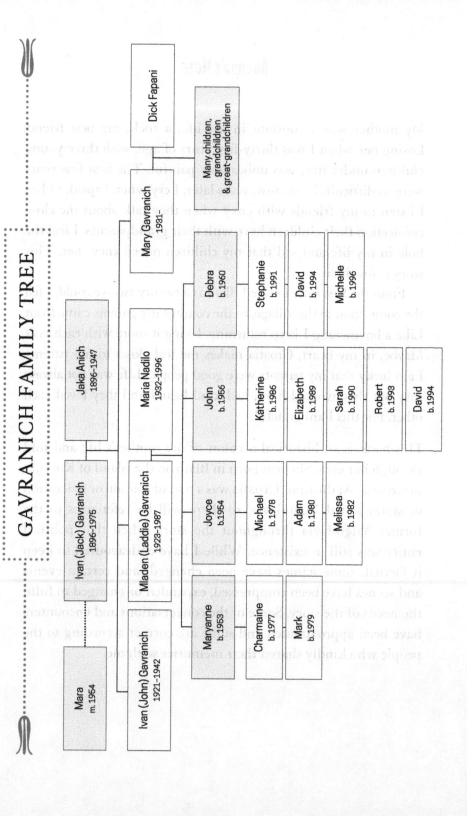

Jaka Anich 1896–1947

Ivan (Jack) Gavranich 1896–1975

Mara m. 1954

Ivan (John) Gavranich 1921–1942

Dick Fapani

Mary Gavranci 1981–

Many children, grandchildren & great-grandchildren

Maria Nadilo 1932–1996

Mladen (Laddie) Gavranich 1923–1987

Debra b.1960
- Stephanie b.1991
- David b.1994
- Michelle b.1996

John b.1956
- Katherine b.1986
- Elizabeth b.1989
- Sarah b.1990
- Robert b.1993
- David b.1994

Joyce b.1954
- Michael b.1978
- Adam b.1980
- Melissa b.1982

Maryanne b.1963
- Charmaine b.1977
- Mark b.1979

NADILO FAMILY TREE

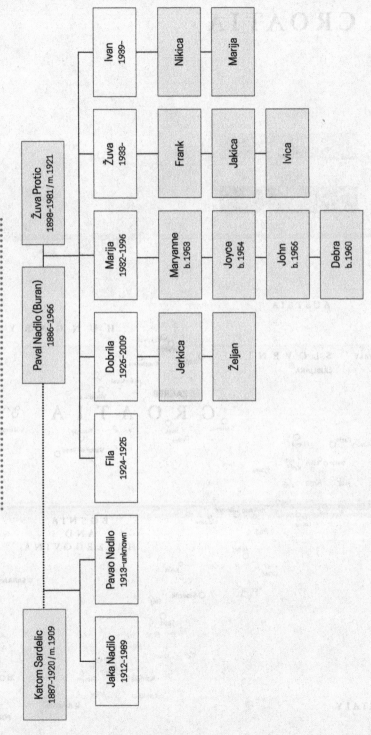

Katom Sardelic
1887-1920 / m. 1909

Jaka Nadilo
1912-1989

Pavao Nadilo
1913-unknown

Paval Nadilo (Buran)
1886-1966

Žuva Protic
1898-1981 / m. 1921

Fila
1924-1925

Dobrila
1926-2009

Jerkica

Željan

Marija
1932-1996

Maryanne
b. 1953

Joyce
b. 1954

John
b. 1956

Debra
b. 1960

Žuva
1933-

Frank

Jakica

Ivica

Ivan
1989-

Nikica

Marija

CROATIA

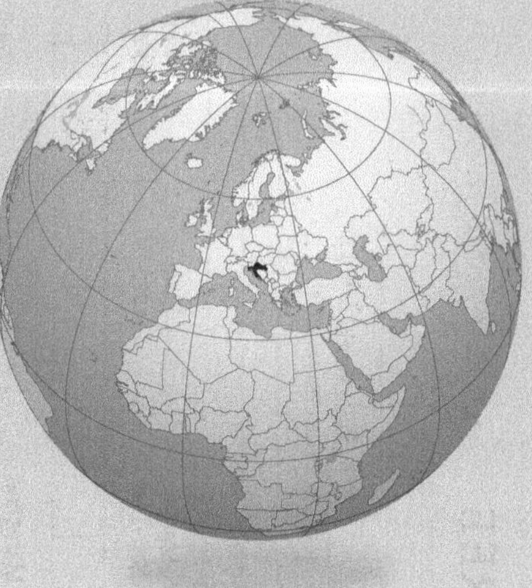

AUSTRIA
HUNGARY
ITALY
SLOVENIA
LJUBLJANA
Cakovec
Varaždin
Krapina
Koprivnica
Bjelovar
ZAGREB
Virovitica
CROATIA
Osijek
Karlovac
Sisak
Pakrac
Požega
Vukovar
SERBIA
Glina
Slavonski Brod
Poreč
Pazin
Rijeka
Stalije
Labin
Krk
Krk
Senj
Slunj
Pula
Kres
Rab
Lun
Karlobag
Gospic
Udbina
Mali Lošinj
Pag
BOSNIA AND HERZEGOVINA
Zadar
Knin
Dugi Otok
Kornat
SARAJEVO
Šibenik
Sinj
Split
Brač
Hvar
Vis
Hvar
Ploče
Orebic
Neum
Korčula
MONTENEGRO
Lastovo
Mljet
Dubrovnik
ITALY
PODGORICA
ADRIATIC SEA

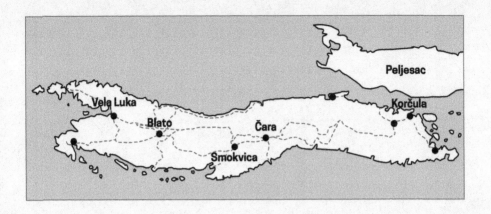

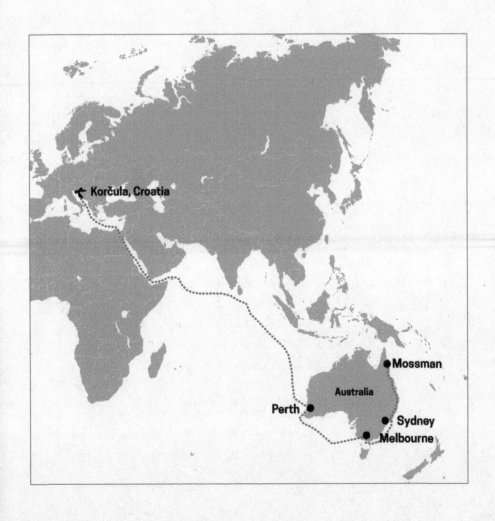

Contents

1

Blato, Yugoslavia, 1950: A proposition

'There is a man from Australia looking for a bride,' Alena blurted, 'from Australia!'

'What are you talking about?' Marija was confused and waited for her friend to regain her breath. Alena had sprinted up the two flights of stairs from the courtyard to the balcony.

'I thought of you, Marija,' rushed Alena in small gasps.

'Who? Wh—'

'As soon as I heard, I thought of you.' A broad smile lit up Alena's face as she poked strands of hair back into her messy bun. 'You might even know the family.'

Alena pulled up a seat next to Marija, who was busy peeling potatoes for the evening meal. Marija glanced over her shoulder into the dark kitchen and the shadowy figure of her mother.

'Why me?' she whispered.

'Well, I heard my mother talking about the procurement. The proxy marriage. She was saying that one of our neighbour's daughters had been selected, but then my mother said that this girl has had too many boyfriends,' she gushed, the words tumbling over each other.

Marija paused, her attention captured.

'I heard this Australian man is fussy, very fussy. He is from here.' Alena hesitated, trying to remember the details she had heard. 'He left as a child over twenty years ago but wants a bride from here.

1

My mother said he wants someone young, someone strong… and someone…' she giggled, 'who hasn't had any boyfriends. That's you.'

'Alena.' Marija blushed.

'Well, it's true. You know it's true. You're so good, you pray all the time and love going to church. You hardly ever go to the dances. And you haven't had a boyfriend. This town is so small, I would know if you had.'

'You said that I might know the family?' Marija asked.

The township, in the middle of an island of Yugoslavia, was small, with no more than five thousand inhabitants, so Marija thought she would at least know of him, or know someone who knew him.

'He's related to the Anić family. A cousin.'

Alena rambled on about the family connection. Marija stood and cleaned her hands on the faded red and green chequered apron tied around her waist. She walked over to the edge of the balcony, rested her palms on the smooth, cool balustrade and looked out over the village. Her village. Blato.

The town filled the valley and climbed part way up the hill on the opposite side. Surrounded by a thicket of trees, a small church perched on the peak facing her, a sentinel guarding the inhabitants. On her left, the sun was setting, casting a rosy hue like a warm blanket on the terracotta roofs. They seemed almost pink. This was her home. She had known some of the young women who had left for countries far away, mainly Australia and America. It was not unusual but was it something she could do? The thought had never entered her mind.

Alena joined her. Marija could smell the sweat on her skin. Like Marija, she had been in the vineyards all day, repairing the trellises for the grapevines. They all worked hard. There was not a lot left after the war, and Blato had suffered dearly. So much destruction and so much pain. Many of her neighbours, both young and old, dead or gone. What future would she have here?

2

'You could escape this,' Alena said, stretching her arm across the township of ancient houses stacked together, some empty and crumbling. 'You know what they say about Australia? So much work, so much money. Just think of it. No chance of war.'

Marija was silent as she thought of her splintered childhood, scarred with memories of bloodshed and war. Images seen that could not be unseen.

'No chance of war!' Alena repeated.

A spark of excitement fluttered in Marija's chest. Maybe. Maybe this is my chance? she thought. They were interrupted by the sound of hooves on the cobbles below. Looking down she could see her father, Paval, and her younger brother trudging up the street as they led the family donkey. Although Paval was in his sixties he still had a full head of hair. He was slightly built and his skin a deep brown from hours spent in the sun. She noticed how stooped he was and how slowly he trod. She looked tenderly from her father to her brother, Ivan, the youngest in the family and the only son. He was eleven, tall for his age, quiet and slim like his father. He always helped after school.

'*Tata*,' Marija yelled to her father.

He looked up. Although tired, his face crinkled into a broad smile that reached his eyes.

'*Tata*, Alena is here with some interesting news. Come up and listen.'

'What news?' came the voice from the kitchen.

Gripping Alena's hand, Marija asked her to stay and tell her parents the story. What would they think? she wondered.

Here she stood, on the deck of a ferry, two years later. Alone. Nineteen years old. The breeze fluttered through her hair, blowing some strands across her face. She brushed them away and gripped the railing, her eyes fixed on the wharf. Her pale blue dress whipped around her legs. She shivered and clenched the railing tighter; her shiny new wedding band gleamed in the soft sunlight of spring. She watched her family, standing among the throng of people crowding the wharf, etching their faces into her memory. Her father seemed so small. He was thin and frail, his weathered face creased with worry. Her younger sister, Žuva, waved vigorously, caught up with the excitement. Off to the side stood Ivan. He was thirteen now. He kept his head down and kicked at the white pebbles on the wharf. This last week he had been quiet, much quieter than normal, she thought. He looked unhappy or maybe, just uncertain. Her mother was not there. She was back in their home working, scrubbing, cooking.

Young children shrieked. Confused and excited by the commotion, they ran up and down the wharf, waving to the departing passengers, their older brothers, sisters, aunts or uncles. Young men on the ferry leaned precariously over the railing, shouting promises of fortune, promises to help make a better life. Some of the women, cheeks stained with tears, stood silent, waving to relatives.

The ferry pulled away and the crowd on the deck thinned as passengers moved inside. Marija stayed there, watching the receding island and noticing, for the first time, its rugged charm. The splash of red roofs contrasted with the azure blue of the Adriatic Sea and the bobbing fishing boats. Many of the old stone houses were damaged from the anger of World War Two. She meticulously imprinted these images to her memory; this was her homeland, her island. Her eyes brimmed with tears.

'When will I see you again? Will I *ever* see you again?' she whispered as she strained to retain the outline of her father. Taking a deep breath, she stood tall, blinked, and set her jaw firmly. She reminded herself that this was an adventure, an opportunity. So much awaited her. She was a proxy bride, a *procura*. In Australia, thousands of kilometres from Yugoslavia, Mladen, her new husband, was waiting. As she thought of his photograph, her heart skipped a beat. He was twenty-eight years old and ruggedly handsome. She pictured him waiting on the wharf for her in Sydney. She would

4

disembark the magnificent ship, and they would travel together to her new home thousands of kilometres north. A home on a sugar cane farm near Mossman in Far North Queensland.

Marija could not visualise her final destination but she did not care. Her home had been ravaged by war. She knew terror and starvation, far more than any young teenager should know. This was her escape, her new beginning.

2

1952: Goodbye Korčula

The ferry rocked as it navigated its way out of the harbour. Marija was on her way to Italy, to the large seaport of Genoa, where an Italian liner awaited.

Standing on the deck near Marija was Marinka. She was a tall, solid woman with a wide face encircled by tight frizzy curls. Her skin was unblemished, smooth like porcelain. She lived on the same street as Marija. Almost neighbours. Marinka had been asked to watch over Marija on this journey. Like Marija, Marinka was also leaving her homeland, but she was leaving with her husband, Ivan, and their two young children. Already settled in Australia was their sponsor, her cousin Ivica. Folded carefully in her suitcase were all the encouraging letters Ivica had written describing their destination, Sydney.

A big city—new, tall buildings, it is full of shops bursting with food; a bridge that looks like a coat hanger across a huge harbour; lots of green parks and strange animals that you would never have seen before, like kangaroos; they hop all over the place, were some of the highlights she had written about in her letters. Before they left the village, Marinka had told Marija that the descriptions of the food had convinced her that this was the right decision. Her children, she said, were intrigued by the strange-sounding animals and had lively discussions about whether they hopped along the city streets or not.

'Can we have one as a pet?' they had asked their mother, jumping up and down and clapping their hands. Marija had looked on, smiling, and wondering what was waiting for them in this new city.

Like all the others who were leaving, Marinka said she was wanting a safe life for her little family. Marija knew that it would be so much harder for her, as a procurement bride, leaving to join a man she had never met. There was no familiar cousin waiting for her, only a husband known solely from a photograph and a handful of letters. Although many young women from their village were taking this step into proxy marriages, what a precarious step it was. This was goodbye. There would be no going back.

'Come, come and sit inside,' said Marinka, as she lightly touched Marija's elbow.

'Thank you, Marinka, but no. You go inside and be with your family. I'll stay here for a while.'

Marija was intent on watching the disappearing island. The island of Korčula was small but mountainous. Those stark hills and their secret caves had hidden the Partisan soldiers during the last war. This mountainous terrain was a reminder of the courage of her countrymen and women. As the ferry motored out to sea, she could still see the carefully stacked stony walls, forming a grid-like pattern on the hills. Olive trees clung to the rocky slopes, their pale green leaves blurring in the distance. These hills encircled the farms, the vineyards, the fig and olive trees and Blato. Will these trees grow in Australia, Marija wondered.

Her mind swirled with thoughts, skipping restlessly from emotion to emotion. She could no longer see her family. Are they still there waving? Or have they returned to Blato? she silently asked. She imagined them opening the large green metal door that led from the cobbled street into the courtyard of the stone house that had been in her family for generations. The door was heavy with rusted edges. It always creaked. She thought of the musky smell of the animals that were kept inside the courtyard. Her family was poor so they didn't have many animals. One donkey, two goats, a pig and four chickens. She imagined her father slowly climbing the stone staircase to the balcony they shared with their neighbours. His knees were stiff. The steps were uneven. Will he stop at the room I share with *Žuva* and Ivan? she thought. Will he look at my empty bed and regret letting me go?

Although her island was now out of sight, Marija decided to stay on the deck. Inside smelt of stale cigarettes and diesel. She inhaled the briny air, her eyes glued on the landscape as the ferry hugged the coastline. It slowly glided by the bleak cliffs of the Yugoslavian mainland, a jagged grey contrast to the blue of the sea. Packed in her small bag were some fresh figs and spicy rice-stuffed peppers, her favourites, but she did not feel hungry. Her stomach was unsettled.

The ferry made stops along the way, collecting more passengers laden with luggage. All the coastal towns seemed like mirror images of each other. She watched the farewells, families clasping each other and tears flowing freely. Marija thought back to her own goodbyes, at the wharf and earlier at her home. My mother didn't shed a tear, she recalled, biting her lip. She suspected her mother was eager to farewell her, relieved to have one less mouth at the dinner table. The assumption that she would send money back to her family weighed heavily on Marija's mind. She knew that her husband Mladen and his father had a sugar cane farm—but were they wealthy? Hopefully Mladen would be a generous man. The man in her photograph had kind eyes. Making enquiries about him, her father had asked, 'Is Mladen Gavranich a good man?'

'Yes, he is,' were the replies from the Yugoslav community in Mossman.

Marija held her breath as she thought of the huge step she had taken. I hope he is. Yes, I know he is. My Jesus will not send me into danger, she decided, her faith calming her beating heart. It was her stoic father whose gentle heart she knew was quietly breaking. She would miss him. She missed him already.

3

1941: War comes to Blato

It was close to five o'clock in the afternoon on 23 April. It was a Wednesday. Although the middle of spring, there was a bite in the air. Sitting just above the treeline the sun glowed over the hills guarding the perimeter of Blato. The small village was an amphitheatre nestled in a valley surrounded by hills of stone. It was a sleepy village waking from its winter hibernation, the spring sun coaxing its residents out of their homes and into its streets.

The main street, Zlinje Ulica 1, dominated the village. Running from east to west, it was a kilometre long and straight, dividing the weaving streets and alleyways. Along the street, mothers with young children in tow would mingle with farmers and their donkeys and carts returning from the farms. Sitting in small groups in front of their homes were old men puffing on pipes and chewing on nuts as they discussed the latest crop of grapes. Stray cats hid in shadows and would devour any crumbs left behind. It was also a place for promenading, especially in the evenings. One hundred and seventeen linden trees, planted more than thirty years ago, bordered the street and controlled the thoroughfare. A couple of little shops were scattered along the street and through the village. Some houses doubled as bars, selling glasses of wine to the locals.

At the eastern end was the school, standing two storeys high, a grey building with tall windows. The afternoon school session had finished and a few students were meandering home in small groups, some scuffing their shoes, most barefoot, swinging bags and chatting with each other.

Marija sat on the concrete steps that led into the school building. She was nine years old. She smoothed the skirt of her floral dress and stretched her legs out, her bare feet jiggling on the bottom step. Beside her sat Žuva, who although nineteen months younger, could have passed as Marija's twin. It was Žuva's first year at school and she was intently reading the book cradled on her lap. Marija tucked her hair behind her ears and leaned close to Žuva, pointing out words and helping her read, their heads almost touching as they turned the pages together. Inside, the school was quiet, almost peaceful, the long hallways silent, teachers sitting at their desks preparing lessons, children entering the doors behind them that led to the school library.

Raising her head Marija listened carefully. She had been on edge these last few days. Her parents had been talking in worried voices and she had caught snatches, not quite sure of their meaning. 'Yugoslavia has surrendered. War is coming to our country.'

From the direction of the seaside town of Vela Luka, beyond the long main street, she discerned noises, ominous noises. Trucks rumbling. Men shouting. The echo of stomping boots. Although still a child, she sensed these were not friendly sounds. The girls shoved their books into their bags and edged closer together. Fear crept icily through Marija's veins as she listened and watched and waited, unsure of what to do next. The sounds were getting louder and closer. Should we run home? she wondered. She wanted to but her body felt paralysed. Straining her eyes, she searched for the origin of these sounds. She did not have long to wait. Rounding the corner, a sea of grey appeared, an army of uniformed soldiers with rifles slung over their shoulders, stern faces under green helmets, boots crunching in unison on the gravel as they marched. Through the narrow main street they advanced, followed by slow-moving trucks. Her heart thumped. There were hundreds of soldiers. Grabbing Žuva's hand, Marija raced up the steps to the school and pushed open the heavy door. One of the teachers beckoned them.

'Quick, girls, come over here. Hurry!'

They rushed towards her, joining the other students in the corner of the library. Some of the teachers crept down from upstairs and wrapped protective arms around the students. The tall narrow windows were closed but they could still see through the sheer curtains. They clustered together. Scared and confused.

Eerily deserted, the town suddenly seemed ghostly. The wind paused and the leaves ceased their gentle chatter. The locals on the street had scattered and Marija guessed they were probably also peering out from behind their partially closed shutters to see what was happening.

The street was long but the army approached rapidly, waving their flag of green, white and red. Marija's pulse quickened. A formidable sight, the army stopped at the town hall opposite the school and a sharp voice barked orders. Marija could not understand the language but she watched, transfixed. The Yugoslav flag, the symbol of her country, fluttered from the pole in front of the town hall. The soldiers lowered it and replaced it with their own, the Italian flag. They cheered as their flag reached the top and dominated the skyline. The wind had found its voice and the flag billowed wildly.

Where are these soldiers from? Who are they? What will happen now? Marija thought, her mind messy with questions and fears. What does this mean for my town? Will we all be put in prison? Will my school shut? Where are my parents? Do they know what is happening?

The teachers were whispering in anxious voices, but she did not strain to hear. She did not want to hear. She was anxious and bewildered too. None of this made any sense.

A section of the army took their orders and marched eastward, towards the next village. Leading them out were the trucks that had rumbled in behind them; some soldiers sat crowded in the covered backs holding their rifles against their chests. Standing motionless at the library window, Marija watched, her fingers resting on the cracked white sill.

'What will we do now?' Žuva murmured into her ear.

'Shh,' Marija said, wrapping an arm around her little sister and pulling her in close. 'Shh, and listen.'

Standing on a step above the army stood their leader. Without raising his voice he commanded silence. His long grey overcoat was buttoned to his knee-high shiny black boots. Golden eagles on black triangles were embroidered on both sleeves. Medals decorated the left side of his jacket. With his hands firmly planted on his hips and his feet apart, he lifted his head slightly, surveying his men. He possessed an air of seniority. His face was swarthy, jawline angular and nose aquiline. A grey peaked military cap, dominated once again by the golden eagle, covered his close-cropped, black hair. Short sharp instructions were delivered in a clipped tone. The soldiers quickly dispersed to carry out their orders, leaving the town hall alone, the alien flag owning the building.

'Quickly, run home now,' said one of the teachers to all the children. 'Now, while it is clear.'

Opening the door with one hand, she guided them out and watched as they raced home trying to avoid any of the soldiers. Slightly uphill on the cobbled streets ran the sisters, scattering the stray cats loitering on the doorsteps, oblivious to the confusion that had descended upon the town. The streets were empty but Marija was sure countless pairs of eyes were watching from behind windows, concealed by lace curtains or sturdy white shutters.

'Mama! Tata!' Marija yelled, as she pushed open the door from the street. The girls scrambled up the stairs and found their parents huddled around the kitchen table deep in conversation with Dobrila, Marija's eldest sister. They did not notice the girls.

'But I have to go. I can't stay. You know I can't stay,' Dobrila exclaimed. 'It's my duty! We have to fight them.'

'But you're only fifteen,' argued her father.

'Yes, but so many of the others are as young as her,' her mother said. 'She will probably be safer in the hiding spots of the hills with all the other young men and women. Who knows what will happen to us now?'

The two girls hid in the shadows, fearful. What do they mean 'hiding in the hills'? What are they talking about? Marija wondered.

Paval half turned and noticed the sisters motionless in the doorway. He sprung from his chair with an agility they had never seen before.

Embracing them both he said, 'Thank our Jesus, you're safe. I asked Goran from up the street to run to the school to find you both. He's a much quicker runner than me.'

And so began the occupation of Blato by the Italians. Dobrila was convinced to stay at home. For now...

4

A village changed

The Italians had been in Blato for almost a week, and the air was heavy with tension. The adults spoke in whispers about this sudden invasion. No one was really sure what would happen next. Doubt and mistrust crept like an unwelcome thief through the streets. Which of their neighbours were aiding the Ustaše, the Yugoslav military branch that supported the fascist Italians? The village was divided.

Hearing the bray of a donkey, Marija knew her father was home. She had been waiting for him. It was late in the afternoon and he had returned from a long day working on his farm. The farm was small, located in the valley between the towns of Blato and Brna. Despite the Italian occupation, the fields still needed tending. The vegetables he grew were needed to feed his family and the grapes and olives were their livelihood.

Sighing, he brushed the dirt off his grey trousers and tethered the donkey in the pen near the chickens.

Marija raced down the stairs and gripped his hand.

'Sit here.' She pointed to the uneven bottom step, shiny and worn from years of footsteps. 'Sit down and speak to me,' she begged, dragging him.

He lowered his weary body and Marija snuggled close. She breathed deeply, the earthy farm smell mingled with his sweat. Clutching his cracked and dirty hand, she ran her small fingers along its many creases. From years of working hard on the farm, the dirt never really seemed to wash away, embedded in the crevices and under his fingernails.

'What do you want to talk about, little one?'

'Tell me the story about Australia again,' she said. This story would take her far away from Blato and the soldiers stomping through their streets, yelling at them with words she did not understand.

She had heard this story many times. When her father was younger, before Marija was born, he had joined the countless men from their village who had travelled to Australia. For a number of years he worked at the mines in Broken Hill.

'Australia is far away from here. Four weeks on the big ship,' he said, stretching out his legs and massaging his sore knee. 'It was not like here in Yugoslavia. Over there was red dirt... everywhere! Grey scrubby bushes, and as far as you could see, flatness, wherever you looked—desert.'

She curled her arms around his neck, closed her eyes and listened, losing herself in the imagery of this faraway land, his quiet, measured voice calming the flutter in her chest.

'We were a long, long way from the sea. The skies were so blue,' he told her. 'Like Blato, it was hot in the summer, so much hotter than here, and freezing in winter. And I worked hard. Long days in the mines.'

'Did you miss Blato?'

'Of course. But it was all right, there were many of us there from our village. We looked after each other. I worked hard so I could send money home.'

'But why did you leave Australia?'

'I got sick. The mines damaged my lungs, and I coughed all the time. I couldn't keep working, so I came back home.'

'Awww, poor Tata.' She stroked his head.

'It doesn't matter. I have all of you.' He tightened his embrace. 'I can work on my little farm. It's not much, but we get by.'

Yes, her father was a good storyteller.

'Please tell me again about Dida,' she begged. The story of her grandfather was her favourite.

15

'But I've told you so many times,' he said. 'Your mother will wonder where I am. I should go upstairs and help her.'

'No, please, Tata, stay,' she pleaded, tightening her grip around him. 'Just this one last story. If we go upstairs we'll have to do chores.'

He chuckled as they both hid from Žuva and any chores that awaited them. 'Well, Marija, I'm not a rich man but my father was. Rich, very rich. But he lost all his money.' He paused, arching his back, stiff and tired from the endless bending in the vineyard.

'How?' she asked.

'Instead of buying property he put all of his money in the Austrian bank. After the big war the bank collapsed, like so many of the other banks, and with it went all of his money. Gone!'

'Just like that?'

'Just like that. Unless...' Paval's voice trailed off.

'Unless what?' Marija asked breathlessly, even though she knew the answer.

'Unless all that money was not in the bank. Family legend has it that my father sold his wine and got gold, a lot of gold, and hid it here, somewhere in the walls of this house. And he died before he could tell anyone where he hid it. Hidden treasure!' he exclaimed.

'Can we look?' she asked. 'It might be over there.' She pointed to the old well in the corner of the courtyard near the animals.

'Maybe, or I think, maybe not. It could be anywhere. Where would we start? This old house of stone could have so many hiding places. We could easily end up digging everywhere and end up with no treasure and also no house.'

'But if we find it we could be rich!'

'No digging anywhere. I am not rich with money, but rich with love,' he said as he gently kissed her forehead. 'Yes. I am—'

A sharp knock on their front door startled them.

'*Apri la porta!*' shouted a voice from the street as the knocking continued.

Marija held her breath, her heart pounding, and shadowed her father as he slowly stood and walked the ten paces through the courtyard. Hesitantly he half-opened the door. Two Italian soldiers stood in the street. One was in his thirties, his face grim. The second could not have been more than eighteen, his blotchy face betraying his adolescence. Although Marija hid behind her father, her eyes were glued to their guns. She had never been this close to a weapon before. The younger soldier waved his gun, motioning for him to open the door fully.

Talking in this foreign language, the older soldier beckoned them closer and kept talking at them, gesticulating, trying to explain something to them. Paval shrugged and shook his head. He understood nothing. The soldier then took a photograph from his shirt pocket. It was faded and worn around the edges as if it had been handled and looked at often. He bent forward and showed it to Marija. It was a portrait of the soldier, a woman and two small girls. The girls wore pretty patterned dresses. They were twins and looked about her age.

The soldier's expression changed as he smiled at Marija and patted her gently on the head, then he pointed at the girls in the photograph. It seemed as if he was trying to tell her that he had daughters of his own and he would not hurt her. She shyly gave him a smile. His gun did not seem quite so frightening now, she thought. Saying a few more phrases that neither Marija nor her father understood, the two men nodded their heads and moved onto the next doorway.

Later that evening, when the family had gathered around the table, Marija told her sisters about the soldier and the photograph.

Her father nodded and said, 'Yes, I couldn't understand them but I think he was trying to tell me that they just want us to cooperate. That they are soldiers fighting a war and that they won't hurt the women and children.'

'Was he scary?' asked Žuva.

'Well, they had guns, so yes, he was frightening. But I think we are lucky that this part of Yugoslavia was given to the Italians,' Paval said.

'What do you mean?' Marija looked at him.

'The rest of Yugoslavia is occupied by the Germans and I hear they are much crueller than our Italian brothers.'

'I still want to join the Partisans,' protested fifteen-year-old Dobrila, her face flushed. 'I don't want to sit and watch these men take our food and houses. I want them gone from our island.'

'Shhh,' whispered her father, looking fearfully towards the window. 'Someone might hear you. We don't know who we can trust. Our own people can be our enemy as well. Don't you forget that.'

'I will go, you know I will go!' Her eyes shone with tears of frustration.

'Yes, when the time is right. Wait and see,' reassured her father. Turning to the younger children he motioned with his arm in the direction of the bedroom. 'It's late, girls. Take your little brother and go to bed but don't forget your prayers. We need our God more than ever in times like these.'

The two sisters knelt before the picture of Blessed Mother Mary that hung above their bed and said their prayers together.

'Marija, I'm scared,' her sister whispered.

'Me too, Žuva.' She grasped her little sister's hand. 'It's all right, we have each other and I'll look after you. I promise.'

The girls snuggled close under the blanket in the bed they shared, their feet intertwined to keep warm. Their two-year-old brother, Ivan, had a mattress on the floor between their bed and Dobrila's bed. He always managed to sneak into their bed and curl up at their feet. Marija tousled his hair with her foot and he giggled. He squirmed while she tickled him with her toes and then he giggled some more. He would be in trouble if he laughed too loudly but this night, Marija guessed, their parents were too preoccupied to notice. Too worried.

Later, long after Ivan and Žuva had drifted off to sleep, their soft snores filling the room with a gentle hum, Marija thought back to the conversation earlier in the evening—the talk of the Partisans. Many young men and women had run off to the hills circling the town. They knew all the hiding spots but she had heard talk that if caught, they would be shot. Her parents revealed little, but Marija was worried that Dobrila would leave and she may never see her again. She prayed fervently that their parents would forbid her and for God to keep them all safe.

At dawn the next morning Paval attended Mass. This was his daily ritual. Sometimes Marija would go with him. Rising above the surrounding buildings, the church tower dominated the village roofline, a guardian watching its sleeping occupants, its ancient bells calling them to prayer. The father and daughter would tread the cobblestones, climb the six steps and enter the church. The exterior of the building was austere, the front façade adorned by a solitary gothic rose window. Kneeling on the stone floor they would bow their heads and pray. Marija felt safe in this church. The Catholic priest was the custodian of this imposing building, the custodian of the souls of this village. Marija would listen as her father whispered his prayers. He prayed for the war to end and for his family to have enough food. He was not alone. Many of the local townsfolk would attend this early morning service, take Communion and beg their God to keep them safe. Following church, Marija would go to school and Paval would walk with his donkey through the countryside to work on his farm.

5

Under occupation

Overnight, life as Marija had known it, changed. Her country was no longer her country. Her town was no longer her town. Like vermin, soldiers had infiltrated the island. As she sat on a wooden stool on the balcony of her home mending the threadbare clothes that were passed from sister to sister to sister, she could hear the unmistakeable *clack, clack* of army boots on the stone-paved roads long before seeing the polished helmets of the soldiers as they marched down her street. They were on the street corners, in the little bars, rumbling past in their trucks, patrolling between villages, always watching and always listening.

Life was not easy in the little town. The locals did not loiter in the streets to chat as they had in the past but kept their heads down while they hurried about their business and then hid behind the safety of their doors. The shadows under their eyes grew darker, their hair grew greyer, their faces more lined, and their pockets emptier.

The Italians took over the hospital, the school and occupied the best houses.

'We are lucky for once. Lucky we're not rich,' Paval said to his family. 'Italians have good taste in houses. I think ours is not up to their standard. Thank our dear Lord.'

Their home was modest and as a result remained their own.

The Yugoslav dinar was substituted by the Italian lira. The people looked on helplessly as their culture was being strangled.

Frank was old. No one quite knew how old. Nor did Frank.

Every day he sat smoking near the shop on the main street. Marija tried to make time to sit with him and listen to him chatter, mostly because she thought he was lonely. He had lost his entire family to the Spanish flu twenty years ago. She could imagine his terrible loss as her own father had lost his first wife Katom to this flu, leaving him with two children, her half-brother and half-sister. Frank was not afraid of the war and often spoke his mind. He leaned forward on his wooden walking stick, his wrinkled face contorted with exasperation.

'They are thieves,' he would mutter to her in a too-loud voice.

Marija looked up and down the street to check who was within earshot.

'One hundred dinar only gets me thirty-eight lira,' he ranted as he shook his fist. 'I have no money but what I have is now worthless.' He would repeat this story again and again to Marija and anyone else who would listen.

'That's not fair,' she would say, letting him vent his frustration and pretending that this was the first time she had heard this story.

Despite the occupation, Marija's life, in some ways, still seemed simple—she went to school, she helped her little sister, she teased her little brother and in the secrecy of the back streets she played with her friends. One of their favourite games was with the stray cats. They would wedge walnut shells on the cats' paws and let them clatter down the cobbled streets, creating a commotion. The cats would hiss, the dogs would howl and the adults would screech at the uproar. Marija and her friends would then remove the shells, run, hide and giggle in delight.

When she went home one night, Marija was annoyed and complained to her father. 'There are no more stray cats on the streets. The soldiers are catching them to cook and eat.'

He laughed. 'Well, if it stops the soldiers taking our chickens, it's better for us. Let them eat the cats.'

Although the Italians had occupied their village, the school doors remained open. Žuva and Marija were relieved that this aspect of their life remained constant. After the morning session, they would walk home for the midday meal. Sometimes they would take lunch to their father, who was working on the farm, and then rush back for the afternoon session.

One afternoon Marija was in the library looking at the countless rows of books on the shelves that almost reached the ceiling. One by one she extracted a book, examined it then returned it to its spot, keeping the ones that piqued her interest. She was allowed five so she was choosing carefully. In the next row she could hear some teachers talking amongst themselves. She stood still and listened.

'Have you seen the latest message from the Fascists?' one muttered.

She did not recognise the voice. Leaning forward, she pressed her ear to the gap in the books, hoping they would not spot her.

'We have one more month to learn Italian. Then we have to teach in Italian,' the first teacher continued.

Marija could hear the annoyed *humphs* and groans.

'We even have to sit an exam. This is a war. What are they doing to us? Making us little Italy? We have our own language,' complained another as the little group moved away from the shelves, their shoes scraping on the stone floor as they left.

Marija had heard that her teachers had to sit proficiency exams if they were to maintain their teaching positions. The soldiers would sometimes patrol the school hallways and abruptly open the door to a classroom to check that Italian was being spoken. The teachers seemed nervous and less tolerant, quicker to discipline than before.

Marija's teacher now rarely approached the class, sitting tensely behind her ink-stained wooden desk, her knuckles bruised from the continual rapping against the hard surface to quieten the chattering pupils. Marija watched with concern as the woman wiped beads of sweat from her forehead. She wondered whether it was the summer heat or anxiety as her teacher struggled with the foreign words. Her teacher looked much older these days.

Learning Italian was a welcome reprieve for Marija, a new challenge and a distraction from the ongoing tension. Her ears were quick to pick up this language that was so different from her own. The new sounds rolled off her tongue and danced from her mouth like a melody. It was not long before she also realised the power that came with understanding this language. She picked up snippets of conversations between the Italian soldiers when she passed them on the streets or in the halls of her school. She felt like a spy as she gave her father any information that would assist the Partisans in the hills. As a curious nine-year-old, she would practise the new words and phrases at home, proud of how quickly she was learning, but her mother's brow would furrow as she listened to her daughter chatter in the language of the enemy.

'Stop it! Don't bring that language into our home,' she snapped. 'Come and help with lunch. Its's almost ready.'

Understanding the relentless stress her mother lived with, Marija stopped talking and finished crushing the garlic. She drained the liquid from the contents of the saucepan, the silverbeet, added the garlic and poured in the olive oil. *Zeje*—same lunch as yesterday and the day before. She looked mournfully at the small bowl of food. There was not much to share amongst them. To distract herself from the grumble of her stomach she silently kept practising and repeating the new phrases she had learnt at school that day.

Summer came and went and the war in Europe raged on. Although an occupied country, the war within Yugoslavia also raged on. On the mainland it was complicated. Both the Communist Partisans and the Četniks, who were the Royalists supporting the exiled King Peter, battled against the Germans, who were supported by the Fascist Ustaše. Yugoslavian history was complex, with centuries of racial conflict and bitterness. Before long, the Partisans and the Četniks were at war with each other. There were many deaths and extensive torture at the hands of their own people as well as the occupiers.

The island did not escape the bloodbath. As the Partisans sabotaged and attacked the Italian occupiers, the soldiers retaliated with brutal reprisals. Houses were burnt, secret meetings were held, Partisans killed and were killed, many were tossed into the local jail, the hospital housed countless wounded, and numerous civilians were murdered. Uneasiness and fear were constant companions. Who to trust? Who was a spy? Who was with them and who was against them? More and more of the young men and women ran off to the hills to join the Partisans.

6

Resistance

'What are you doing?' Marija asked her mother, who was busy sewing black hessian bags.

'It's to darken the windows,' she answered, keeping her eyes on the task.

'Why?' Marija moved closer and stood behind her mother, peering over her shoulder.

'The curfew.'

'What's a curfew?'

'It means we all have to be inside our house from five o'clock every day until seven o'clock the next morning. And we can't let any light be seen outside. Everything has to be black.'

'Inside the house at five? That's not fair.' Marija scrunched her face. 'It's still light at five. I like to play in the street. Why do we have to do this?'

Her mother looked up at her and sighed.

'It's the war. The Partisans are causing too much trouble, sneaking into the town at night. Do you see all those messages painted on the walls of the houses? Those messages against the Fascists. Do you think that's us?' She continued her sewing, stabbing at the bag with her blunt needle.

'No,' Marija snickered, trying to imagine her mother in the dark of night with a paintbrush and bucket, defacing the walls. 'Of course, it's the Partisans,' she exclaimed, her chest swelling at the thought of her neighbours and cousins as courageous warriors, fighting back against the occupation. 'Aha.' It dawned on her. 'So the soldiers want to make sure there is no one out at night so they can catch the Partisans if they come down from the hills.'

Marija knew that many families supported the Partisans and she listened to the village grapevine that fed the stories of the strife and commotion caused by this fearsome band of warriors. Whispers of Italian trucks being intercepted on lonely roads and the Partisans stealing back their cargo of oil or wine, that had been stolen from the townspeople by the soldiers. Stories of Italian trucks destroyed with crude homemade bombs. She overheard her mother telling her aunt that the Partisans would cut telegraph poles to stop messages getting through. They would also ambush and cut the throats of the Italian soldiers when the soldiers were few in number and least expected it.

Marija shuddered when she thought of these deaths and thought back to the photograph the Italian soldier had shown her and her father, the photo of his wife and children. Surely other soldiers also carried photos of their loved ones who were back in Italy worrying about them. Marija tried to reason with herself. But this is war. She tried to make sense of it. God taught us to love one another, to not harm others and to forgive, always to forgive. But this is war. Are the rules different in a war?

She had heard her father say, 'The Partisans are like a thorn in the flesh of this occupying army, a nasty pebble in the Italian boot.' She often thought of the Partisans and the guerrilla warfare they were embroiled in. They were not soldiers; before the war they were farmers, students, accountants, teachers. Her village had raised an army, and even if they were only thorns or pebbles, at least they were doing something. Her neighbours, sisters in their twenties, were also Partisans. When Marija spoke to their parents she could see the anguish that lurked behind their composed faces. She knew she was not alone when she feared for their safety.

'Don't worry, little one,' her father reassured her one evening. He had entered the dark bedroom to kiss the children goodnight. Žuva and Ivan were already asleep. Marija was kneeling by her bed praying and her father noticed the tears trickling down her cheeks. The bed creaked as he sat on the edge and raised her chin to look into her eyes.

'I'm worried about our neighbours. Are they safe?' she asked, as she wiped the tears from her cheeks with the back of her hand.

'The Partisans are a good army, very disciplined. They look after the young women and make sure they're safe.'

'But how? The Partisans are sabotaging the Italian soldiers. I know.' She couldn't help it. The tears kept trickling. 'At school I hear the teachers talk about what our Partisans are doing.'

'Marija, the leaders of the Partisans are tough but good people.' His voice was firm and convincing. 'Do you know that it is stricter in the mountains than even at your school? They have lots of rules they must obey to be part of this army.'

He gently squeezed her arm. Her tears subsided and as she finished her prayers with a sign of the cross, she sat on the bed beside her father. He pulled her in close to him.

'They look after each other, especially the girls. There are many, many girls, some very young, in their army.'

'Yes, I know.' She felt better. Her father would not lie to her.

'They are brave…' He paused, then said, 'but they need our help'.

Marija looked up at him. 'But you're already helping them. All the people on our street are.'

'But you must never tell anyone how and when we help them as there are traitors in the village. We must be careful,' he said in a whisper.

She felt the tension in his voice and shivered, wanting desperately for the war to be over. She would do anything to help.

As Marija and Žuva were children, the soldiers did not suspect them when they started to help the Partisans. Messages detailing the movements of the Italian soldiers on the island would be written on small notes and twisted into the scarf that encircled

Marija's hair. Sometimes they were even cleverly clipped beneath the pins that held her hair in place. When she went to the farm to give her father his lunch, she would discreetly deliver these notes, which he would pass on to the Partisans in the hills.

One afternoon as the sisters raced home from school to collect the basket packed with their father's lunch, they found one of their elderly neighbours, Branko, sitting in the kitchen with their mother. His black beret covered his rounded balding head, its peak pulled low over his scraggly grey eyebrows. He puffed nervously on his pipe while their mother sat at the table listening to him. Her dress hung loosely on her thinning frame. She had a grey scarf in her hands.

'We have an important job for you today.' His voice was low and hoarse. They could barely hear him. 'It's for our cause.'

He beckoned young Žuva to stand close to him. She crinkled her nose, probably smelling the staleness of his nicotine-tainted breath mixed with the garlic he must have eaten at lunch. A fit of coughing racked his body. Too old and unwell to work on his son's farm, Branko helped the Partisans in any way he could. He carried their cause close to his heart as his youngest son was one of them. When his coughing ceased he extracted a flag from the bag at his feet and wrapped it inside the scarf. It was a Partisan flag with a red star in the middle. His hands shook as he twisted it carefully so no bright colour could be seen, and then meticulously tied this scarf around Žuva's waist.

'What will we do with this?' Marija asked, but she was fairly sure she knew the answer.

'Your father will know,' said Branko. 'Don't let the soldiers see this. It's for the Partisans. You girls must be careful.'

'Yes. Be careful,' repeated their mother as she wrung her hands. Marija knew that her mother worried about the fate of the entire family if they were discovered.

The girls were ready, and without a backward glance they stepped down the flight of stairs, opened the front door as silently as possible and scurried down the street, around the corner and out of the village.

Marija's heart fluttered. Her eyes darted left, right and then left again. Watchful. Wary. If they were caught, they would be shot. She hoped that her little sister was too young to realise this.

'What will we say if the soldiers stop us?' asked Žuva.

'What we tell them every time they stop us. That we're taking our father his lunch, which is true,' replied Marija, holding up the basket she gripped with her sweaty hand. 'See?'

Today's lunch was soup. Her stomach grumbled as the spicy aroma teased her nostrils. It was like an old friend, this grumble, a constant companion always by her side. A reminder of her hunger. As they rounded the corner, they saw a group of soldiers striding towards them, their rifles ready.

'Look, Marija, soldiers!' Žuva stopped and pointed to the men in the distance.

Marija breathed through her rising panic and pushed her sister's arm down.

'Keep walking! Act normally and we'll be all right.'

Žuva fidgeted with the scarf encircling her waist.

'Žuva!' she hissed. 'Stop fiddling with it. No one can see it.'

She wished the flag was not so red, not so bright. Why didn't they wrap it in a red sash around her waist? Why did they pick a grey sash? Sometimes adults aren't that clever, she thought anxiously.

As the men passed the young girls, one stopped.

'Where are you girls going?' He pointed his rifle at them. His face was pinched, his eyes cold and menacing.

'Just… just taking lunch to our father,' Marija stammered, her smile frozen.

He lifted the cloth and sniffed, then stared at the young girls, his eyes narrowing. He called back one of the soldiers who had marched ahead.

'*Antonio, vieni!* Look what we have here.'

Marija's leg trembled under her dress. She gripped her sister's hand. Do these soldiers suspect? Are they playing with us? were the thoughts rushing through her mind.

'Ah, Marco, this food smells delicious. *Dov'é il cibo buono, eh?* Mamma mia, how I miss my mother's cooking.'

As the men complained about the quality of the rations they received, they absentmindedly waved the girls on. The girls quickened their pace, trying not to run.

'We are true Partisans,' Marija exclaimed once out of earshot.

Her chest puffed out with pride at their narrow escape.

'Lucky they didn't take our lunch too,' Žuva said. 'I'm so hungry.'

They hurried onto the track, the trail winding through the valley to the farm. They passed neighbours' vineyards, olive trees and vegetable patches and as always, they waved at the people who were working in the fields. Approaching the farm, they could see their father in the middle of the field, bending to remove leaves from the vines to let more air flow through them and to expose the bunches of grapes to the sun. It was a warm day in May. High in the sky, the sun beat down mercilessly. Marija beckoned her father to their usual spot under the nearby fig tree.

'Come and cool down in the shade,' she called out, as she spread the checked cloth on the ground in between the gnarled roots of the old tree. He stretched backwards several times before lowering his slight body to the ground, leaning against the grey trunk and wiping his sweaty forehead. Shaded by the large green leaves he glanced upwards at the ripening bluish-red fruit.

'Look, girls, these figs are ready to pick. We must do this before the soldiers notice them too.'

Marija sighed as she unpacked the basket. There was not much lunch. There was never enough food for their large family. Unwrapping the blanket, she removed the lid from the ceramic dish, careful not to spill the precious contents. Today's soup was *brudet*, with more broth than fish. Oil swirled through the rich tomato soup, speckled with black pepper. Their noses twitched. As usual their father shared it and the three of them huddled together as they took turns to slowly ladle the soup into their mouths, savouring every mouthful.

Looking furtively over each shoulder, Marija leaned in and whispered in her father's ear, 'Branko has given us a flag for the Partisans'. She was not sure if she was more excited or more frightened.

'Where is it?' Paval asked, peering into the empty basket.

'Wrapped around her waist,' she said, pointing to Žuva.

Glancing around him, he hastily untied the scarf, extricated the flag and hid it down the front of his shirt before retying the grey scarf around Žuva's waist.

'What will you do with it?' she asked.

'Just wait. You will see.'

When they had finished their meagre meal, the girls hugged their father and raced back in time for their afternoon school session.

❦

The following morning, the small town awoke to the night's effort of the tenacious Partisans. The sleepy grey curtain of night lifted to expose slogans painted on many of the white-washed walls in the village. Large crimson letters, like stains of the Partisans' spilt blood. *Long Live Tito. Death to Fascism. Freedom to the People.*

The fog dispersed revealing a Partisan flag on the hilltop above the village.

As they walked to school barefooted as usual, Žuva pointed to the hill. 'Look, Marija! There's my flag.'

'Žuva, shh,' warned Marija, glancing around to see if any soldiers were closeby. 'You can't say things like that.'

Although worried about the soldiers, Marija's secret burned proudly in her chest as she watched the locals whispering to each other: 'Have you seen the flag? Have you seen the slogans? The Partisans had a busy night.'

Furious, the newly appointed Italian Commissioner summoned the villagers to the town piazza. He struggled as he hoisted himself onto the small stone wall surrounding the loggia, the covered building at one end of the piazza. Instructing his soldiers to retrieve the flag, he shredded it in front of the crowd.

Standing high, his rotund body shook as he spoke in a menacing tone: 'Who was responsible for all of this?' He pointed at the graffitied buildings with the index finger of his black-gloved hand. 'Who? Some of you must know!'

Žuva trembled as she hid behind Marija, clutching at her dress with her small fists.

'It's all right. They can't find us,' Marija whispered. 'Don't worry.'

'Who did this?' He bellowed once more, his jowls wobbling. 'And the flag. Who?'

The silence was interrupted by shoes scuffing and rattly coughs. Marija could barely believe that she and her sister, two ordinary young girls, had instigated so much anger with the part they had played with the flag. Trying not to gloat, she noticed the reactions of the surrounding crowd—a clenched fist here, a suppressed chuckle there. Her father would be so pleased to see this angry little man and despite him, the glimmer of hope amongst their people.

He would probably say, 'Serves him right. This is our town. This is our country. Leave us be.'

The Commissioner's face reddened as his voice escalated. He didn't look healthy, Marija thought. In the short time he had been here, she'd noticed that he was getting fatter. Maybe from all the food he was stealing from the locals. All the pigs he was slaughtering and feasting on. She looked around at the local people. They were all getting thinner. Her eyes were drawn once more to this little man now shaking with rage.

'Well, we have captured and shot many of you. We have found a man carrying another flag and destroyed it. You do this again, I promise you, the whole village will suffer!'

He shook his fist again, angry with their audacity. He would know they were assisting the Partisans. Marija had heard from her parents that he was also fearful, as a number of attempts had been made on his life. Even though he kept arresting and executing Partisans and civilians, even though he kept burning their houses, these guerrillas kept up their sabotage and their attacks. He shook his head and muttered to himself as he stepped down from the loggia and strode back to his headquarters, keeping his soldiers close for protection.

7

1942: Raising the flag

A nother year had passed and the Italians still occupied their village. Hundreds of troops had arrived and three tanks had rumbled onto the island. The boats were confiscated, robbing the people of their fishing livelihood. More locals ran to hide in the hills. There had been deaths, so many deaths. Villagers were often taken from the prison to the graveyard and executed. Some as retribution for the Partisans activities. Some... just because. No discrimination between men and women, between young and old. Graves with no funerals. Houses randomly torched. Those suspected of assisting the Partisans were massacred, their houses destroyed. Marija was now ten and she often heard her parents and others talking about the horrors and tragedies. When will this war end? she wondered.

It was six in the evening on 6 November. The houses were shrouded in a winter cloak of darkness. No glimpses of life could be seen through the blackened windows. There was no one on the streets; the locals being captive in their own homes, forbidden from stepping out their front doors for fear of execution. Marija sat at the kitchen table with Žuva as they worked on their home-work. The candle stub between them threw a pale, flickering light. Rain drizzled on the roof and as the wind howled Žuva shivered and moved closer to her sister. Stone houses were so cold.

A sudden volley of gunfire followed by distant shouts made the girls jump to their feet.

'Mama, what is that?' Marija said.

'Wait, we'll creep out and look. Don't let any soldiers see us.'

The family snuck onto their balcony, pressing their backs against the rough wall to shelter from the icy raindrops and the eyes of the soldiers. On the hill behind their house a fire was blazing, flames leaping high despite the rain. Then a flash of light shone on the bell tower. Marija's hand flew to her mouth. Flying provocatively from its top was a large Partisan flag, much larger than the one that Žuva had smuggled to the Partisans. Marija smiled wryly at the bravery of the Partisans.

'That flag looks like the handiwork of Kuzma Gavranić, from the tailor shop,' her mother muttered. 'I hope he and his family will be safe. Who knows what might happen to them.'

She herded her family back indoors before the soldiers spotted them. They huddled inside and listened as more shots and yells continued into the night.

∞

The following morning the Italian Commissioner was livid. He positioned his guards on the streets with an order that no one was allowed to leave their houses. Flames crackled from the hillside as houses burned. One was the Gavranić house. A coincidence? Or maybe paying their price for helping the Partisans.

'So,' the Commissioner snarled, 'you have done this again. Flown your flag. Well, if you behave like children, you will be punished like children.' He marched to the sturdy wooden door of the church and padlocked it shut brandishing the metal key. He did the same to the adjoining bell tower.

'Your church is closed. No more Mass,' he announced loudly to the pairs of eyes he must have imagined would be watching from the surrounding houses, before turning and stomping away.

'It doesn't matter,' Marija's father said to them all as they sat in the kitchen. 'He can lock our church but he can't stop our prayers.'

8

1943: The return of the rebels

Peoples of Yugoslavia: Serbs, Croats, Slovenes, Montenegrins, Macedonians and others! Now is the time, the hour has struck to rise like one man, in the battle against the invaders and hirelings, killers of our peoples. Do not falter in the face of any enemy terror. Answer terror with savage blows at the most vital points of the Fascist occupation bandits. Destroy everything that is of use to the Fascist invaders. Do not let our railways carry equipment and other things that serve the Fascist hordes in their struggle against the Soviet Union. Workers, Peasants, Citizens and Youth of Yugoslavia... To battle against the Fascist occupation hordes who are striving to dominate the whole world.[1]

This was the official call to the people of Yugoslavia on 4 July 1943 from the leader of the Partisans, Josep Broz, known simply as Tito. Right under the noses of the Italians, the Partisans passed this important message from brigade to brigade, from village to village.

∞

Dobrila held the crumpled message in her fist. She was hot and sweaty from working in the fields. She had read it and reread it, almost memorising the words.

'Perhaps when they see this, they will let me,' she said to Marija.

---

1   https://www.historylearningsite.co.uk/world-war-two/resistance-movements/the-resistance-movements/the-resistance-movement-in-yugoslavia/

She beckoned her parents and sister into the corner of the bedroom, away from the spying ears and eyes on the streets outside.

'Look at this message. Look! From our leader,' she exclaimed.

'I know,' whispered Paval as he took it from her. 'I have already seen this. I think we all have.'

'Well?' She stood tall. 'I'm seventeen and a half. I want to go and help. You said—'

'No,' Paval said, his jaw set firm. 'Not until you are eighteen. You are still too young.' He ran his hand through his hair and glanced through to the kitchen, making sure no one was listening. 'I know, I know there are many young girls fighting, girls younger than you, but I don't want you to go until you're eighteen.'

'All right, so you will keep your promise?' Dobrila asked, her eyes darkened with resolve. 'I'll be eighteen in February. You don't know how hard it is to sit by and do nothing while the Italian soldiers act as if this is their town, their country.'

'Shh,' Paval said as he held her shoulders. 'It's hard for all of us but we're doing what we can. Your time will come.'

Marija agreed with Dobrila but was scared for her and truly hoped the war would be over by then.

On a cloudy day in September, Marija woke to the ringing of the church bells. Confused, she and her family wandered into the streets, joining their neighbours. The lock on the door to the bell tower had been wrenched off and someone was ringing the bells, the sound reverberating through the narrow streets.

'What is happening?' people were asking.

Italy had surrendered! The church bells in each village rang loudly and continuously, the message echoing throughout the tiny island. Triumphantly the courageous Partisans returned in daylight to their towns. Despite being dishevelled and gaunt after months of hiding in caves high in the cliffs, despite wearing shabby, ill-fitting uniforms taken from fallen soldiers, they marched proudly, wearing their *titovkas* firmly on their heads. The red star on the front of these green side caps named after their leader, Tito, was symbolic of their struggle. They raised clenched fists in the proud Partisan salute as they entered the main street and greeted the hundreds of townfolk, young and old. The fighters were encircled and hugged by the family they had not laid eyes on for so long.

Marija and Žuva held their little brother's hand as they pushed through the dancing, singing people and under the twirling flags. Ivan was now four. He hid his head and clasped his sisters' hands, frightened by the commotion. The sisters found their neighbours and wrapped their arms around them. They had all returned, thinner and older, but alive.

'We need to open the jail,' urged a young Partisan, her eyes glowing with zeal. The crowd followed, roaring above the ongoing ringing of the bells.

Eventually, the crowd climbed to the crest of the hill behind their village, to the cemetery, the community paying respect to those who had made the ultimate sacrifice. Stone walls encircled the graveyard as if trying to keep the souls safe. Grieving wives and mothers clothed in black could finally sob openly.

Long into the evening the emotions continued. High above them the moon illuminated the village, shining down on the festivity of freedom. The adults sat together, drinking, slapping each other on the back, hugging, crying, and singing. The children ran and played. Marija perched contentedly beside her parents, listening to the endless stories of bravery, hanging on every word.

Gradually, the Italian soldiers were quietly sent back to their country by the Partisans, not imprisoned. Marija heard that the boats carrying them left from the seaside town of Vela Luka. After stopping briefly at the prison on the small isle of Lastovo, they departed to Italy.

'We are free,' Marija clapped her hands together, her face radiant when her father finished telling her this latest news.

'Ah, no, sadly, no,' he replied. 'The Italians have gone but the war has not finished. The Germans are still in our country.'

'So the Partisans still need to fight?' Her shoulders sagged.

'Yes, now more than ever,' he said wearily, his eyes clouding. 'A storm is coming.'

In the days that followed, the Partisans patrolled the villages and controlled the entire island of Korčula. It was not large. Forty-seven kilometres long and eight kilometres wide. It was a welcome reprieve after two years of Italian occupation. The Partisans' weapons were old so they claimed the weapons, trucks and ammunition left behind by the Italians. Their firepower was intensifying, Tito's numbers were multiplying, and with them grew confidence. The killings had stopped. The Partisans had seized control of the islands and large stretches of the coast.

On the mainland they were still fighting, desperate to prevent the Germans from moving towards them.

Dobrila was almost eighteen and her parents had relented. Marija and Žuva sat on their bed and looked at their sister.

'The uniform looks good on you, Dobrila,' Marija said. She meant it. Her sister looked so grown up, so serious. 'Here, let me,' she insisted as she placed the *titovka* on Dobrila's head, making sure the red star faced frontward. She wrapped her arms around her, holding tightly. 'Be safe.'

'Come back to us at the end of this war,' whispered their father when he walked in.

Dobrila hugged him, then told them what was awaiting her that night. Under the blanket of darkness, she and the other recruits would sail to the mainland, navigating through the islands of the Adriatic Sea to the Bay of Kotor in Montenegro, known simply as Boka. There she would begin her training to become a code breaker for the Partisan secret service.

9

Autumn, 1943: Hope arrives

It was mid-afternoon and the sun was almost setting, dropping the temperature into single digits. The Partisans from Blato had been summonsed to the town piazza to meet some important soldiers. Many locals joined them, talking excitedly and stamping their feet to keep warm. Petar, the local Partisan leader, arrived on his black stallion. The horse had galloped hard and was foaming at the mouth, its muscular flanks trembling. Petar's chest was puffed with pride as he dismounted and stood with his people awaiting the arrival of the special foreign guests. Marija and Žuva had heard the talk in the streets about these British soldiers who had landed on their island. Word travelled quickly, especially regarding newcomers. Curious, the girls stood in the growing crowd, watching and waiting.

'Why are they here?' murmured a man standing behind the girls. 'I heard they were in Korčula the last few days. Someone said the Padre was looking after them.'

'I hope they bring good news,' his friend replied. 'They might be able to tell us what's happening on the mainland.'

Leaving behind a trail of grey smoke, a small blue Italian car beeped its horn as it arrived from the direction of the nearby village of Smokvica, coming to an abrupt halt before the assembled crowd. Out stepped a tall, pale, clean-shaven man dressed in uniform with a cap perched lopsidedly on his head.

'This is Brigadier General Fitzroy Maclean. British,' Petar proudly informed the crowd. 'And Sergeant Duncan and Sergeant

Smith.' He pointed to the other men who had stepped out of the vehicle.

The large crowd cheered at their arrival. Maclean climbed onto the ledge of the loggia at the end of the piazza and waited for everyone to settle. A few nuns stepped forward and threw flowers at their feet, welcoming them to Blato.

'We are very pleased to be here on your beautiful island,' Maclean said in his broken Yugoslav. 'These past few weeks we have been on the mainland, in the Bosnian mountains behind enemy lines.'

'How did you get behind the enemy lines?', asked a young Partisan woman, her hands on her hips.

'By parachute.' He paused, formulating the words before speaking. 'Late at night from a low-flying plane.' He demonstrated this with his arms. 'And hoped that I would not land in a field of Germans.' He pulled a small, battered dictionary from his side pocket. 'And I brought this with me. But I speak Russian so your language is not too difficult,' said Maclean. 'And day by day I think I am getting better. You agree?'

The locals laughed at his accent and attempt at their language and then bombarded the men with questions.

'What is happening on the mainland?'

'Will the Germans be invading here soon?'

'How will we defend ourselves?'

'Have you met Tito?'

'Do you know our cousins in Sydney? Do you like to dance?' a cheeky Partisan piped up.

Raising his arm to stop the verbal barrage he began, 'We have met your great leader, General Tito. He is a good man, a brave soldier.'

The roar and fist pumps encouraged him, and he continued. 'We, the Allied Forces have been giving money to the Četniks to fight the Germans—'

Interrupted by jeering and scowling, he patiently waited for the raucous crowd to quieten down. 'But my leaders are looking at helping your army in our fight against the enemy and—'

'We have no ammunition, no guns, only what we have taken from the Italians—'

'We need more. We need support from the air,' interjected another fighter.

'Yes. We want to help. I am trying to talk to my leaders to work out what we can do—' continued Maclean before his speech was terminated.

'Enough,' the Partisan Commander said. 'You have met my army and some of my people here. That's good. Now it's time for us to eat and drink. You will come to the dance tonight. You must meet everyone, all the village.'

Old men with crinkled faces sat on oak barrels puffing on their pipes and tapping their feet to the beat. The folk music echoed off the stone walls of the rustic barn on the outskirts of the town. Marija's pleas of, 'Please, please can we go? The whole town is going,' had been successful and she joined the other children skipping and spinning on the dirt floor. The shutters were bolted, closing out the bleak wintery chill. Hiding behind the hills, the town was sheltered from the *bura*, the gushing wind that blasted from the hills and then out to sea.

Local wine flowed freely. Some were skulling little tumblers of *rakija*. In one corner was a stooped old man. His body shook and his coarse salt-and-pepper hair swayed rhythmically as he blew into a wooden pipe of a strange looking musical instrument resembling a bagpipe. The shrillness filled the air. One of the young Partisan girls who could speak English gripped a British soldier by the hand and pulled him up to dance.

'I will show you,' and she proceeded to teach him the steps of a traditional dance. As he struggled, she chuckled and persisted.

At the opposite end of the barn, away from the dancing, the leader of the Partisans was deep in conversation with Maclean. Marija was curious about these foreigners and wandered over, lurking behind and listening.

'Tell me of our General,' enquired Petar as he fixed his gaze on the soldier.

'We spoke a lot. I like the man—,' began Maclean.

'Yes…yes. He is courageous. Did you know that he has been outlawed by our government, and called a traitor?' Petar scoffed. 'And the Germans, they have been trying to capture him; but no, not yet, that will never happen.'

Seeming to enjoy the discussion with this fearless Partisan leader, Maclean continued, 'General Tito told me that at the beginning, in the summer of '41, they tried to work with the Četniks, they fought side by side, but by the end of the year they were fighting each other. But you know, he is so true to your cause, the cause of Communism. And do you know what he told me?'

'Tell me. You must tell me.'

More men dragged their seats closer, leaning in to listen, straining to hear above the loud music and the laughing of the dancers.

'He said to me that the more village people the Germans shoot and the more villages they burn, the more Germans he will kill and the more bridges he will destroy.'

'Yes!' the men roared in unison. Despite the cost to civilian lives, their loyalty was unshakeable.

'Come, British soldier, you will dance with me.' The intense discussion was interrupted by a pretty Partisan woman, who dragged Maclean up to join the festivities.

'I am very, very bad at dancing,' he protested.

Tossing her head back she announced: 'Tonight I teach you'.

And the soldiers danced amongst the crowd, the pairs twirling, skipping and clapping. Tonight, hope was palpable. The presence of these British soldiers had buoyed their spirits.

Near the door and beside his neighbours, Paval sat with his wife. Marija returned and sat beside them and her little brother.

'Do you know where Dobrila is now?' Marija asked her father. 'Do you think she's safe?'

'She's tough. She's a fighter and will return to us. I'm sure of it.'

He forced a smile and started tapping his foot and clapping in time to the music, urging Marija to do the same.

They all watched the flurry of activity that brought the barn to life, the couples hopping and twirling, faster and faster. Their family friend, Mladenka, was teaching one of the soldiers.

'I think I've got the hang of this,' Sergeant Smith yelled to his mate as he spun Mladenka, her dark hair floating behind her.

As he grabbed her, he dislodged a red Italian hand grenade attached to her waistband. It flung sideways, hitting the side of the barn.

'No! Bomb!' Mladenka shrieked and dived behind a nearby chair pulling the soldier with her.

For one or two seconds, time stood still. Then came the blast of chaos. The music stopped and the crowd screamed and scattered, diving for cover. Marija grabbed her young brother, throwing him to the ground and shielding him with her body. Luckily, the dancing was in the corner of the barn and the stone wall absorbed most of the explosion. The smell of cordite lingered as the smoke cloud dissipated.

Excited voices filled the room as the crowd gathered to examine the damage—a few flesh wounds here and there but no major injuries and luckily, no fatalities.

'What the...' exclaimed Maclean to his friend.

'What the hell was she doing with a grenade attached to her waist? She could have blown us all up,' said Smith.

'Actually,' whispered Duncan scanning the room, 'If you look carefully, they all have their weapons on them. Every single one of them.'

Mladenka stood and motioned for the music to restart. This was just one grenade in a long war.

She clutched the soldier's hand commanding, 'We'll keep dancing, but this time be careful. Don't touch my bomb.' She smirked with a mischievous sparkle in her dark eyes as she pointed to a second grenade attached to her waistband.

'What a bang of a night,' Smith yelled over to his friends as he twirled her, more cautious this time.

The villagers enjoyed their night of distraction but bubbling below the celebrations, however, ran an undercurrent of anxiety. It was hard to imagine that across the narrow strait of water separating this island from the mainland, the Germans were gathering. The harshest part of the war was yet to reach them. Split had fallen and the Germans were coming. It was inevitable.

10

The fall of Blato

On the mainland the fighting continued as the German army advanced on their march to the coast. In Blato the Catholic infant school became a hospital. Instead of teaching the little ones, the nuns nursed the wounded brought from the mainland. Marija watched these quiet, devoted women tending to fighters, whose faces were filled with pain, some with legs hastily splinted with bloodsoaked rags, bandaged heads, many with severe injuries, such as amputations. Often their injuries were too severe for them to recover. Fearful, she would scan for familiar faces. With every new female Partisan brought in, her heart would hammer against her chest. Is this Dobrila? Thankfully, no. Where is she now? Nobody is sure, Marija would think. She noticed the similarities in the expressions on the faces of the Partisans—the fervent glow of their eyes. Commitment to their cause.

How many more people have to die? Marija thought, as she helped the nuns, running errands for them.

Dull winter sunlight struggled through grey clouds. With a basket of freshly scrubbed clothes at her feet, Marija draped the garments over the line on the edge of the balcony. Hearing the unmistakeable roar of fighter planes, she dropped a damp towel to the ground and leant out for a clearer view. A number of German Stukas buzzed overhead, the black swastika instantly recognisable on the tail of the aircrafts. They flew so low she could see the pilots in their cockpits. Her stomach sank. It was just as her father had warned—terror had arrived. It was 30 November, 1943. The Nazis were here.

She watched in horror as the fighter planes turned and thundered back, releasing bombs on the unsuspecting seaside town of Korčula. Bomb after bomb whistled through the air. Although she was kilometres away, in the centre of the island, she could feel the earth rumble as the bombs found their targets and imagine the scream of the children, the cries of their mothers, boats sinking and houses collapsing.

Terrified, some of the besieged locals fled to the islands of Vis and Hvar on boats provided by the British. Marija heard that their destination was El Shatt, the refugee camp in Egypt. Others dashed inland, some coming to hide in Blato.

'I don't know why they come here. Our town will fall too,' Paval said to his family as they watched the arrivals.

Enemy planes continued to circulate above the island. More bombs fell. The harbour of Vela Luka and its fishing boats did not escape the wrath of the German bombs. Meanwhile, the Partisans who had been fighting on the mainland retreated to Korčula where they fortified the damaged buildings as best they could against a German invasion. Paval had told his daughter that they could not fight the might of the German onslaught, and indeed, once established on the mainland, the Germans, set about capturing the islands one by one.

One evening in the bitter month of December, most of the Partisans left the island. Taking the wounded with them, they slipped away in boats from the seaside towns of Vela Luka and Pregradica to the neighbouring island of Hvar. Marija heard her parents whisper about the vulnerablility of their village and the dread of the inevitable.

Korčula fell on Christmas Eve 1943. Marija and her younger siblings huddled with their parents in the main bedroom. The bitter wind blustered through the narrow streets, rattling the shutters. The bare branches trembled. There was no moon. The stars hid, maybe afraid of what was to come. With most of the Partisans gone and the local rebels returned to the hills, no one remained to protect them. She felt afraid and alone.

They knew that the Germans were on their island. Messages were relayed when the army reached the village of Smokvica, fifteen kilometres away. Blato was next. They did not know what to expect from these soldiers. They had heard stories of their cruelty. Marija's father bowed his head. He trembled as he hugged his family and led them in prayer.

'We are together. We will pray. It is in God's hands,' murmured Paval as he pulled his family closer. His faith was unflinching. It was all he had.

At nine in the evening, the enemy arrived. Marija trembled as she heard the staccato of the shots. What or who were they shooting? Her father had extinguished the small candle and they hid in silence under their flimsy cloak of darkness. Surely, everyone is hiding, she hoped; please no one be outside. Gripping her rosary beads, she prayed silently. Outside in the street she could hear quick, sharp orders in a foreign language, interspersed with more gunfire. Then there was quiet. There was no one to fight back. Disconcerting stillness.

∞

Waking from a fragmented sleep just before dawn, Marija wondered whether she had slept at all. She disentangled herself from the blanket she shared with her sister, and tiptoed on the cold stone floor into the kitchen and peered through the frosted window. In the greyness of the departing night she could see a new flag flying from the tower—blood-red. In the middle was a black swastika on a white circle. As it flapped, the swastika spun as if hypnotising her. She shivered as she recognised this symbol from the planes that had flown overhead in the preceding weeks but kept watching and listening, wondering whether there had been much damage from the night before.

The streets were empty. A ghost town. Then shouts and the rhythmic sound of many boots on cobblestone pierced the stillness, drawing closer. Stretching up on her toes to peer down, not daring to open the window, she saw soldiers marching up her street. They clattered past, a sea of grey helmets; soldiers in grey-green uniforms with long coats. She thought how lucky they were to have these coats. How warm they must feel. She shivered again, watching their new occupiers, the German Military. The Wehrmacht.

She glanced across at the bell tower. There would be no bells calling her to church this Christmas.

Marija crept back to her bed and curled up next to her sleeping sister, wrapping her arms around her to stay warm, to find comfort, wondering what was next, but too tired to pray. Closing her eyes, she wished for the nothingness of sleep, hoping it would be devoid of the nightmares that had plagued her. Her thoughts drifted to her sister, Dobrila. Where was she? Would she be able to stay safe?

11

1944: Danger at sea

'Shh, be quiet,' whispered Tomislav as Dobrila and her fellow fighters stepped aboard the blue fishing boat. Night's blanket concealed their secrets. Stowing their weapons carefully beside their feet, the four young soldiers began their perilous journey seawards. Their training as code breakers on the mainland in Boka had finished. It had been rushed as there was no time to waste; their skills were needed. Dobrila felt nervous as they manoeuvured silently out of the bay and threaded in between the islands, all now occupied by the German military. All fallen, except for their destination, the furthest island from the coast, the island of Vis. Questioning the Partisan sailor transporting them, one of the young women asked tentatively, 'What is happening on Vis?'

'You have been to Vis before?' he replied.

She nodded.

'You would not recognise it,' he said proudly as he looked ahead, slowly steering the little vessel. 'The olive trees in the valley are gone and instead they have made a landing strip. A big one.' He took his hand off the rudder and stretched both arms out wide. 'It was built in eight days. Only eight days. And you should see it. There are British everywhere, and trucks, jeeps, fighter bombers coming and going. Right under the noses of the Germans.' He snickered.

'We're working with the British? How?' Dobrila asked, wondering what awaited her.

On the horizon Tomislav saw a yellow speck. A light from an approaching vessel.

'Quick, hide,' Tomislav hissed. He killed the motor while they flattened themselves in the hull of the boat. Without the constant chug of the motor, all they could hear was the gentle lapping of the sea against the boat, their jagged breathing in the cool air and in the distance, the sounds of the German language and their boat coming closer. Their searchlight skimmed the waters surface in a wide arc.

As the minutes crept by Dobrila's legs began to cramp but she dare not move them. The enemy boat moved past them without the Partisans being detected. Tomislav exhaled loudly and informed his passengers that they could sit up. Their journey resumed.

'You asked about the British,' Tomislav continued, stretching his arms backwards. 'Well, we have become used to each other. They didn't understand our ways at first, but now, now they can see how brave we are. What fierce fighters we are.' His eyes glowed as he told these young Partisans of his role in this war.

'We go out at night, like pirates, and raid the German boats. We steal the ammunition and food they're bringing to the mainland. You should see the good food we get! We watch where they're burying mines on the islands, and at night we go dig them up and steal them,' Tomislav said. 'I think they're scared of us.'

Hanging onto every word, the four young Partisans listened to their enthusiastic comrade.

'And it's good. The Allies have dropped radios to all our groups of fighters.'

Now that the coast was clear, Tomislav paused to light a cigarette. As he languidly puffed, the grey wisps disappeared into the night and their little boat motored further away from the coast.

'How did they do this?' his impatient audience insisted.

'The Allies come from Italy and fly down low. Our people light fires so they can see where to drop supplies. They even took some of our men to Africa to train them and so our soldiers are flying planes too, bombing. My cousin, he is one of them,' he boasted, amused by the reactions of the young recruits. 'They have even put our red star over their circle on the side of the plane. Wait till you see them. They're our planes now!' His smile broadened, his white teeth glinting in the moonlight.

The quiet chatter continued, distracting them from the peril they faced weaving in between these occupied islands.

'Are there many of my people with the Partisans? I'm from Blato,' said Dobrila, gripping the edge of the rocking boat while watching the shadowy shapes of the islands glide by. Blackness was everywhere. Adrenaline coursed through her veins as she thought of what lay ahead.

'Blato?' He shifted his gaze towards her. 'Aha—one of my best friends on Vis is Frank. Frank Petković. You know him? He is from Blato?'

Dobrila pondered. 'Yes, I think I know the family, but I can't be sure'.

'Well, he was caught by the Ustaše two years ago and sent to the concentration camp up north. Sisak, I think. He escaped and walked all the way to the sea, hundreds of kilometres. He's with us on Vis and like me he's a pirate!'

'And are there others from Blato?'

'Yes, you will meet them all. There are hundreds of us Partisans there.'

Dobrila was eager to hear more and kept up with her questions.

'And our General, is he there? We heard that he was nearly captured.'

'They tried to catch him when he was in the Bosnian mountains, but he escaped. Don't worry, he's safe. In a cave high up in one of the mountains on Vis. Look, we are nearly there.'

He pointed to the approaching island. It was small with craggy cliffs. Tomislav steered the boat to the northern end so that he could enter through the tiny inlet. Dobrila could barely make out the outline of two ancient, crumbling forts perched high on the rocks on either side of the bay. Tomislav slowed the boat to an idle.

'Okay, we have changed the secret signal. I hope they remember this time and don't shoot at us,' Tomislav laughed as he flashed his torch three times, the sign to indicate they were *naši*, one of theirs.

Dobrila looked towards where her island of Korčula was, hoping that all her family was still alive.

12

Blato, 1944: Retribution

Marija felt the intensity of the war escalating. The Allied planes flew in increasing numbers over her house. Sometimes low and deafening. If she peered closely, she could count the bombs on their wings. Later, she would see them return from their missions, minus their bombs. Some of the planes were not so lucky. She watched one returning, coughing and spluttering with smoke trailing behind. Fearful for the pilot she was sure she could see, she watched it pass over her island, stall and then drop into the sea like a stone from the sky.

That evening as her parents huddled in the kitchen, Marija hovered and listened. When her parents spoke in hushed tones she knew they were talking about the war, and their words were not meant for her young ears. Even though it frightened her, she was hungry for knowledge.

'He was a young American, the pilot,' Paval whispered to his wife. 'The plane crashed near Vela Luka. He drowned.'

'I heard about the British pilot rescued near Lovište. His plane went down and he was floating in the sea attached to his parachute. Two women rowed out and rescued him.'

'Brave women. Lucky pilot that there was a boat hidden nearby that could help him,' muttered Paval. 'So dangerous if they got caught.' He turned and noticed Marija. 'Come, little Marija,' he beckoned and cradled her against his chest in a warm hug. Marija could feel that he desperately wanted to shield her and her siblings from the horrors that were going on around them.

Life in Blato under the Germans was harsher than under the Italian occupation and the soldiers were brutal. The curfew remained and Ustaše leaders were appointed. With the school still closed, Marija and Žuva spent their days helping their parents on the farm or in their home.

One Thursday, Marija was with her father on their farm picking bunches of purple grapes from the gnarled vines entwined on the trellises, carefully placing this precious produce in the baskets at their feet. Approaching on the road from Blato, an enemy truck rumbled to a stop beside their field.

'Marija, here they come again, either to take our food or ask about the Partisans,' Paval whispered. 'I'll talk. You say nothing to them.'

The two soldiers jumped down from the truck and glanced around before striding over. They were both young, with pale eyes and blond hair barely visible beneath their steel helmets. They halted in front of the farmer, pointing their lugers, ready and menacing. When they barked out some questions and commands, Paval stopped his work and listened. He could understand some of their words. Suddenly a yell from the trees behind them pierced the stillness.

'Brzo! Spremi se!'

Paval ducked and dragged Marija with him to the ground. Unlike the German soldiers, he understood the words, 'Hide quickly.' They heard the crack of bullets being fired from behind them. The bullets whizzed over their heads and thudded into their targets. One of the soldiers locked eyes with Marija, his expression reflecting his disbelief as his body toppled backwards. His pistol dropped to the ground.

The deafening crack of the gun shots echoed through the valley. The young soldiers lay lifeless on the soil, eyes open but unseeing, legs crooked, crimson blood creeping through their vests. Trembling, Marija clasped her father. It was not the first time this had happened but she still trembled.

'*Brzo!*'

Two young men and a girl, barely a woman, emerged from their hiding place amongst the trees.

'*Brzo!*' they shouted again, urging Paval and Marija to move quickly.

Paval helped carry the bodies to the truck. Marija collected the weapons from where they had fallen and handed them to the young woman, who accepted them without uttering a word.

Marija recognised her. She had been a few years older than Marija at school. She looked thinner now, but strong. She half smiled and nodded at Marija before turning to join her comrades. The Partisans disappeared with the truck and the bodies, melting back into the hills. Frantically, Paval kicked at the soil and rocks to conceal the bloodstained ground. Marija stood still, trying to process what she had seen. More death.

Untethering his donkey, he and Marija hurried home. They pushed open the door to their courtyard. Marija's mother, Žuva, was sitting on the bottom step, elbow deep in water, scrubbing at the clothes in a metal bucket between her bare feet.

'Why are you home so early?' she asked.

Paval shook his head and placed a finger against his lips. She froze, dread seemed to engulf her body.

Wordlessly, Paval gathered his family and took them downstairs to hide with the animals. He knew what would follow. Retribution.

This little family stayed silent and waited. Marija held her breath as she squeezed herself into the back corner of the stable, feeling the rough wall through her thin blouse. She lowered her head to her knees, curling her slight body into a ball, and wished she was invisible. Her feet began to cramp. It seemed like hours but was probably only minutes. Her parents squatted in front of the children, shielding them. And then it happened. Through the thick walls they heard the yells of the soldiers in the streets outside. Angry roars. Marija tried to calm her breathing as she silently whispered her prayers.

'Please, God, have mercy. Please, God, save us. Please, God, let no one die.'

Her body shook as she heard the shrieks outside. Unsuspecting locals were randomly selected from the streets or dragged from the closest houses. Fifteen was the number. Fifteen Yugoslavs killed in retaliation for every slain German soldier.

'Please! No! Please have mercy on us. We've done nothing wrong.'

The civilians were lined up against the stone walls. Even though her eyes were closed, Marija could not shut out the images.

'Please, I beg you, I have small children,' wailed a mother's voice.

The soldier hesitated, not wanting to shoot this terrified, innocent woman.

'Shoot her or I'll shoot you!' his superior commanded.

Marija crushed her ears with her sweaty palms, trying to block out the horror, the realisation that she recognised the woman's voice. A staccato of shots.

The sound seemed to go on and on. Tears slid down her cheeks as she heard the screams. Executed. She could picture the bodies on the ground, the blood splattered on the whitewashed walls behind them. This was war. The brutality and unfairness of war. Marija wept as she stayed hunched over with the animals. How much more could her little town endure?

13

Hunger pains

Marija was always hungry. The German soldiers would raid homes and take the food, slaughter the animals. She knew that some of the locals hid their smoked ham in their chimneys but the Germans, like rottweilers, would sniff it out. Occasionally she would see a group of soldiers eating plums in the street. She would hide, her stomach rumbling, as she watched them. When they left she would rush over to gather the seeds they spat on the ground. Inside these seeds were tiny kernels that she would eat and share with her siblings. She grew thinner. Shadows appeared beneath her dark eyes and her stomach was always empty. She tried to forget the hunger by working hard on the farm.

❧

'Look up, Marija.' Her sister Žuva nudged her as they both dug at the hard soil. 'Look, let's eat them,' she urged, pointing at an almond tree nearby.

'They're not ripe,' Marija said, as she glanced up and then kept working.

'But I'm so hungry!' moaned Žuva, rubbing her belly. Their family had no food. They sometimes collected grass and boiled it for soup, their mother adding salt to hide the bitter taste.

When they did have food Marija would watch as her parents would encourage them, saying: 'Eat it all, we've already eaten'. She knew they lied.

Marija looked up once more at the yet-to-ripen fruit above them.

'I'm hungry too,' she agreed. 'All right, let's eat them.'

They collected the fuzzy peach-like fruit that had yet to develop a hard shell and devoured the soft jelly-like centres. They ate handfuls and handfuls, enjoying the sweet nutty taste. Hours later the two sisters lay side by side in their bed, whimpering and clutching their distended stomachs. Their distraught parents bent over them.

'Do you think it's the measles?' their mother said, with her hand on their foreheads. 'Four children died this past week.' Her voice was edged with concern. An epidemic was sweeping through the village.

'I can't see any spots.' Paval lifted Žuva's shirt and checked her stomach.

Žuva groaned. 'Don't touch my tummy. It's so sore.'

As tears trickled down Marija's cheeks, she confessed.

'Almonds? You ate how many green almonds? The whole treeful?' her mother, Žuva, exclaimed. 'No wonder you're sick. I don't feel sorry for you girls at all; you should know better.'

She stomped out of the room.

Paval chuckled as he hugged the girls.

'Your mother isn't angry, just relieved you won't die. Now, I bet you won't ever do that again.'

'No,' they said together.

He sat by their beds talking to them, holding their hands and telling them stories to distract them from their bellyaches.

After a while, he cleared his throat and tightened his clasp on their small hands. 'Little Danica Tulić lost her mother yesterday.'

The girls stopped their weeping and listened. This family lived close by and they often played with four-year-old Danica, a sweet little girl with thick, dark hair and large, inquisitive eyes.

'Her mother was walking to their farm to get vegetables for lunch. She was rushing and took a shortcut.'

'Was it a mine?' asked Marija.

They knew of the mines that were scattered randomly, concealed just beneath the surface.

'Yes, she stepped on it. I heard she lost her leg and her arm and part of her face too, I think. Terrible.' He bowed his head and shook it slowly. 'They had to carry her on their donkey to get to the doctor, but she had lost so much blood there was no hope for her. She lived only three days.'

Marija's heart tightened, thinking about the little girl who had lost her mother. A sore belly was nothing to cry about.

'So, you girls must be very careful when you walk to the farm,' Paval said. 'Make sure you stay on the path.'

'Yes, we know, Tata,' they replied in unison.

14

18 March 1944: Taken

It was seven in the morning. Winter had lingered and Marija shivered as she tiptoed amongst the animals, checking under the clucking chickens, hoping for eggs. She was grateful they had not been taken by the Germans. Raising her head she heard in the distance the crunching of footsteps, the harsh yelling of the soldiers as they hammered on each door. She froze, wondering what was being said. The racket intensified until they thumped on her door and slid a folded note underneath it. Intrigued she knelt on the chilly stone and smoothed it out to read the message.

All males from fourteen years and older must report to the town piazza before 8 a.m.

Her eyes smarted with angry tears as she raced up the steps, the message crunched in a ball in her fist.

Her parents were busy in the kitchen. They read the paper that Marija thrust at them.

'At eight? That's soon,' whispered Paval, his jaw clenching and unclenching.

'What does this mean? What'll happen to you?' Žuva clung to her husband. 'We'll hide you. You can't go.'

'That's crazy. They'll kill all of you if they find me hiding. They know there's a man in this house.'

For the first time during this war Marija thought she saw defeat in her father's face. It was momentary. Paval pursed his lips together, swallowed and then hugged his children and his wife, not knowing if he would see them again.

'Where are you going?' asked Ivan, rubbing his eyes.

The commotion outside had awoken him. He was five, already tall for his age with sombre brown eyes and fine brown hair. Marija listened in silence, her face creased with concern. Who will work the farm? Who will keep us safe? Are they going to execute the men?

Many of their neighbours had been executed. The cemetery was a patchwork of fresh mounds, brown dirt hiding the murdered corpses. Trembling, she hugged her father tightly, feeling his heart thudding through his worn shirt.

'Be brave, little Marija,' he said, his mouth close to her ear. 'Look after the family.'

She nodded and tried to ignore her mother's sobbing. Holding the heavy door ajar, she watched him depart, his head high and shoulders straight. Without a backward glance he joined the other men, some with walking sticks, some limping, as they all made their way to the town piazza. There were not many men left in this village. Only the old, the injured and the very young remained. By eight o'clock they had all assembled in the centre of the town. They stood in silence, warily watching and waiting, unsure. No one dared to ask questions. Young boys, barely into their teens, shuffled their feet and coughed nervously as they glanced away from their weeping mothers.

'March!' shouted a German officer, pointing in the direction of Smokvica. 'Now!'

From her balcony, Marija hugged her little brother and held her breath as she watched the procession of civilians trudge eastward on the narrow road leaving the village. She stifled a cry when she saw her father. He was neither healthy nor strong. She tried to comfort herself with the thought that at least it was not the middle of winter when his persistent cough seemed harsher. Soldiers marched behind them, rifles ready in case of a surprise attack from the Partisans. She watched until they disappeared from sight. She tightened her embrace on Ivan, grateful that the small boys remained.

As the days passed, news filtered back to the village that these men and boys were working for the Germans, rebuilding bridges, building bunkers. Marija missed her father. The house seemed soulless without his quiet encouragement and steadfast faith.

Where is he now? Will they feed them? she thought. There were now no men, young or old, in their village. She had heard that some had escaped and were in the hills. Is my father one of them? Is he safe? Marija could only hope.

15

The battle of Blato

Marija was studying the drifting clouds, trying to imagine what they resembled. Today they seemed menacing. All she could conjure from their shapes were monsters, not flowers or hearts. She was trying not to look down at the gruesome sight near the main piazza. Hanging from a tree with a noose tight around his bulging neck, his dark eyes lifeless, was Antun, one of the young Partisans. He had lived nearby and was an older brother of one of her friends. Antun had been captured near Vela Luka by the Germans and the Ustaše. He had been tortured and killed. His body had been hanging for three days, as a lesson.

She had heard whispers that trouble was brewing. There had been fighting in the neighbouring islands. Warplanes had spliced the sky. That morning she had seen the planes, roaring low and dropping bombs. So close. Too close. It looked as if they were bombing Vela Luka, the town on the western coast of her island, less than ten kilometres away.

Her cloud watching was disrupted by a grenade whizzing through the air and exploding at the feet of the two German soldiers who were standing on a corner across the road. She leapt up, her heart thudding, and peered down the street. Fighting commenced. The Partisans were attacking the invaders. Confusion spread. The children in the street scattered, searching for shelter. From her balcony she could see Mara Posinak running. Nine years old, Mara was slight with cropped dark hair. Her white dress flapped furiously as her little legs sprinted. Marija knew her family well. They lived on the opposite hill. Her father, Petar, had been the Mayor of Blato before the war. Like her own father, he had been taken by the Germans. Marija gripped the balcony edge and stood on her tip toes leaning as far over as she could.

'Run for cover, Mara,' she yelled. Mara pushed open the door of the nearest house. 'No!' screamed Marija. 'Not that one!'

Marija knew that Germans occupied that house. Startled, Mara looked at the soldiers standing inside with their guns cocked. She froze, squealed, then turned and ran back into the street. Bullets were whizzing past. Marija scrambled downstairs, pushed open the door and yelled.

'Quick! Mara, quick! In here!'

Marija grabbed her hand and dragged her in, slamming the door behind her. Outside the walls they could hear the explosions of grenades, the *rat-tat-tat* of gunfire. Shouts and screams filled the air. Marija's mother and siblings scurried down the steps and joined the girls hiding amongst the animals.

'What's happening?' Mara asked with her hands over her ears.

'It's the Partisans from Vis,' Marija's mother said as she brushed the straw away, finding them a place to sit. 'It looks as if they're trying to recapture the island.'

The Partisan brigades had amassed an armada of two thousand fighters, a third of them women. The battle was also raging in Smokvica. Chaos and confusion spread throughout the island as the Germans fought back. Marija had heard all of this from listening into whispered conversations between her mother and other local women. She also knew that families had fled, scurrying to get onto boats at Pregradica, trying to make their way to Lastova and Vis.

Day became night and still the battle continued. Mara, Marija and Žuva distracted each other by chatting and telling stories as they hid behind the high walls, ducking their heads when an explosion was close by. They shooed away the chickens that were scratching at the dirt and pecking at their toenails.

'Did you hear what happened to my brother Petar and me last week?' Mara asked.

The sisters shook their heads. Mara's face lit up as she recounted the story.

'Well,' she took a big breath and began. 'We were out at the farm. My mother had sent us with food. We always hide it in the cottage for the Partisans. In the hole in the wall as usual. Then we were playing a game outside and it got late.'

'Oh, no. The curfew,' murmured Marija.

They both knew how harsh the Germans were. If caught outside after curfew you would be shot, no questions asked.

'Yes. The curfew. We knew it was late but we weren't sure how late. We raced home. Petar had to keep waiting for me as he's bigger and faster. We thought we were safe.'

'And were you?'

'No. We were almost home and were running up our street when a soldier saw us. He yelled, "Stop or I will shoot"!'

'What did you do?' asked Marija, holding her breath.

'Panicked and kept running. There was no way we were stopping. He would've shot us anyway. We ran as fast as we could and prayed that he was a bad shot. And he was,' Mara smirked. 'Our mother nearly killed us too.'

Behind them the evening sky lit up with the phosphorescence of explosions. Artillery thundered. The streets were under heavy shellfire. Marija guessed that everyone in her village would be hiding, each hoping their own house would not be targeted. The fighting was fierce. It dragged on and on, and Marija lost track of time. She sipped on the water from the well and dozed when she could. She wondered whether Dobrila was out there, fighting in the streets. She blocked this thought from her mind.

After two days there was quiet. They waited until they could hear their neighbours whispering in the streets before they were brave enough to open the door and peek out. It was eerily still. She saw bodies strewn amongst the rubble. The Partisans had withdrawn.

With this battle over, Mara fled home and Marija and Žuva crept back to the farm, hoping to gather food. They averted their eyes as they tiptoed around the corpses scattered on the streets, on the roads, in the fields. Partisan bodies mixed with Germans. Some had limbs missing, congealed blood, faces disfigured. There was a stench of death. Marija quickly glanced at each female Partisan corpse they passed, hoping it would not be her sister.

'They look scary,' said Žuva. 'Their eyes are open. It looks as if they're watching us.'

'Well, do you want to go and close their eyes?' asked Marija. 'No!'

Marija had seen many dead bodies by now, but the horror never left her. The numbness. Yet she could not find it in her heart to really hate these men. Thoughts ran through her mind. Some look so young. I wonder if they really wanted to be here fighting. Were they like me, wishing they were still at school?

There were too many dead. Some were buried in the fields where they fell. Marija and her family were told later that three hundred Germans had been killed and five hundred were taken to Vis as prisoners. The Germans were not defeated but they had retreated to Korčula and the other towns. The Partisans celebrated a successful battle.

A friend of Marija's mother came to the house one morning and told her that the fighting was moving into Serbia and Tito's Partisans were gathering there. As the local Partisans attacked more, the Germans grew crueller but the locals could sense that the enemy were weakening as more and more American and British planes flew overhead. Planes with red stars too. Thousands of leaflets dropped from low-flying aircrafts scattered throughout the island and fluttered to the ground; leaflets from the Allies urging the enemy soldiers to surrender to the Partisans. The Germans were spread thin and retreating.

Eventually, the township of Blato was liberated by the Partisans and returned to the people.

'Be careful. Stay hiding. Don't go out,' the Partisans told the fearful villagers. 'The Germans are still here. We know they are on the other side of the island at Pupnat and near Korčula. They could still come back.'

As the Germans were fleeing there were still shootings and killings. Trucks of German soldiers still rattled through the island. The Partisans remained alert and guarded their village and their people as the battles continued to rage on the mainland.

Finally, in May 1945, the Germans surrendered in Yugoslavia. It was over.

But the hate was not over. The Yugoslav groups throughout the country persisted with vengeful bloodletting against each other. Gruesome acts were committed against their own countrymen, building on the hostility that would continue in the years that followed.

As the wounded shuffled home, they were met with buildings destroyed, farms stripped, animals slaughtered. The people were starving. It would be a long road to recovery. Marija watched from the balcony, listened for news that filtered through her neighbours and waited and waited, hopeful that her father and older sister would return.

∞

Finally, Paval came home. With the other surviving men, he limped into his village.

His clothes were torn, or maybe just worn, at his elbows and knees. The grey cloth hanging off his emaciated frame was discoloured with months of dirt. He paused at the edge of the main street leading into Blato, astounded that the trees remained unscathed, defiant amid patches of rubble. His eyes glazed over as he glanced at his countrymen, shadows of the men they were.

Putting his arm around the man next to him, he pointed. 'See Petar, we're home. We survived and so did the trees.'

His friend nodded shakily. Paval looked into the hollow eyes of the man who was once the Mayor of this town. He knew him well. Before the war they had spent many hours together discussing and making decisions for their community as Paval had been a councillor alongside him. Paval was in charge of the winery section of the Council as well as working his farm. Those times seemed so long ago. Like this town damaged by war, Petar too had been damaged, a head injury sustained during his captivity in Dubrovnik.

Paval patted his friend's bony shoulder and said, 'Go and find your family. They will want to know you are safe.'

He watched as his old friend and colleague shuffled with the other men towards the hillside on the northern edge before turning to hobble up the well-worn incline to his own house, unsure of what awaited. As he passed some rubble he wondered if his house would still be there. And his family? Turning the corner, he was relieved to see the large stone house, intact.

He knocked feebly at the door and tried to call out to those inside, but his voice was hoarse, barely a whisper. He knocked again. Finally, the door opened, and there stood his son. Paval could see the confusion in his boy's young eyes.

'Ivan, it's me, your Tata,' Paval said, as he stooped to wrap thin arms around his youngest child.

'*Mama, Marija, Žuva! Tata se vratio doma!*'

The family shrieked as they gathered around him. Tears streamed down their faces. He looked from face to face. Dobrila was still missing. He began to speak her name but his wife stopped him, shaking her head.

'No,' she said. 'We know nothing of her yet. We can just wait, like we waited for you.' Helping him up the steps into the kitchen, she pulled out a chair, motioning for him to sit.

'Are you hungry?' She asked as she looked in the direction of their empty cupboard.

Paval followed her glance and gently squeezed her arm. 'It's okay, Žuva. My stomach is used to not eating so don't worry. Just some water, please.' Marija watched him drink, holding the glass with hands calloused from hard labour. She tried not to look at his bare feet that were wrapped in bloodstained rags.

Her family tried to piece their lives back. Their father did not speak of what he had suffered. He simply told Marija and Žuva that he considered himself one of the lucky ones. He was alive. They waited and waited, until, finally, Dobrila returned, her *titovka* firmly planted on her head, her eyes still on fire. She had survived. Their family was whole again but life would never be as it was.

Bit by bit the village licked its wounds. During the war many families had fled to the safety of the refugee camps in Egypt—mainly women, children and the elderly, leaving the men to defend their land. Some returned. Some stayed in Egypt; Marija was told that they weren't convinced the war was over, and were fearful that the Germans would one day return. Some became refugees in other countries. Years of starvation took their toll on these frail frames. The bodies of the killed Partisans who were buried in the fields where they had fallen were exhumed and taken to the cemetery to be mourned and receive a deserving burial. Many were still missing. Damaged buildings were being rebuilt. Mines were still hidden, killing or maiming unsuspecting locals. Marija thanked her God again and again that her family and her home were spared.

16

A new nation emerges

Although the war was over, their country was on the path of change. Their new leader, Tito, set about establishing his communist government, striving to restore order and pull the splintered people together. The Monarchy had ended and, in 1945, Tito proclaimed the Federal People's Republic of Yugoslavia, uniting the six republics of Bosnia and Herzegovnia, Croatia, Macedonia, Montenegro, Serbia and Slovenia, as well as the two autonomous provinces within Serbia, of Kosova and Vojvodina. This republic was a mixture of ethnicities and faiths. With his communist government established, he still had the Catholic Church to contend with.

Marija looked and listened, fearful for her future, the future of her country and her beloved religion. Her school reopened but the war had stolen her education. She was now thirteen and her chance for attending the primary school was over. As she led their donkey on the daily ritual to labour on the farm, she would avert her eyes as she passed the school, not wanting to see the eager students with their books. It was unfair.

A favourite part of her day was late in the afternoon, after she had returned from the farm and before she was called on to help with the household chores. She would sit at the little table on the balcony and watch as the sun crept towards the horizon.

Sitting there one afternoon, she beckoned her little brother.

'Come, Ivan,' she said pulling a stool close to her, 'sit down. I'll help you with your reading.'

He didn't need to be asked twice. Racing over, he plopped on the stool beside her.

'I wish I could go to school every day,' he said as he opened the green soft-covered reading book, titled *Početnica I Čitanka* (Writing and Reading). He flicked the pages to the middle and pointed to a drawing. It was of three young children wearing felt hats with stars.

'They're wearing their titovkas,' he said.

He began to read, moving his index finger along, under each word: *Maricu asked Simo: 'Why do the soldiers of our army wear a red star on their caps?' Simo tells her.* He read slowly, hesitating at the harder words. *'The star is a sign of freedom. All who fight for freedom wear a red star. Our Partisans also fought for the freedom of the people. They expelled the—'*

Ivan paused, looking up to his sister for help.

'Traitors,' she said.

He nodded and continued. *'...expelled the traitors by fighting. A large number of fighters fell in the struggle for freedom. That's why we wear a star hat. We brought food to the fighters. That's why the Ustaše killed my brother Branko. Glory to the fallen freedom fighters.'*

Ivan turned to the next page with a flourish and grinned at Marija.

'You are such a good reader,' she said, patting him on the knee. 'I don't think you need any help.'

'No, stay.' He moved his stool closer, absorbing her calmness. After studying the picture of the man hammering nails, he began. *'Cedin's father is a worker in a nail factory. The Germans destroyed the factory. Our workers repaired it quickly. They know...'*[2]

As her brother kept reading aloud, Marija's mind drifted back to her school years. She remembered her last day of school at the end of Year One. She was worried when her teacher had asked to see her parents. I am good. What is this about, she'd wondered. But her teacher had told her parents that their daughter was very clever

2   *Početnica I Čitanka*, published in Zagreb, 1947.

and should skip a year level. She remembered the glow of pride as her father patted her on the head and said, 'You are a good student, Marija'. She looked back to the book her brother was reading. These books were so different; each page mentioned Tito, the Partisans or the war-memories still fresh in her mind. These students are seven or eight years old, she thought, wouldn't it be better if the books are about cats and dogs and flowers? Why fill the heads of the young with the ugliness of war?

'So do they still teach you about God?' she asked when Ivan had finished the page.

'Yes,' he said as he hurried onto the next story in this newly printed textbook. 'But something strange happened the other day.'

'What?'

'My friend in the Infant School told me they said, "Praise be Jesus" to the Sisters like they do every day. Just like I did when I was at that school. He said that there was a man from the government in the classroom who said in a serious voice that they should be brought up in a fighting spirit. The Sister has gone now.' Ivan seemed confused by this, but quickly lost interest and kept reading.

Marija had also heard of this. The two Sisters were told they were no longer needed as teachers at the Infant School. She had also heard that religious teachings had been stopped in the higher grades and would soon be banned from all schools. Her cousin, a priest, whispered to her parents that soon religion would only be taught through the churches.

'This is not good. People may be too scared to bring their children to the church to learn about God,' he had said.

Marija still remembered the uproar in September 1945 when most of the Catholic priests throughout Croatia had read out a letter from their bishop to their congregations. In it, the bishop demanded rights for the Catholic Church in this new Republic. Some priests had been too nervous to read it, fearful of possible repercussions. This letter had led to the imprisonment of their Church leader, the bishop. Marija didn't understand who had betrayed whom, but she felt the grumble of anger and the roar of reprisals. World War Two had ended but these were still uncertain times.

∽

The few shops in the village that were not damaged reopened, and the main street welcomed back the men, those who were left, to reclaim their seats out on the footpaths, leaving vacant spaces for fallen friends. Marija saw her father and their neighbour, Branko, deep in conversation, sitting slightly away from the others. She went over and joined them, sitting quietly beside Paval. She knew that many of the adults around her were still too nervous to discuss politics in this new 'equal' society. They never knew who was listening, and who they could trust.

'Paval, are you sure you won't join the Party?' Branko often asked this question.

'How many times can I tell you? No.'

'But life would be easier for you, for your family. You will be able to get a pension when you are older.'

'So, you're asking me to betray my God?' Paval shook his head. 'Never.'

Marija's father watched on as others benefited, but he often said to her that he didn't care as he maintained his daily ritual of attending Mass, working on his farm and thanking God that his family had survived the war.

Marija was also grateful that she worked on the farm and not for the Government, so she could attend church. She found comfort being surrounded by the congregation, heads bowed fervent in prayer. In the local church, the main altar was adorned by a marble sarcophagus that held the relics of St Vincenca, the protector of Blato. It was frequented by men with walking sticks and women in black, past caring and defiantly holding onto their faith. Marija would clasp her glass rosary beads and rest her eyes on the statue of Our Lady of the Rosary, then shut her eyes to block out any distractions, whispering her rosary again and again.

The population of her village continued to dwindle. Boats left, carrying hundreds of men who had survived the war. Some families followed to join them.

'So many from our village are leaving,' Marija said to her father as they sat on the bottom step at the end of a long day. 'I heard that another boat left today.'

She was tired. Her dress was streaked with dirt and sweat. Her boots were scuffed and bound together with string. In front of them was a large wooden basket half full of freshly picked bunches of grapes. Absentmindedly, Marija plucked some and nibbled on the dark purple fruit. She wiped her face as she tried to stop the juice from dribbling down her chin and further staining her already marked dress. It was the end of August and the days were long and hot.

'This has happened once before, you know. After the last big war—1924 or 1925—I think,' Paval said.

'Ah, the phylloxera,' Marija said, referring to the insect that destroyed many of the grapevines, paralysing the economy of her small town. This was before she was born but she had heard her father and his friends speak about it.

'I think one day over a thousand of our people left from Pregradica. Whole families gone.'

'Well, Tata, it's happening again. Our town is getting smaller and smaller.'

She watched the departures with curiosity. What faraway lands were they going to? She had listened to the talk of Australia and South America. She still often asked her father to tell her of his time in Australia. Broken Hill, where he had worked, sounded so strange, so different. But he had returned to Blato. These families were going for good. Many of the houses stood empty, like mausoleums, rooms full of memories and stories but with no one to tell them to the next generation.

She watched the proxy weddings. Young brides standing beside their cousins or neighbours, saying, 'I do', committing to strangers thousands of kilometres away. She wondered how these women felt. She thought they looked frightened.

'She's getting a chance of a better life,' her father would say about each of the brides. 'And at least it is with someone from our village.'

17

1951: Dressing for a new life

'I'll help you.' Žuva held up the white satin dress while Marija placed a hand on her sister's shoulder to steady herself as she stepped in. Together they guided the gown over her slim body, careful not to damage the outer layer of floaty chiffon. Marija threaded her arms into the long, sheer sleeves. Žuva then pulled the dress firm and fastened the row of covered buttons that moulded to the contour of Marija's spine. The neckline delicately circled the base of her neck. Žuva retrieved the gold chain necklace and arranged it at the front of the dress.

'How do you feel?' she asked her sister.

Marija chewed on her bottom lip, not answering. She was eighteen, almost nineteen. They were in their bedroom. Her mother and Dobrila were fussing over her too.

'What beautiful material this is,' her mother said, feeling the fabric. 'Mladen must be rich to have sent all this fabric over. There's nothing like this here. Australia must be a wealthy country.'

'The dressmaker did a good job. It fits you well.' Dobrila stood back and admired her younger sister.

'Lucky you're the same size as me, Žuva. It'll stay here for when you marry,' Marija said.

'No, don't talk about me. Today's your wedding day. You look like a princess,' Žuva beamed.

Dobrila lifted the veil off the bed and pinned it to the top of Marija's head.

'Use lots of pins, Dobrila. My hair's so fine, I don't want it to fall off while I'm walking down the street. Everyone will laugh at me.'

Dobrila checked that it was firm and then lifted the tulle in the air and watched as it floated back. Dobrila was twenty-five and had married five years ago. Her husband, Frank Petković, was a brave Partisan soldier from Blato who had been based on Vis.

'Everything going well?' Paval tapped at the half-closed door. He pushed it a little wider and as Marija turned to look at him he said, 'You look so beautiful!'

'Tata.' She moved towards him and hugged him.

'Careful. Don't let your dress catch on any of his buttons,' warned her mother.

Finding his voice, he whispered, 'Are you sure that you want to do this?'

'Of course, she wants to do this! What are you trying to do?' her mother, Žuva, said.

Small and bird-like, Žuva's hands fluttered as she fussed and fiddled with the white tulle veil, adding yet more pins to secure it.

'It has to happen,' she muttered, shooting a menacing glance at her husband. 'She will be better off. She will have food.'

Standing tall, Marija calmly smoothed the satin dress across her stomach and touched the simple gold chain that rested just below her neck. She swallowed and pursed her lips together before a ghost of a smile crept across her face.

'Yes, Mama is right.' Turning to look at herself in the mirror, she tucked a stray strand of hair behind her ear. 'Of course, I want to do this.'

'Well, that's fine, good.' Her father took a deep breath, exhaled and continued, 'You look like an angel'.

Marija's eyes misted.

'I still can't believe this is happening.' He cleared his throat, perhaps trying to hide the quaver in his voice. 'And you'll be leaving us soon.'

'I know. But it's good, isn't it?' She wanted his reassurance.

'Yes, yes. You'll have a better life. I know. Go and finish getting ready. I'll wait for you downstairs.'

Paval turned, shuffled unsteadily down the stone steps then lowered himself onto the bottom step. His head told him this was a good thing but why was his heart so heavy? Was it fear that she was leaving for a land so far away? He had heard stories of proxy marriages failing, leaving wives abandoned in faraway lands. He sighed at the thought of such uncertainty and of never seeing her again. Reaching into his pocket, his weathered hands fumbled with the rosary beads as he whispered his prayers, praying her life would treat her well. A better life than she had had until now.

18

A family character reference

While he sat waiting for his middle daughter and praying, his mind drifted back to that day he had returned from the farm and first heard about Mladen Gavranich, a young Blato man who had emigrated as a child with his family. A farmer seeking a bride from Blato.

'What do you think, Marija?' he'd asked after listening to Alena, who had told them about the man, Mladen, who was looking for a bride from his own village. He put his elbows on the table and looked into her eyes. 'Do you think you would like to go to Australia?'

'Well, I don't know.' She hesitated and glanced away. 'It's something I have never thought of before.'

'It's a long way,' he said.

'I've heard what the others have said. The girls who have gone. I know it's far away.' She looked unsure. 'But it's safe. And lots of opportunity. A rich country. You know—you've been there.'

'Yes, yes, I have.'

'You'll have more than you have here, Marija,' her mother said. 'At least you'll have food on the table every day. You won't be hungry.'

'But you're only almost eighteen. Are you ready to even think about this?' Paval studied her face.

'Tata, you know Mara—Mara Posinak? She's going and she's fifteen.'

'Yes, yes, she's only fifteen. If she can go, you can go,' her mother insisted. There was a lengthy pause before her mother continued,

'Marija, you should think seriously about it. These chances don't come every day.'

Marija looked across at her friend, Alena, and asked, 'What do you think?'

'Yes. I think you should go. Do you want me to get his address?' she replied, a grin spreading across her face.

Marija didn't reply but looked at her father earnestly. 'I don't know what to do. I think I could help you all. I could send money back to you.'

Paval shook his head. 'No, this is not about us. It's about you. Do you want to go?'

'Well, I don't know. I would like to know more about him. His nature. And… and of course, what he looks like. Well, just to see if he looks… all right.' She looked down. She seemed embarrassed to be enquiring about something that seemed trivial, so superficial.

'I'll get his address then.' Alena answered her own question. 'I can ask my mother for it.'

'I agree. Let's start and just write him a letter,' Paval said.

'What would I say?'

'Tell him about yourself and your family.'

'We will have to have some proper photographs taken, to send him. He'll want to know what you look like too,' her mother said.

'Tata, so you think this is a good idea?'

'No, not yet. I will ask the Anić family about him. His uncle lives here and they have family in Mossman.'

'Mossman? Where is Mossman?' Marija asked.

'It doesn't matter where it is. It's Australia. That's all that matters.' Her mother beamed.

Paval decided to visit the Anić family to gather background information on this possible husband for his daughter. As he sat beside Franko Anić on their patio looking over the town, Franko's wife, Frana, poured brewed coffee from the red enamel coffee pot. They waited for the ground beans to settle to sludge on the bottom of the small ceramic cups. It smelt bitter. It smelt good. He declined their offer from the little bowl of sugar that sat on the white tablecloth; sugar was scarce. They chatted for a little while, the weather, the economy, the shortages. Then he questioned Franko.

'Tell me about your nephew, Mladen Gavranich.'

'Aha. Alena has told you. Yes. He's looking for a bride. Alena told us that she thought of your Marija.'

'Mmm. What do you know about him, about his family?' Paval sipped at his coffee. It tasted even better than it smelt.

'My younger sister, Jaka, was his mother. She married Ivan Gavranić.' Franko started.

'Which Gavranić family? There are many Gavranić families in Blato.'

'Gavranić Rado. You would know of them. Ivan was the only boy, with many sisters. I don't know, six or seven. But I know Ivan was the only son.'

'And they are from here? From Blato?'

'Yes... yes, his family is from here. My sister married him in 1920. She left Blato with her young boys over twenty years ago.' His eyes watered. 'But... but she died three years ago.'

'How?' Paval questioned. 'From what?'

Franko shrugged. 'Who knows? She was young. Fifty-one. It happens.'

He urged Paval to eat one of the sweet *kroštule* that Frana had placed in front of him.

'*Jedi*, Paval. It is good.' Frana pushed the floral plate closer.

Ivan reached for the *kroštule* and bit into the sweet biscuit, the thin pastry crunching and dissolving in his mouth.

'Her husband, Ivan, went first to make money. I didn't know him well. A big man, Ivan Gavranić. My brother, Antun, went as well. To the same town around the same time.'

'Mossman? I heard that's the name of the town.' Paval did not really know where this town was.

'Yes, Mossman. It's the top of Australia somewhere. After a few years Antun bought a farm, sugarcane, together with Ivan but, you know, it didn't work out. Antun never said much, but I think he was a hard man to get along with, that Ivan.'

'Difficult, you say?' Paval shifted uneasily in his seat. 'And his son, Mladen? He is like his father?'

'Oh, no, Mladen is a good man. Antun and his wife, Ema, have the farm behind them and they know Mladen well—'

'Yes, I write to Ema when I can,' interrupted Frana. 'We're good friends. She speaks of the family. Don't worry. Mladen is nothing like his father. Nothing.' She sat down with them and poured herself a coffee.

'Does Ema know Mladen well?' Paval needed as much information as possible about this man who might marry his beloved Marija.

'Yes, of course. From when he was a little boy. Jaka and Ema were good friends here in Blato. The three of us were all good friends as children and then as sisters-in-law. Jaka and Ema went on the ship together to Australia.' She turned to her husband. He shrugged.

'It was a long time ago. I don't remember. I think that's right. Ema was on the ship and so was Jaka with her two boys, Ivan and Mladen. I think Mladen was three or four then.'

'He has a brother?'

'Yes.' Frana paused and looked away. 'Well, no. Very sad story. Ivan was twenty-one, a few years older than Mladen. A gentle man. Quiet—' said Frana.

'Frana, no.' Franko raised his hand to hush his wife. 'That broke his mother's heart.' Franko hesitated. 'My poor, poor sister,' he whispered.

Paval paused, unsure, and then continued 'But Mladen?'

Frana continued. 'Ema talks well of him. He works hard on the farm. He is very good at sport. I think they play tennis or something like that in Australia. Yes. Yes, he is a good man.'

Paval's heart relaxed a fraction. These were good people and would speak the truth.

'He has a younger sister. Mary is her name, I think. Ema speaks well of her too. So that's a good thing,' Frana added.

He had heard enough. They sat a while longer and spoke of politics and the grape season.

19

A message from Australia

The first step of this proxy marriage process was the exchange of photographs. As there was no professional studio on the island, Marija travelled to the mainland city of Split. Mladen's uncle, Franko Anić, accompanied her. She was excited to board the ferry and although she desperately wanted to stand on the deck in the briny breeze, she remembered her mother's instructions and stayed inside. That morning she'd taken particular care with her clothing and her hair, so she perched on the bench near the window, facing forward so she could watch the approaching mainland, pushing her nose as close as possible without messing her neat hairstyle. The cliffs rising up behind the city looked so severe and almost bare, she thought.

As she stepped off the ferry she asked if they could look at the city.

'No, there's no time,' replied Franko. 'We need to find this man and get these photographs done in time to be back for the return ferry.'

From the harbour it was not too far. They climbed several winding streets that zigzagged up the slope behind the bell tower. The photographer greeted them at the door of his little whitewashed house and ushered them in.

I'll wait out here,' Franko said.

The photographer seated her on the green cloth-covered stool in his dusty back room. Her hair was swept off her forehead, tucked neatly behind her ears and resting on her shoulders. Her outfit was elegant but simple, a pale blue dress with tightly smocked shoulders. Her gold chain, earrings and borrowed brooch completed the picture.

'Don't look at the camera,' the photographer said. 'Look over my right shoulder into the corner of the room. Turn your head slightly and smile. No, don't smile too much.'

So many instructions. She coughed nervously as she fidgeted, smoothing the wrinkles in her dress and crossing and uncrossing her ankles.

'Don't worry about where you put your hands and feet. I'm only photographing your head and shoulders,' he reassured her.

How many dinar will this cost Franko? Or rather how much will it cost his nephew, Mladen, she wondered.

The photographer knew his trade. When the photographs were finally developed and delivered, her thought was: Is that me? I look so glamorous! Do I really look this pretty in real life? Marija studied the image of this young woman with a captivating half smile and alluring dark eyes. Her image.

Mmm, this photo will definitely do! How can he not want to marry me when he sees this? she thought. She posted the photographs and waited nervously for photographs of Mladen to arrive.

∞

'Marija, Marija, a letter for you,' her sister screamed, racing into the house gripping a thick envelope with blue and red stamps in the corner.

Marija came out from the kitchen and she dried her hands on the apron.

'Hurry up,' urged Žuva. 'Open it, or I will.'

Marija hesitated, fearful. She wondered what this Australian man would look like. What if he's ugly? Would her mother still insist on this marriage? Holding her breath, she ripped open the envelope. Inside was a letter and two photographs. Marija pulled out the photographs first and cautiously turned them over.

'Žuva, look at him.' Marija's eyes sparkled.

'Oh, Marija, he's definitely not ugly.'

They both studied the photographs of the young man. In one he was standing and wearing a double-breasted suit, his face serious. The second photograph featured only his head and shoulders. In this photograph he wore a half smile.

'Yes, he'll do. I'm going to Australia. Goodbye, Žuva.' Marija joked and waved to an invisible audience as she walked into the kitchen holding the photographs. 'Mama, do you want to look? I would like to marry him!'

Her mother turned, her face beaded with sweat as she stirred the soup on the stove.

'He hasn't seen your photographs yet. What if he doesn't like you?' she warned her daughter.

'He'll like me,' retorted Marija, frowning.

'Of course, he will,' Žuva followed her into the kitchen.

'Show me.' Marija's mother peered through her cataracts at the two photographs. 'Mmm. Very good looking. You like the look of him?'

The knot in Marija's stomach loosened slightly. She knew that the opportunity was too good to turn down. A ticket to Australia. A ticket to leave Yugoslavia. A husband. After the war, many men had left and many of those who remained were damaged. At last, she had an image of the man she was to marry. She sighed with relief. At least he wasn't ugly.

'Yes, Mama. I *do* like the look of him.'

'She's getting married. She's getting married. Off to Australia!' Žuva danced around Marija, grabbing her hands and skipping with her. 'I wonder if he's got your photos yet?' she giggled.

'You just sent the professional ones from Split,' her mother stated rather than questioned as she returned to her stirring.

'Um…' Marija hesitated, looking to her sister for support.

'What, Marija? What did you do?' Her mother scowled.

The two girls looked away.

'Marija?' she repeated, her voice louder.

'Tell her,' said Žuva, stifling giggles.

'Well, I… well I thought that I would put in some other photos too.'

'And?'

'I sent him the photo of me on the beach at Pregradica.'

Her mother stopped stirring the soup and glared at her.

'That photo in your swimming clothes? The one where you can see all your legs?'

'Uh-huh,' Marija mumbled.

'Marija!' She turned back to the stove and stirred furiously. 'If he says no, it's your fault.'

'Don't worry, Mama, he'll love the photo. I look good.'

And he did. The photographs did the trick. A flurry of letters crossed between the continents. Short letters from Mladen. Long ones from Marija.

Marija couldn't contain her excitement every time she received a, very infrequent, letter from Mladen. The flimsy envelope that arrived in today's post was edged with the red and blue border, and in the corner was a blue rectangle with the words 'BY AIR MAIL' and 'PAR AVION' in smaller letters underneath. She went to a quiet corner near the chickens and sat down. The stamps had a profile of a man with rather large ears. Her father had told her that he was their king. She was puzzled that they had a king in Australia. She took her time as she extricated the letter, smoothing it out on her lap before starting to read. Mladen was not a prolific letter writer, and when he did write, they were short sentences about the farm, sometimes about the weather, and always about all the sports he played. At the end of this one she read:

Come and live with my family. See if you like me and then marry me here. I have seen some of the Italians do this in Mossman.

Is this a formal marriage proposal? she wondered. She read it again just to be sure. Yes, she thought, it was definitely a proposal. She knew her family would not be surprised but she didn't want to rush inside and tell her parents immediately. She wanted to savour the moment, this delicious secret, and wait for the right time to break her news. All her family would be together at lunch on Sunday. Her sister, Dobrila and her husband Frank would be visiting from Korčula. Could she wait that long? She decided she could.

Marija looked at everyone gathered around the table. As usual, her father was at the head of the table, her little brother at the end and her mother and younger sister on one side. Dobrila and Frank squeezed next to Marija on the other side. An old stone cooking pit in the far corner kept the room warm, especially during the bitter winters. The cracks in the stone walls were almost disguised by the many years of soot and dust from the fire. Floral drapes hung to the cement floor to hide the well-used pots that were stacked neatly in the tight little corner. To the right was a tall wooden cabinet, the glass panels decorated by curtains with cream lace edging. This familiar room was the hub of the old house. Paval poured glasses of wine made from their grapes. They all spoke over each other, hands waving, except for Paval who, as usual, was thoughtful and quiet. Breaking through the commotion, Marija spoke up.

'Mladen has asked me to marry him!'

The chatting and the hand-waving stopped as all heads swivelled in her direction. Her sisters jumped to their feet and rushed over to smother her with hugs.

'Oh, Marija, this is such good news!' Her mother cried. 'What did he say?'

'He asked me to come to Australia and live with his family. He said that if I like him, we can get married.'

Amidst the laughs and chatter Marija's father was silent, considering the news.

'You realise, Marija, there is a problem.'

The women paused.

'What problem?' Marija asked.

He took a deep breath and exhaled slowly. 'Yugoslavia is a Communist country.' He drummed his fingers on the wooden table as he collected his thoughts and then explained to her. 'You are not free to come and go as you please. You cannot just leave this country. From what I know, you must be married to Mladen before you can go.'

'That's not a problem,' retorted Žuva, his wife. 'It will just have to be a proxy marriage. It happens all the time. You must write and tell him this. I'm sure he will still want to go ahead with the wedding.'

'Marija,' her father continued, 'if he agrees to a proxy marriage, this is a big decision. Going to Australia.'

'Yes. I know, Tata.' Marija said.

'There will be no father, no mother, no sisters, no little brother—'

'She knows. She knows,' his wife interrupted, annoyed, her eyes narrowing. 'What are you doing? Are you trying to talk her out of it?'

'It's a long way away. You might never see us again.' He was determined to ensure Marija realised what may lie ahead.

'I don't think I could ever be brave enough,' ventured her younger sister as she sipped her pinkish wine. 'I think I will just stay here and stay poor.'

'You know that it's a proxy marriage, so when you see him, if you don't think you can live the rest of your life with him, you can annul the marriage straightaway. That will be allowed in the eyes of our church,' her father explained.

'Paval, no. You can't tell her that.' Looking at Marija, her mother said, 'You must make it work. It would bring shame on our family if it didn't. You can't come back.' She folded her arms across her chest. 'And the church has nothing to do with it, Paval.'

'I know. It's all right. Don't worry. It will work. It *will* work,' Marija repeated, telling herself not to be afraid. She had made her decision months ago when she first saw Mladen's photograph. She *would* make this marriage work. She gazed out the small kitchen window. All she could see were the houses of the village creeping up the hill.

'This is my chance. I think it's my destiny.'

20

1951: The wedding

Marija paused at the top of the stone steps that hugged the outside wall leading down to the courtyard of her home. Her eyes rested on her father, who was sitting on the bottom step. She could hear him mumbling his prayers softly as he clutched his worn rosary beads. She thought that today he somehow looked older and tired, his shoulders sagging and his hair thinning. He was wearing his best and only dark suit, hidden beneath his black winter coat.

'I'm ready,' she said eventually, noticing that her voice sounded distant, not like her own.

Holding her dress in one hand she cautiously descended the uneven steps, careful not to let the chiffon sleeves catch on the sharp edges of the stone wall. Her father stood and took her hand to help her down the last few steps. With his spare hand he pushed open the towering door that led onto the street. They stepped outside. The family followed. They walked, a procession, to the town hall. It was Friday, late afternoon. The children were out from school and surrounded them, skipping.

'A wedding! A wedding!' they yelled.

The locals stepped in behind and followed the family, passing the town piazza and the church.

'It's not fair,' muttered her mother, as she glanced left at the gothic building that dominated the town piazza, casting a cool shadow over them.

'Shh, Žuva,' Paval said to his wife and stared straight ahead.

'People will hear you.'

'I don't care.'

'Well, you should. It's a small town. We must be careful,' he whispered, as his eyes darted from side to side. 'Our leaders, our government are communist now. We must not forget that.'

'I just wish our daughters could marry in our church, just as we did and our parents and their parents.'

'Darling, Žuva, it's not legal,' he said. 'We must be patient. With time, things may change.'

When they reached the town hall, Marija hesitated under the arches of the doorway. She could see her proxy groom waiting inside, standing at the far end of the dark cavernous room, snatches of the fading light struggling to penetrate the opaque windows. It smelt musty, of papers and ink, nothing like the incense and candles of her church. Her groom wore a white shirt and black tie, and a dark double-breasted suit. He was fidgeting with his tie as he waited near the long desk, scattered with papers.

He looks nothing like my Mladen, who's waiting for me in Australia, Marija thought, her mind going back to the photographs he had sent her. Photographs of a handsome man with crinkly dark hair, a broad face and smiling eyes. A man she had never met but was marrying today. Waiting for her here was Kuzma, Mladen's first cousin, who lived in this village. His proxy. She tightened her grip on the cluster of flowers in her gloved hands and walked towards him with steady steps. Kuzma straightened. This was a serious task, standing in for his cousin at his wedding.

'Are you nervous?' he whispered to her when she reached his side.

'No, not at all.' She looked up at him: 'Excited'.

'You look beautiful. My cousin is a lucky man.'

She blushed. Although the village was small, she didn't know Kuzma well. They waited for the official who was shuffling papers at his desk. He was an old man with grey hair and bushy eyebrows. He gathered what he needed and stood before them peering through his glasses at the single page in his leathery hands and began reading the marriage vows in a surprisingly strong voice, pausing for emphasis at certain parts and glancing at the couple over the top of his spectacles. The bride and proxy groom repeated their vows. Behind them sat Marija's family. Her mother wept noisily, dabbing her white handkerchief at her watery eyes. Marija was unsure whether it was from sadness or joy, perhaps both.

As Kuzma slid the golden band onto her left ring finger, Marija held her breath. She wasn't sure how to feel. Excited? Scared? Overwhelmed? Yes, she decided she definitely felt overwhelmed. They signed the papers, and the ceremony was over. It was a blur. She was married. That was it. They walked out slowly and posed in front of the town hall for photographs. Marija held her bouquet close to her chest to hide her rapid breaths as she lined up with the five men in black suits, a mixture of her relatives and Mladen's. No one smiled. The children played in the background, running up and down the steps. It was over. No wedding reception. No speeches. No gifts. Just a small get-together.

At the end of the evening, Marija thanked her husband's cousin and bid him goodnight. He leant forward and kissed her on both cheeks.

'You will make a good wife for my cousin, I am sure. This lucky cousin I don't know.'

'Thank you, Kuzma. I am the lucky one.' She truly believed this.

She told her family to make their way home as she hooked her arm through Žuva's.

'Let's walk for a bit. I'm not ready for sleep,' she said.

They wandered through the quiet main street, and passed the large school building.

'Well, Žuva, we didn't get a chance to finish school here, did we?'

'No. The war stopped all that. You're so smart, Marija. What would you have been if you could have finished school?'

'Hmm.' She stopped in front of the school. It looked as if it were asleep, the long windows, like eyes, were closed. Peaceful. She remembered sitting on the steps with Žuva the day the war came to their town. It seemed so long ago.

'Even if I had finished school here, I don't think I could ever have gone to high school on the mainland. Our parents could never have afforded that. But in my dreams, I think maybe a teacher, a home economics teacher. I love sewing and cooking, but especially sewing.'

'Yes, I could see you as a sewing teacher.'

They resumed their stroll.

'Oh, Marija, do you remember that time when you were little and you took our mother's material. The material she was going to use to make my dress?'

'How could I forget? I cut it up and made dresses for my doll. And then got scared and hid them under our bed.'

'Our mother yelled so loudly at you and smacked you so hard when she found it, the woman next door thought you were being killed.'

'That's right and our dear neighbour made our mother even madder when she told her that she should be happy to have such a talented daughter who could sew so well.'

The girls giggled as they remembered their mother and her flushed face screeching at Marija for cutting up her precious material.

'Yes, no dress for me but at least your doll looked nice.'

'For me to be a teacher—that's all gone'

'But look,' Žuva turned her sister's hand over and admired her ring. 'You're married.'

'It seems so strange, but yes,' she looked down at the gold band, 'I'm married'.

A few people walked past them wishing her well. Her white dress shimmered in the patchy moonlight.

'Do you know how long it takes to get your visa and everything you need to go?'

'Yes. Months and months. I hear almost a year, sometimes more.'

'So *slow*, this government.'

'Shh.' Marija glanced behind her, to check if the passers-by were out of earshot. 'I wish I could just go now—I'm ready.' She looked around her at her small village. 'It's so silly waiting. I just know the young boys are going to tease me and ask me where my husband is.'

'Well, you can tell the truth. He's waiting for you in Australia. And tell them how lucky you are. You're going to Australia but they're staying here in Blato.'

'I'm going to tell them I'm going to Australia where I can eat as much bread as I want.'

'Stop it, Marija.'

'But, Žuva, I hope that's true. It's what I've heard.'

The thought of bread made her happy. They walked the length of the street and then turned right to curve back up to their home, passing the stone houses, some in darkness, others with lights glimmering through the shutters. She knew most of the inhabitants. Everyone had lived here with their families for generations. Her mother and father's parents, grandparents, great grandparents.

They pushed open the large door to their property, not wanting to wake anyone, and quietly climbed the steps into the dark house. Žuva unbuttoned the back of her sister's dress and helped her step out of the garment. Marija ran her fingers along the smooth fabric. Even in the dark it seemed to catch a moonbeam and glimmer. Such beautiful material, she thought, as she folded it carefully and gave it to her sister.

'I won't need this dress in Australia. You have it for when the time comes for you to marry.'

Žuva hugged her. The young women stood there for what seemed like an eternity. What an extraordinary wedding day. She wondered if her husband had remembered that today they were getting married. Will he have had a drink to toast them? she wondered; and what time is it in Australia now?

A few days later Marija ambled down the main street. It was early afternoon, and the town was nearly deserted. Most people were home having their midday meal. She tried to stroll but it was hard to keep her legs from striding out as her heart hammered in her chest. Her father had organised a very special event for her, but it was an event that could go terribly wrong. She had hardly slept the night before. She kept walking until she was at the edge of the village, near a small church. She walked on a little while before looking over her shoulder and ducking into a nearby street to double back. She was wearing her oldest dress, a patched farm dress. She didn't want to attract any attention. Reaching the church, she glanced over her shoulder, pushed the door open slightly and slid in. The windows of the small building were shuttered; she stood still, waiting for her eyes to adjust to the darkness.

'Ah, good. You're here,' a deep voice said from the shadows. 'Did anyone see you?'

She shook her head.

'Then come here and we'll do this quickly.'

In front of the simple altar of this humble church stood her cousin, Don Ivo Protić. He had returned to Blato as the chaplain a few years ago. Beside him stood Kuzma, her proxy groom.

'We'll now make this marriage sacred in the eyes of our God.'

Marija stood beside Kuzma, facing the priest. Everyone quickly said their parts. If caught, no one could imagine the consequences, but Maria had heard she could be prevented from leaving.

Don Protić completed the service with the sign of the cross and smiled.

'There, Marija, God now recognises your marriage. The sacrament has been completed.'

'Thank you. Thank you, so much.'

'Now go. Leave separately. May God go with you.'

Marija struggled to keep from singing to herself as she returned home with a spring in her step.

21

A chat after church

It took many months to finalise all the paperwork required for Marija's journey abroad. Australia needed a health certificate and a visa. As Marija waited for the paperwork to be processed, she kept working on their little farm, helping her parents. She was also right about the young boys in the village. They did tease her.

'You've been married for ages. Where's your husband?'

She'd shoo them away, after calling back, 'Waiting for me in Australia with buckets and buckets of bread! Hah!'

She watched as other young women trod the same path as her, many of the young Blato men in Australia writing to their families, asking them to find brides.

One Sunday Marija was walking home from church and saw Mara Posinak who was also a proxy bride. Although only fifteen, she had married Antun Bačić in December 1951 and was also waiting for her paperwork. Linking arms, they wandered down the main street, linden trees shading them, nodding to the people they passed. The street was busy at this time of day.

'You know, we'll be related.' Mara told Marija.

'I heard that. Tell me again how that is.'

'Well, it's complicated and I get confused. Your father-in-law's sister, Marija Gavranić, is my husband's mother. My mother-in-law. Marija Bačić.'

Marija nodded. 'So, my husband, Mladen, and your husband, Antun, are cousins.'

'Yes, through his father,' Mara said, 'and your late mother-in-law's mother, Jaka, and my mother, Žuva, are sisters. They're Anić.'

'So, you're Mladen's cousin too!' Marija's face lit up.

'Yes! Your husband is *my* cousin through his mother and my *husband's* cousin through his father. So, he's a cousin to *both* of us. This is so confusing,' Mara said.

Marija laughed. 'Yes, too confusing. This is what happens in a small village—we're all related.'

'No.' Mara's voice was edged with concern. 'You understand that I am not related to my husband. *We're* not cousins.'

Marija kept chuckling. 'I understand, don't worry, I understand. But it's nice that we'll be related. I've married your cousin.'

'Yes. Antun's farm is at the top of Australia too. I hope we see some of each other when we get there.'

Marija hugged her. 'I'm sure we will. We'll make sure of it.'

'Tell me, did you have a secret church wedding?' Mara whispered. 'I heard talk.'

Marija looked around her before whispering back, 'Yes, but please don't tell anyone. It could be dangerous.'

'So you're legal in God's eyes,' Mara said, almost enviously.

'You should do it too. They don't write it in the church records; the Party has no way of finding out. Just do it when no one sees you, and in one of the smaller churches.'

'Maybe, but I think it's too dangerous,' Mara said as they reached the end of the street. 'Will I see you at the dance tonight?'

Mara loved to dance, and with the war over, there were many dances in the halls.

'No, Mara.' Marija laughed. 'I don't go to the dances. I'd better run home. Žuva will be waiting for my shoes so that she can go to church.'

'All right. Well, bye, new dear cousin.' Mara kissed her on both cheeks as was the custom, and hurried home.

22

1952: Goodbye Blato

It had been over a year since Marija's wedding when, finally, the documents had progressed through the various offices of her government. The papers had been stamped and signed while she had waited patiently. This process could not be hurried. But now it was time. She was leaving the next day.

Although it was March, the winter chill lingered. Marija shivered in the cool shadows in her bedroom as she folded her few items of clothing and placed them in the brown suitcase that lay open on her bed; and her meagre dowry, one embroidered tablecloth folded neatly and a few doilies, which was all that could be spared. Her rosary beads and bible were tucked in one corner. She closed the lid and clipped it shut, wrapping a belt around the suitcase as one of the clasps was not secure, and pulling it tight before fastening the buckle. This small suitcase had a long journey ahead of it.

Everyone was busy. She was alone. She checked her papers one more time. Opening her blue travel document, she glanced at the photograph stapled there before closing it, her throat constricted. She quickly slid it into the safety of her white handbag. She was ready.

Sitting on the bed, she took the time to survey her bedroom, the room she shared with her siblings. She had lived in this old stone house her entire life. It was basic but strong. Despite them now living in a communist country, religion was still very important in this house. Holy pictures hung from the walls alongside framed photos of Tito. The rooms smelt of smoke, sweetened by the fragrance of drying grapes and plums. She thought about what awaited her. It would be a long trip, and now it was time to go. Nothing waited for her here.

She had visited her sister Dobrila in Korčula and spent a week with her there. Marija had realised that the only meal she knew how to cook was *zeje,* the vegetable dish of silverbeet and potatoes and any other green vegetables from their garden. Their source of food was from their farm and they very rarely had anything else to eat. Dobrila had been tasked with teaching her younger sister other dishes so that she could cook for her new husband. Marija had then said her final goodbye and thank-you to her eldest sister. All the cousins had been farewelled. Her friends had been embraced. Her neighbours Marinka and Ivan, who lived close by were travelling on the same ship, emigrating with their little family to Australia, to Sydney. Her father had spoken with them and organised Marija's cabin to be adjoining. Marija guessed that they would understand her father's anxiety.

'Yes, yes. Sure. We'll watch over her all the way. There's no need to worry,' Ivan had reassured Paval. Marinka had put her arm around Marija and smiled at Paval.

Stepping out onto the balcony, Marija's skin warmed under the soft sunshine. Sprawled before her was her town: the picturesque church on the crest of the hill opposite, on her left was the steeple of her own dear church. The line of trees bordering the main street were a splash of green dividing the town while wisps of smoke curled from neighbours' chimneys. The occasional bark of a dog or sound of hooves on the cobbles disturbed the peace of the morning. Glancing over, she could see Jelkica, her neighbour, hanging the washing on the line strung up on her balcony. Jelkica saw her and the women waved at each other.

Nothing had changed for many years, although far fewer people lived here now. There were more empty houses; so many of her neighbours had left, some for America, some for Australia. Some worked hard and returned, but only some. Most stayed in their new countries. This would be her too. She would have a new country. Her mother's words echoed in her mind and she knew that no matter who or what awaited her in Australia, there was no coming back. She was leaving the next day—on a one-way ticket.

23
Rattling through Yugoslavia

Awakened from her reverie by passengers jostling and pointing excitedly, Marija spotted the bustling port of Split in the distance. Towering above the city was the solitary bell tower, undamaged from the war. A symbol of hope. As the ferry approached the city, Marija could see the wide esplanade that fronted the busy harbour and the imposing sandstone walls and gates of the Diocletian's Palace. Our history is with the Romans, she thought ironically. Our history has been with so many different cultures.

Marinka found her.

'Collect your suitcase and come with us,' she said.

Eventually the ferry moored at the far end of the harbour and the gangplank was lowered, secured to the wharf by thick twisted ropes. Marija followed Marinka, her husband, Ivan, and their two excitable children, Tomislav and Anja. Holding the railing with one hand, she struggled to carry her suitcase and handbag in the other as she walked down the gangway, stepping carefully in her sturdy brown sandals; they were worn but well cared for. She felt guilty wearing them as she had shared them with her sister Žuva. They only had the one pair between them and they were their Sunday church shoes. Marija would go to the early morning Mass and Žuva would go to the evening one. What will Žuva wear now? Marija wondered, surprised she hadn't thought of this earlier.

'We need to find the station to catch the train to Genoa,' Ivan said.

Hurrying down the footbridge, the passengers blended into the masses on the wharf of this once beautiful but still damaged, city. Memories of the war confronted their senses. Charred remains of proud buildings waited patiently to be rebuilt. Here and there were those that had escaped the wrath of bombs or mortars. New buildings were emerging amidst the destruction.

The wharf was a hive of activity. Long wooden trestle tables were laden with glass bottles of golden olive oil, stacks of freshly baked loaves of bread and leafy green vegetables. Women in mourning black with tired faces and dark headscarves stood, hands on hips, guarding their produce. There were many women in black, widows after the war. Some women were bustling through the market carrying woven baskets crammed with their purchases. Men with fedora hats loitered at the tables lining the pavement, watching the activity, smoking and talking.

Marija thought back to the last time she had seen this city, two years earlier when she was almost eighteen, to have her photographs taken. That seemed so long ago. So much had happened since then.

Staying close, they followed the crowd and made their way towards the station adjacent to the wharf, to the train that would transport them to Italy. Marija's pulse quickened. She had never been on a train before. On the grey steel tracks stood the charcoal-black train, with its long line of carriages, but the presence of armed soldiers of their national regime made Marija feel uneasy.

Rushing to find their carriages, passengers checked numbers with their tickets. The steps into the carriage were steep so children were lifted in and the elderly helped up. Frail women in black dresses with faces ravaged by time and war clung to the arms of their adult children. Men in loose suits carried bulky brown suitcases secured with wide belts and shouted impatiently at their wives and children. Women in heavy coats with large buttons herded children and constantly checked behind them, ensuring they had left nothing behind.

Once on the carriage, Marija relaxed and rested on the hard wooden seat. With her suitcase tucked safely underneath and her handbag secure on her lap, she took time to look around her. The family settled themselves and the children squealed with excitement, jumping up and down. More passengers crowded onto the train. A sense of urgency pervaded the scene. Travellers like herself mingled with stern-faced soldiers and peasants tightly clutching clucking chickens under their arms.

Ivan slid the grimy window down to encourage the cool evening breeze to dilute the stale air inside. Marija cupped her chin in her hands and rested her elbows on the wooden sill and watched and waited.

With a piercing whistle the train soon coughed and spluttered to life, grey plumes of smoke spewing from its smokestack. Out of the station it lumbered carrying its human cargo.

As they left the city and rattled through the countryside, Marija watched curiously as the train travelled through the large collective farms. The land and the people looked grey and grim, silhouetted in the fading sunlight. Rusted abandoned locomotives captured from the German Army and riddled with bullet holes stood on the sidings, a reminder of the cheerless decade before.

Marija, whose life had been centred on her small island of Korčula, was fascinated by this large country. Wide-eyed, she gazed out as the countryside rolled by. Removing her sandals, she curled and uncurled her toes in her thin stockings. Marinka unpacked some food and fed her children, inviting Marija to join them.

Shaking her head, she said, 'No, thanks, I'm not hungry. I'm watching my country.'

Yugoslavia seemed like such a large land, complex and varied in both its history and its landscape. As the train rumbled inland, the sheer Dalmatian cliffs and the deep blue sea were left far behind. Through the mountains of northern Yugoslavia, the train clattered, stopping at stations, loading and unloading luggage and passengers, platforms buzzing with activity. The train carved its way through the thick humid forests of Slovenia and rattled past farms peppered with the occasional spring blush of flowers. The scenery was so different from her own island. Ancient churches high on hilltops dotted the landscape, many scorched and desecrated.

Her thoughts drifted back to her father and the many hours they had spent together discussing their homeland. Her homeland, so loved and yet so complicated. A deeply religious man, a staunch Catholic, she remembered his anguish of being under communist rule. They often spoke of President Tito and the role he had played during the war, uniting the Partisans to fight the invaders. What a brave leader he was and what a disciplined guerrilla army he had led. How hard they had fought against impossible odds. Her father's eyes would cloud over when he spoke of the internal conflict, the anger and fighting between the rival groups in Yugoslavia—the communist Partisans against the royalist Četniks and the fascist Ustaše. Neighbours murdering neighbours, betrayals and deep burning anger. So much mistrust.

'You know that we probably murdered more of each other than the Italians and Germans did,' he told her.

As a child she understood little and now as a young adult she realised she still understood little.

'Why so much hatred between us? Can't we all just be Yugoslavs?' he would softly ask. 'Our country has suffered too much pain.'

She would nod in agreement. And then they would discuss their beloved God and the world would seem a brighter place.

It was a long trip and Marija noticed the passengers around her drifting off to sleep on their narrow wooden benches as the train slowly rattled through the night. She was weary too, and shifted in her seat to get comfortable. Eventually, they reached the border and, with a protesting screech of wheels, the train shuddered to a halt, waking her and her fellow passengers. They had arrived in Trieste, a city with a history almost as convoluted as Yugoslavia's. Like so many of the European countries at this time, borders were fluid, fought over and bargained with. A beautiful Italian gem on the seaside, Marija had been told that Trieste was a neutral state under United Nations protection, divided between the United States, British Allies and Yugoslavia.

'We are in Trieste and need to change trains. Have your papers ready,' instructed Ivan.

Marija blinked the sleep from her eyes, stretched her aching body and buckled on her sandals. As she retrieved her documents from her handbag, her father's words echoed in her mind.

'Do not lose these,' he had told her many times before she left.

Walking nervously through passport control, Marija was jostled by the other travellers. Self-consciously she pulled her old coat closer to hide her plain dress as she watched the fashionable Italian women with their elegant fur coats and high heels. The train station was rowdy. Vendors with their carts displayed plump oranges and bottles of wine in wicker baskets. Intrigued, she listened to their shouts, surprised that she could remember snippets of the language taught to her at school when the Italians had occupied their village. She found her seat on the next train to resume her journey.

Finally, after many tiring hours of sitting as the train made its way through the northern Italian countryside, passing towering snow-capped peaks, rustic villages, fields of spring flowers and vast blue lakes, they arrived at their destination, Genoa. The real adventure was about to begin.

24

Farewell Europe

The scene that greeted Marija's eyes was chaotic. Genoa was an ancient city wedged between the Mediterranean Sea and the sharp mountains behind. A sixteenth-century lighthouse guarded the entry to the port. The landscape ran vertically from the harbour to the mountains. Crooked streets fed into the harbour; the wharves congested with people. Shady-looking men leaned nonchalantly against the grubby shop walls, in front of which were open-air stalls, cramped close on the narrow streets and footpaths. Matronly looking women were cooking over steaming pots or selling trinkets to the never-ending flow of passengers and sailors. Following the war, Genoa was an open city and was flooded with illegal immigrants. The air, heavy with the odour of seasoned brick and sawdust, intermingled with the salty air and the seductive fragrance of sizzling fish and deep-fried vegetables.

'Are you hungry?' Ivan asked.

Without waiting for a reply, he reached into his coat pocket and handed some lira to the woman cooking at one of the stalls, receiving some deep-fried sardines in return. Inhaling the savoury oily smell, Marija gratefully nibbled on them as she walked, realising that she had not eaten for many hours. They were small and tasty, like the ones she had eaten at home. Crunching the tails, she licked the salt off her lips.

'Mmm, they're good.'

Ivan stayed close to her side, his face grim with paternal concern. As the family walked along the streets, she noticed heads turning, some men openly leering at her.

'Stay close to us. It's not safe for a young woman like you here in this city. It's different from home,' Ivan said.

This little group from Blato stayed with the crowds from the train, as they walked towards where the liner was docked. Below the weathered timber boards of the wharf, the turbulent sea sloshed and slammed against the shell-encrusted pylons. Marija gripped her suitcase and handbag, treading carefully so as not to trip.

Swirling like the current below, the men, women and children surged forward. This ship could not be missed. It towered above the buildings on the wharf, casting a shadow that stretched up to the alleyways. It was magnificent. The MV *Australia* looked new and modern, its hull pearly white, encircled by a thin blue stripe. The funnels were canary yellow with a blue top and the Italian flag was proudly fluttering from the mast.

Marija glanced up at the flag and flinched, her thoughts flashing back to when she was nine years old and first saw this flag of the occupier. Although the images were blurred by the years, she vividly remembered how she felt. Her chest tightened as she recalled the day the army had marched into her town. It was not so long ago that her country was at war with Italy; yet here she was in Italy, about to board this grand Italian vessel. Locking her memories away, she forced herself to think only of what lay ahead.

The ship was truly beautiful as it stretched the length of the harbour, the footbridge seeming to anchor it to solid land, chaining it to the dock. The open decks towered above the sea below as the waves splashed against the white hull. Joining the line of passengers snaking along the edge of the wharf and winding back on itself she waited patiently. Standing at the far end of the wharf, at the entry onto the footbridge, an Italian sailor in a crisp white uniform crosschecked names on a passenger list with their proffered tickets. Marija quickly retrieved her ticket from her handbag and gripped it firmly. Her husband had sent the money to pay for it; it had seemed a small fortune.

'How many of us on this ship?' asked Marija to no one in particular as she gazed in awe at the sheer size of the vessel that was to be her home for the next six weeks.

'Hundreds,' was the reply from a young man standing close by. 'More than eight hundred, I've heard.'

Looking around at the waiting passengers, she noticed that some seemed tired and anxious while others looked excited; some were alone while others were surrounded by farewelling family. She heard the chatter of different languages. Listening carefully, she could pick out words in Italian; knowing the language may come in handy on the boat, she thought.

It seemed everyone was dressed in their Sunday best. The men wore hats, black suits, starched white shirts buttoned up to the collar and down to the cuff and perfectly knotted ties. Some of the suits seemed ill-fitting as if they were borrowed, or as if the wearer had lost weight—probably both were true. Leather shoes were shiny even if old and cracked. The women wore calf-length dresses or skirts with their sensible shoes, the children, long socks and shoes. So much variety, some in fashionable new clothes and some in old. Many of the crowd were young men, mainly Italian, excited about the prospect of a new country. They had been promised jobs by neighbours who were already in Australia, jobs on farms—sugarcane farms in the sweltering far north or fruit farms in the cooler south. Young, handsome and strong, they squatted in groups in the long line and chatted, smoked and laughed loudly about what lay ahead, confident in their youth and masculinity.

The boarding process was tedious, stretching on and on, as did the shadows cast by the ship. Some of the children ran and played on the wharf, befriending other children under the watchful eyes of their parents. 'Keep away from the edge,' warned the mothers, gesticulating with their arms. Crying babies on mothers' hips added to the loud buzz. The sun started to sink below the horizon, orange melting into the violet sea.

At last, it was Marija's turn. She followed Marinka and her family.

'Your name?' said the Italian sailor.

'Marija Gavranich,' she answered, showing the ticket that was stamped 'Second Class Passenger'. It sounded strange saying that name. No longer was she Marija Nadilo. Yes, she reminded herself, she was married.

The sailor flipped noisily through the pages, scanning for her name. Marija waited anxiously, holding her documents, hoping that everything was in order. He ran his finger down the page until it reached her name, then read it out aloud, struggling with the pronunciation.

'Passenger 311 Gavranich Maria, Alien, C/o J Gavranich, Cassowary Valley via Mossman.'

She wondered why her father-in-law's name, Jack (Ivan) Gavranich, was marked against hers. Why wasn't she 'care of' Mladen Gavranich? Her heart skipped a beat—she hoped the wedding papers were authentic and that Mladen was indeed her husband. It was then that her name caught her eye. Marija was spelt differently—Maria without a 'j'. The Australian way. She made a mental note that from this day onwards she was Maria, not Marija. This decision, although small, made her feel different, a little less foreign and maybe, just maybe, a little more Australian.

With her name checked off, she finally walked up the long gangplank onto the deck. Marinka waited at the top for her while the two children skipped ahead with their father. Maria could see that Marinka was tired; it had been a long two days for them all.

'Watch the children,' Marinka called out to Ivan, who was walking ahead, searching for their cabin.

Turning to Maria she said, 'Let's go and find our cabin and rest'.

Although Maria was also tired, excitement coursed through her veins. Everything on board was so shiny, so new, so large, so modern and so different from everything in her village. Tilting her head and gazing up, she could see small white lifeboats suspended near the top deck. Passengers bustled around the two women as they pushed through the swinging doors into the main lobby. Smelling of fresh wax, the brown vinyl floors were gleaming and spotless. Staff in white uniforms hurried past, preparing the ship for the start of its journey. Urgency fused with expectation.

Adjacent to this main lobby Maria could see a number of rooms—a hairdressing salon, a doctor's surgery and a room with a large sign on the door: 'Emigration Office'. All the signs were in English and Italian. Not able to read English, Maria tried to decipher some of the Italian words. Spanning the entire room was a wall of glass through which she could see comfortable-looking orange chairs clustered around coffee tables. Windows lined the long room and through them she could glimpse the sea. She later discovered that this was the second-class lounge. Rocking slowly back and forth with the motion of the boat, Maria gazed around her in amazement. To one side of the lobby were stairs cordoned off with the sign 'First Class' swinging on the chain and an officious looking man guarding this entry.

They made their way to the lower decks and found their cabins. When Maria opened the door of 28A she was surprised to see a woman lying on the top bunk. She was humming quietly to herself and smiled when she saw Maria.

'Hello, my name is Katica. It looks as if we're going to get to know each other well this next month,' she said, as they both scanned the tiny room fitted with bunk beds and not much else. '*Really* well!'

After introducing herself, Marija discovered that Katica was from Smokvica, a village not far from her own—a pretty village that clung to the side of a steep hill, and was much smaller than Blato. Her cabinmate was chatty and confident, and was also a proxy bride, with a husband waiting in Sydney. She had also been on the same ferry from Korčula and train to Genoa, but they had not noticed each other in the crowds.

Their conversation was interrupted by Marinka tapping gently on the door and popping her head around the corner.

'Ooh, this is tiny,' she said. 'We're just next door and we share the bathroom with you.'

Marinka's room was larger. A double bed with a starched white bedspread occupied most of the cabin. Beside the window was a bunk bed like Maria's, an aluminium ladder secured at one end and a railing at the top for safety. The children were already bouncing on the top bunk and giggling. They had never seen a bunk bed before. The two cabins were connected by a shared tiny cubicle containing a toilet, shower and wash basin.

Before long they heard the long, deep blast of the ship's horn reverberating through the walls of the cabins. Joining the crowded deck, the passengers leaned against the high railings to watch as the ship slowly exited the harbour. Clinging to the rails, most of the passengers were waving, some to the families waving back from the wharf, some to nobody in particular, maybe simply waving farewell to Europe. A soft blanket of darkness enveloped the city. On the wharf the silhouettes that crowded beneath the glow of the lampposts grew smaller as the ship glided out to sea. Soft sobs were interspersed with excited chatter.

Maria didn't remain long on the deck; she had already said her goodbyes to Europe. Returning to her room, she unpacked her few items of clothing, and slid her suitcase under her bed, the bottom bunk. Colourful paper lira notes were hidden carefully with her documents. She looked at her Certificate of Registration booklet once more. It was not a passport but it was her entry booklet to Australia. Its bright blue cover had a number on it: 284956.

She opened it again and studied the securely stapled photo of herself. Below it was a description.

Height: 5 ft 7 ins

Build: medium

Eyes: brown

Hair: brown

Her eyes stared back at her, open and warm above her smile. Yes, she thought, it's a nice photo. On the opposite page her details had been written in blue ink by the official in the Blato Town Hall. Her new surname, 'GAVRANICH, was in capital letters, and all the rest was cursive. She remembered holding the pen and signing it, awkwardly, hoping she would not smudge her new signature. 'Arrived in Australia on' and 'Port of' had blank spaces awaiting a date and a name.

The surname was Gavranich, not Gavranić. She had been told that the English pronunciation was different, so many immigrants added 'h' to the end of the names so the name would end in 'ch' not the harsh sounding 'k'.

What a strange language, she thought, feeling slightly overwhelmed at the prospect of having to learn it. How much English do I know? she pondered. Nothing, none at all. She laughed. 'Oh, dear, what have I got myself into?' she said to herself.

Her husband had sent her some money for the trip. She counted the Italian notes. What would she buy? she wondered, as she'd never had her own money before. Money had always been scarce in her family; they existed mainly on what they could grow on their farm and their little vineyard. Carefully, she tucked the notes into her documents once more and hid it under her clothes in the drawer.

'Why don't you wash your face and come to the dining room?' Ivan yelled through the open door. 'We're all hungry and tired. Dinner's being served.'

At the thought, Maria's stomach rumbled and she realised that she had barely eaten during the whole journey.

'Katica, are you hungry?' she asked her cabinmate, who had just walked in.

'I'm always hungry—there was never any food in our house.'

Maria knew exactly what she meant. The six of them climbed the narrow stairway, holding the rail as the ship rocked side to side, before entering the large dining room that echoed with the chatter of hundreds of passengers. Young men from the third-class dormitory sections, deep in the ship's bowels, mingled with the second-class passengers. Their excited talk was accompanied by extensive arm gesturing, so typical of Italians, Maria thought. The first-class passengers were seated on the next level. Maria looked around: starched white tablecloths covered circular tables and bright overhead bulbs threw a dazzling light over the large room. Smartly dressed waiters in their spotless white uniforms merged seamlessly into the picture, each armed with platters of steaming food. Wafting out from a nearby galley was a combination of aromas, some sweet and others savoury. Chefs' voices shouted above the clattering of pots. Stretched along the back wall was a long table covered with food. The passengers formed an orderly line for their dinner. A basket of bread on the table edge caught her eye. She had not eaten bread for so long. Her family couldn't afford the prices at their bakery and flour was expensive.

She tried not to stare but Marinka noticed, and subtly pushed the basket towards her. 'Eat some. Enjoy this. The good Lord knows how much we've suffered.'

Holding her plate close, Maria moved slowly along the length of the table. Her face reddened as her stomach started a low grumble, getting louder and louder. She was sure everyone could hear it. She had never seen so much food. There was spaghetti, fried fish, meat balls, crumbed veal, salads, soups, vegetables—so many foods she hadn't tasted or even seen before. Will it be like this every day? she wondered as she layered more and more onto her plate.

They found a table and Maria dragged her chair in close. Copying those around her, she discreetly covered her lap with the napkin. She noticed that there was a small bread roll on a plate beside each knife and fork. As she already had bread on her plate she slipped this roll into her pocket for later. Then she began her meal starting with her favourite, the chunk of white bread. As she chewed through the crunchy crust, she felt pinpricks of guilt as her thoughts drifted back to her home. What would her family be eating?

She pictured them sitting around the old wooden table with its worn tablecloth covering the cracks and marks. There would be a large bottle of olive oil near the vinegar and salt in the middle of the table. Would it be *zeje* again tonight? The staple food of silver beet, potato and any other green vegetables they could grow, with lots of sea salt, olive oil and garlic. Perhaps tonight they would be lucky and have *brudet*. There would certainly not be any baskets of bread or pots bubbling with meat balls and spaghetti.

'Did you know there are shows and bars and dances on this boat,' Katica whispered to her. 'The Italian men were telling me. I was going to meet them after dinner. Come with me; it'll be fun.' She winked.

Maria shook her head. 'No, I'm tired. I'm going back to rest.'

After the meal she returned to her cabin on her own. Cocooned in her narrow bunk bed, she propped herself up on her elbows and spread out some paper to write to her family. The words tumbled onto the page as she wrote of the adventures of the last two days. Scribbling furiously, trying to recall all the images, the muffled sound of a softly crooned lullaby in a deep melancholic voice filtered through from the cabin next door. Stopping her writing, she listened to Ivan singing to his children. This was the same lullaby her father sang to her and her siblings when they were children, the familiar words haunting, yet strangely soothing.

Later that night, curled up in her bed, Maria pulled the crisp white cotton sheet up to her chin and rested her hands on her stomach. It was fuller than she had ever known it to be. She thought of the tasty soup she had eaten that night and recalled the grass soup she had sometimes eaten during the war when she was a child.

Tilting rhythmically the boat rocked her. I hope it doesn't get rougher than this, she thought as she held the side of her bed to stop slipping. Absentmindedly, she twirled the wedding band around her finger and wondered when Katica would return. Through the little window the sea was black velvet stitched seamlessly to the silken night sky. The moon glowed, leading the way for this majestic ship steaming its way halfway round the world, leaving Europe far behind. And so Maria drifted off to sleep, her dreams intermingled with a kaleidoscope of the colours and fragrances of the days that had passed.

Blato, on the island of Korčula, Croatia.

Maria on the farm near Blato, Korčula, 1946.

Maria as a teenager on the beach, Korčula, 1948.

Maria's childhood house, Blato.

Maria's father, Paval Nadilo-Buran, 1920s.

Photo Maria sent to Mladen, 1950.

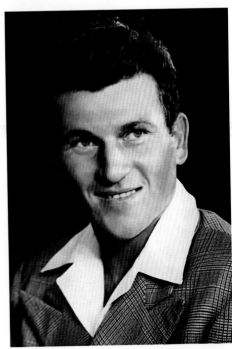

Photo Mladen (Laddie) sent to Maria, 1950.

Church and bell tower, Blato. Photo courtesy Blato Tourist Board.

The Croatian wedding. L to R: Mr Gavranić, Paval Nadilo (Maria's half-brother), Maria, Franko Anić, Kuzma Anić (proxy groom), Frank Petković (Maria's sister Dobrila's husband), Blato, 1951.

Maria's wedding in Blato with Kuzma Anić (proxy groom), 1951.

Laddie and his sister, Mary, 1949.

The Gavranich farm in Cassowary Valley (near Mossman).

Wedding celebration when Maria arrived in Australia, 1952.

Maria and Laddie, 1953.

Laddie and Maria, 1952.

Maria and her youngest daughter, Debbie (flower girl at Mossman Debutante Ball, 1965).

Maria and her children at Tinaroo Dam, mid-1960s.

Maria and Debbie ready for church (in front of beach house, Newell Beach), 1966.

Gavranich family, 1974.
Back row: Maryanne, John, Joyce;
front row: Laddie, Debbie, Maria.

Maria and Laddie, 1975.

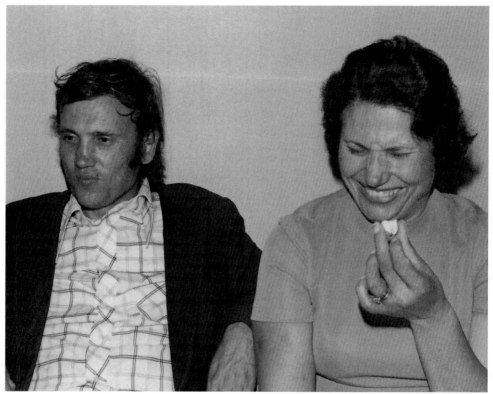

Maria with her brother Ivan, Split, Croatia, 1974.

Maria and her sisters (Dobrila and Žuva) with their mother, Žuva, Blato, 1974.

Debbie in Blato traditional costume, 1983.

Debbie visiting the old house in Blato, 1983.

Debbie's wedding. Back row: John and Joyce; front row: Maryanne, Debbie and Maria, Cairns, 1990.

Laddie at tennis, Esplanade Courts, Cairns, 1986.

Maria in Croatia with her brother, Ivan and sister, Žuva, 1995.

Maria, one month before she died, with grandchildren (Michelle, Stephanie and David) at Michelle's christening, 1996.

25

A dilemma in Egypt

The overhead bunk creaked.

'Oh, my goodness, what a night! My feet are aching,' groaned a voice thick with sleep.

Stirring in her bed, Maria was perplexed. Where am I and who is that talking? she wondered. Glancing around, she realised that she was not in her own bed and remembered that she was on a ship, forging its way to Australia. Through the porthole above her head, she could see the sun rising, a golden orb streaming across an expanse of endless blue, with no land in sight.

'What time did you get in?' she asked.

'Late. I don't know how late. Those Italian men are gorgeous, and they can really dance.'

Katica yawned and stretched her arms back to touch the wall behind her small bunk.

'How can you understand them?'

'Hmm. Yes. It's a problem but you don't need to talk much when you dance. My hips did the talking!'

She wiggled her hips at the memory causing the bunks to shake.

'Hey, careful,' Maria said.

'My Italian's not good but it's getting better. I can remember a fair bit from the war. I definitely need to practise it.' Katica giggled like a schoolgirl. 'You know the two men I was dancing with? Well, they saw you sitting near me at dinner; they want you to come dancing too.'

She leaned over the edge of the bunk, her hair framing her upside-down face.

'No,' Maria said. 'I'm definitely not a dancer.' She pulled the sheet over her face to escape Katica's stare.

'Oh, come on. I'm going to drag you along anyway.'

'Katica, we're married. We have husbands.' Although muffled, her voice still sounded determined.

'I know that. I'm almost sorry I'm married. But we're on this boat for a month. There's nothing wrong with a bit of dancing. Let's make the most of it.'

'I don't think so. I still don't think it's right.'

'We'll see. Come on, let's go and get breakfast. I'm excited by all that food.'

Maria agreed and sprang off her bunk, making sure not to hit her head on the bunk above, and managed to dress while negotiating the steady to and fro pitch of the boat.

The ship glided onwards across the Mediterranean Sea. The first week passed with nothing but unbroken blue. The dining room with its endless supply of food was Maria's favourite place. She discovered that there was a bread roll beside her cutlery at each meal, so she collected them, slipping them into her pocket and hiding them in her room. She finally realised that there was no need to hoard them—there would be bread every day, at every meal. Sheepishly, she showed Katica what she had hidden in her drawer: twenty-one bread rolls, some showing signs of mould.

'I thought the food would stop,' she said, embarrassed.

'I understand.'

One morning, Katica and Maria heard the squawking of seagulls. Leaping from their bunks, they peered through the porthole and in the distance, behind the flapping and swooping birds, they saw a strip of coastline.

'Let's go upstairs for a better look,' said Maria excitedly, clasping Katica's hand and dragging her out of their cabin.

The young women stood on the wide deck amongst the other passengers who were crowding for a better view of this curious land ahead.

'So, this is Egypt,' Maria said, as she overheard the conversations around her. 'You know, this is where a lot of families from our island hid during the war.'

Katica nodded, her eyes glued to the approaching city.

'I know. For Smokvica too,' Katica responded. 'My cousins even came here after the war because they didn't really believe the war was over. They thought the Germans were coming back.'

Their ship was approaching Port Said, a sizeable city at the entrance to the Suez Canal, the man-made waterway, the shortcut to the Indian Ocean.

As the MV *Australia* neared the harbour, Maria looked at the impressive building that dominated the docks. Tall arched windows enhanced the exotic beauty of the wide, white two-storey building, topped with three teal domes.

'These buildings look so strange, so different from the buildings at home. And what trees are those?' Maria pointed to the trees in the foreground.

'Date palms. I heard the fruit is tasty and very sweet.'

'Buy? Buy? Very cheap,' yelled the men bobbing in their small rowing boats alongside the ship.

Contrasting to their white tunics and brimless kufi hats, Maria was struck by the dark colour of their faces.

'Look, Katica. Those men are so dark. Why is that?

Katica laughed at Maria's naivety.

'What? Why are you laughing?'

'That's the colour of their skin.'

'Really? They are naturally dark brown?' Maria turned to watch the men in the rowing boats a little longer. Having never left her little village, she had only ever seen other Europeans.

'Come on, ladies. Come with us,' roared a tall lean Italian man as he wrapped his arms around Katica's waist and nuzzled his face in her hair.

He and his brother were both handsome in a roguish way. Hailing from the northern part of Italy, they were on their way to the sugarcane fields of Australia, excited to make their fortune and relieved to leave postwar Europe.

'Mario, of course we'll come,' Katica exclaimed, with a mischievous glint in her dark eyes.

Katica had revelled in the social life laid at her feet. Away from the claustrophobia of her small village, the watchful eyes of her mother and the unrelenting drudgery of labouring in the family vineyard, this voyage was like a vacation for her. Unlimited food, nightly dances and good-looking, fun-loving handsome young men. Confiding to Maria, she had admitted that she was quite smitten with Mario.

'What about your husband? You're married,' Maria had argued, concerned for her friend.

'I know,' Katica said, 'but it was like a thunderbolt. The moment I saw him I couldn't help it. Crazy! And you know that Giovanni, his brother, really likes you.'

Maria had accompanied Katica, under protest, to some of the dances but had declined offers to dance, preferring to sit and watch and talk.

'Giovanni said he likes me? But why? How? I have hardly spoken to him.'

'You don't have to speak.' Katica had arched her eyebrows knowingly.

Maria frowned and pushed that thought from her head.

The four of them climbed off, Maria still protesting while Katica and the two young men gripped her wrists firmly.

'It'll be fun. We have a few hours. Let's get off this ship.'

With many other passengers, they descended into the small boats that ferried them through the hordes of boats with men selling a dazzling array of goods, depositing them at the docks. There was plenty of time to explore the harbourside while the ship's crew restocked supplies for the next stage of the journey.

The scene that met Maria's eyes was even more amazing than the chaos of Genoa. Lining the wide esplanade were rows of local men squatting in white tunics and shouting, touting their merchandise, the like of which she had never laid eyes on before.

Walking slowly, browsing, she stopped, selecting pieces of jewellery, turning them over and marvelling at the rawness of the colours, most with a common theme—the scarab beetle. This jewellery was so different from the delicate filigree earrings or the simple gold sleepers that the women from her village wore.

'My sisters would love these,' she said to the little group.

'Then buy them.'

'No. They're not necessary.' She clasped her little purse tightly, her lira folded neatly inside. 'I don't want to waste my husband's money.' She looked at Giovanni as she emphasised the word 'husband'.

On through the rambling crowds, they strolled. Men sat on their heels, pounding rhythmic tunes on goatskin-covered wooden drums, others tempting the passers-by with offers of aromatic foods. Smelly camels led by men in long robes wove between them, and a jumble of nationalities surrounded them. French, Italian, English, Egyptian—a mixture of languages, cultures, and dress. So incredible, thought Maria. A potpourri of people so completely different from her own homogenous village.

Katica and Mario loitered behind, holding hands and sneaking secretive kisses. Giovanni remained close to Maria, his hand on the small of her back, gently guiding her through the crowds. He was tall with jet black hair, close cropped, leaving his long fringe veiling his hooded eyes. Maria felt uneasy when he would cease his chatter and silently stare at her. This day he talked nonstop, recounting stories of his life, making jokes and vividly describing what he saw around him. She found she could understand a lot of what he was saying. His energetic gesticulations when he spoke was entertaining. An amusing character, he was quick to make Maria laugh.

Glancing backwards he whispered, 'The lovebirds have dis-appeared'.

'Oh, no! What is Katica doing?'

'She is in safe hands with my brother.' He grinned, raising his eyebrows.

Although concerned about Katica, Maria enjoyed spending time off the ship to wander around this strange city. There were so many different sights, smells and tastes to saturate her mind and her senses. So much to write home about, she thought.

As the day drew to a close, the passengers reluctantly reboarded the ship. Solid land had been a welcome relief after the incessant rocking. As the group waited in line, Giovanni showed Maria the gift he had bought for his mother.

'She cried so much when we left. We'll send her this.'

He proudly held up the pair of earrings, the dangling green scarab beetles sparkled in the sun. 'They told me that green means new life.'

'They're beautiful,' Maria said, 'so unusual. They'll make her smile.'

'No, she was crying so much when we both left, I think she is still crying. I can feel it in my bones,' he said, sadly.

With the city behind them, the ship took its turn amongst all the freighters gliding through the narrow Suez Canal. It was busy. Maria relaxed in a blue-and-white striped canvas chair on the deck and watched, mesmerised by the length of this waterway, Africa on one side and Asia on the other. My father would be so interested to see this, she thought. Stretching for miles was an unbroken line of desert. So hot. So dry.

Pulling up a deckchair beside her, Giovanni lowered his angular body into the canvas and passed her a plate of food.

'Thank you. I was just too tired to go down for dinner, and I wanted to watch this.' She accepted the plate of steaming hot food with a broad smile.

'I wondered where you were when I saw Katica alone; well not alone—she was with Mario.'

They ate their meal in silence, watching the scenery slipping by. Maria twirled the spaghetti around her fork that rested on her spoon, copying the way she had noticed the Italians on the boat eating their national dish. As she raised the fork to her mouth the pasta slipped off into her bowl. She retrieved it by noisily slurping the strands into her mouth, rich tomato sauce splashing messily on both cheeks.

'I'm so clumsy!' she laughed, embarrassed.

'No, you're not. You're perfect,' Giovanni said as he leant over, wiping her face with his white handkerchief.

'Maria,' he faltered, his eyes locking onto hers, 'you're breathtaking. You're the most beautiful woman I have ever seen.'

'Stop!' Maria was startled. She definitely understood what he was saying and held her hand up in protest.

'I can't help it. This little time that I've spent with you, you've stolen my heart. I know you're married but, Maria, you don't even know this man. You've come to know me a bit. Annul this marriage.' Dramatically dropping to one knee he pleaded, his handsome face earnest. 'Marry me. We can run away together. We can elope.'

'No, Giovanni. What are you saying! I barely know you,' she blurted. 'I definitely don't love you.'

'But I think—'

Maria cut him off.

'Giovanni, I don't love my husband as I don't know him either. All I know is that I'm married. I am his wife and that is the life I'm going to. I'm sorry, but this is crazy!'

She stood abruptly, her plate sliding off her lap, splattering spaghetti onto the wooden deck. Ignoring the mess, she rushed to her room. Her head was spinning.

She pushed open her cabin door. It was unlocked. Huddled on the floor was Katica sobbing hysterically, her arms hugging her knees to her chest. Her face was obscured by a tangled mess of curls.

Startled by Maria's sudden entrance, she looked up, her face blotchy and wet with tears.

'What's wrong?' asked Maria forgetting her own problems and crouching to the floor beside her.

Rocking backwards and forwards, Katica was distraught.

'I don't know what to do.'

'What do you mean?' Maria asked, suspecting that she already knew the answer.

'I love Mario. He is everything I've ever wanted. He is handsome. He makes me laugh. I can't believe it. I'm so happy because he has just told me that he loves me and wants to marry me.'

Her sobbing intensified.

'But you're already married.'

'I know,' howled Katica. 'But I'm only twenty-two. I'm young. My husband in Sydney is thirty-five.'

'So?'

'I only married him to escape Yugoslavia. I don't know him. I don't love him. He's not even good looking. You've seen his photos. He's old, and short, and ugly.'

Placing her arm around her cabinmate's shoulders, Maria paused, collecting her thoughts and searching for the right words to say next.

'I know, it's hard. But what choice do we have? We have committed ourselves. Our families expect us to make these marriages work.'

'Yes, I know all that, but I don't know what to do.'

Maria was quiet, thinking of her own family. When they farewelled her, it was a final goodbye. They expected her to make a new life with her husband. Thinking about Katica, she felt guilty that her husband was young and handsome.

'Do you want to hear something funny?' Maria asked.

Hiccupping with sobs Katica looked at her through a film of tears and nodded.

'Well,' Maria began, 'Mario's brother just proposed to me a few minutes ago.'

Katica's eyes widened with disbelief and then both girls burst out laughing.

'Goodness, what a pair we are. And?'

'There's a big no! I'm married.' She stretched her left hand out showing the gold band secured on her ring finger. 'See?'

'So you really think I should stay married, too, and not ask for an annulment?'

'It's your life, Katica. I can't tell you what to do—you must decide.'

'My family will disown me if I run away from my husband. But that's exactly what I want to do. I want to run off with Mario.'

Maria's heart ached as she hugged her friend who kept repeating over and over again, 'What should I do? What can I do?'

Katica continued to weep as Maria tucked her into her bed. Quietly, Maria murmured her prayers as she lay in her own bed, exhausted.

'God, give Katica the strength to do what is right. God, give me the strength to give her good advice. And dear God, just one more thing, please don't let any more Italian men fall in love with me.'

26

Aussie siblings

'Have you got it all organised?' Laddie asked as he lowered his tired body onto the front stairs of the large Queenslander. His grey shirt and loose navy shorts were marked with grease and sweat and his limbs were grubby with the brown dirt from the farm. Packing the tobacco deftly in the cigarette paper, he licked and sealed his rollie before securing it firmly between his lips. He withdrew a match from the Redhead matchbox in his shirt pocket, lit the cigarette and inhaled.

'It's almost done,' answered Mary, his sister.

Although she was eight years younger, they looked alike; both had thick dark curls, high cheek bones, strong noses and wide laughing smiles. She waved away the smoke as he puffed on his cigarette and blew it at her.

'It's not until the fourteenth, anyway. That's next week. Friday night. You'd better make sure you get home from the paddock early that day and have a good wash. Look at you. You look filthy and smell awful.'

'I can scrub up pretty well.' He moved closer and put his arm around her shoulder.

Mary moved away, crinkling her nose. 'Hey. Stop it.'

'It's amazing to think that you're twenty-one today, old girl.' He poked her playfully in the ribs. 'You're an adult now, key to the door. You can vote.'

She rolled her eyes. 'Yeah, so much to look forward to.'

'Nah, your party will be good fun. How many you got comin'?'

'About fifty, by the look of it.'

'The old man said he's going to hide a ten shilling note somewhere for a treasure hunt. I'll believe that when I see it.' Laddie raised his eyebrows.

'Yeah. How about we both try and find it and split it when we do.' Mary chuckled, her dimples deepening. 'I still can't believe that you're married, and she'll be arriving soon. I wonder what Maria is like, apart from being beautiful, you lucky devil.'

Laddie stared ahead, deep in thought. Stretching out in front of him were paddocks, green seas of rippling sugar cane, darkening as the sun dipped behind Mount Demi. Still visible above the growing cane was the flat corrugated-iron roof of the small grey barracks where the cane cutters lived during the harvesting season.

It had been a big decision searching for a bride from his hometown of Blato. He was very Australian—he had grown up here. Even though his name was Mladen, he was known as Laddie because the locals struggled with the difficult pronunciation, and anyway, Australians were famous for shortening names and words, usually adding an 'ie' or an 'o' on the end.

He could recall hazy images of old stone houses and cobbled streets, but really, he barely remembered the village he had left as a very young child. He wondered what she would think of this house, made of wood and set above the ground on sturdy stumps. It would seem so new and different from what she was used to. He knew that her family had a small vineyard. He wondered what she would think of this sugar-cane farm. The crisp northern hemisphere winter would be the opposite to the suffocating blanket of humidity of the North Queensland summers and the endless days of monsoonal rain.

'I hope she's tough enough to cope with all of this,' he murmured, more to himself. 'I hope my two favourite girls will get along.' He smiled down at Mary and hugged her again, gently this time.

'We will, it's okay, I know we will. She'll be the sister I've never had,' Mary said with a determined glint in her dark brown eyes.

'I'm excited.'

'Well, that's good. Me too. But first let me sing Happy Birthday to you.' He burst into song, dragging her to her feet and waltzing her around the front yard while she giggled helplessly.

'Why are you so good at dancing?' she asked.

'Because I am,' he said as he spun her faster.

27
Cassowary Valley, 14 March 1952

Mary scrubbed the timber verandah floors until they gleamed. Party lights had been strung the length of the verandah that stretched along the front and one side of their farmhouse. After weaving the row of rainbow-coloured lights in and out of the wooden louvres, she flicked on the switch, stood back and smiled appreciatively.

She pushed open the casement windows and opened all the louvres, trying to entice a breeze. Although it was the middle of March it was still muggy. At least the wet season was over and there was no talk of any cyclones in the Coral Sea.

True to his word, Laddie arrived home early and was helping her set up. They'd placed a long wooden trestle table down the length of the verandah and scattered chairs around in small groups, leaving enough room for the dancing and the games. Her aunt, Teta Ema, and her 'adopted' mother, Mrs Coates (Coatsey), had spent all day in the kitchen helping her prepare the feast. The chickens were cooked with crispy golden skins, and the spaghetti, oozing with rich spicy tomato sauce, smelled divine.

Standing in front of the mirror, Mary brushed her thick dark hair, the curls resting on her shoulders. She twirled around in her pretty blue party dress, watching the skirt billow like a sail. Stopping, she smiled at her reflection, happy. As she fastened her necklace, her thoughts drifted back to the woman who had given her this piece of jewellery, her mother, Jaka. What would her mother think of her? Would she be proud? It was five years since she had died, leaving Mary a vulnerable sixteen-year-old. Mrs Coates from the farm next door had stepped in, as best she could, to be a mother figure for her. But Mary missed her mother dearly. Kind, gentle and softly spoken, her mother had been a good woman, she remembered, a loving mother who died too young, just fifty-one. She had heard whispers that her mother had died from a broken heart, never really recovering after John's death. Mary had been a child when her eldest brother had passed in such tragic circumstances. No one really spoke about it. Since her mother's death, Mary had been the woman of the household, the sister, the daughter. It was not easy. It was lonely but her remaining brother, Laddie, had been her rock. He was so outgoing, full of fun and always had a joke or a trick up his sleeve. He made life bearable. He made her smile and she felt lucky to have him in her life. She swallowed hard and blinked.

Tonight wasn't the night for sad memories. It was her twenty-first birthday party, and she could already hear the rumble of vehicles as they drove up the curved dirt road that connected Lower Cassowary Road to their house. She glanced at her reflection one last time before racing outside to greet the arrivals. Shiny Holdens, sparkling from their latest wax, lined up next to dusty farm utes and jeeps. Roars of laughter and slamming of car doors echoed in the still of the sultry evening. Standing between her father and her brother at the front door of the verandah, Mary welcomed her guests with warm hugs.

When everyone had arrived, Laddie announced that it was 'time for games'. Guests kicked off their shoes like a bunch of excited children. True to his word there was a treasure hunt and Jack had indeed hidden a ten-shilling note somewhere on the property. Glancing at his sister, Laddie winked as if to say, 'I don't believe it, but he did it!'

'It's hidden outside somewhere,' Jack bellowed in his deep voice.

Everyone scattered, squealing and racing each other around the large property.

'I hope it's not in the shed somewhere,' yelled their cousin, Elsie. 'I might get bitten by a snake in there.'

'You'll probably stand on a cane toad instead. There's heaps in there.'

'Yuck,' uttered the young teenager as she decided not to enter the dark shed. 'It's too creepy in there anyway. I might stand on a nail or something.'

They looked on drums, under buckets, near water tanks, behind sheds. There were so many hiding spots.

'I found it!' shouted Pat, one of the guests.

'Where?'

'It's here on the tennis court, hidden in the rolled-up tennis net.'

The lights from the verandah streamed across the red cement tennis court behind the house. Waving the ten-shilling note above his head, he grinned excitedly.

'You lucky bugger,' someone said.

Another guest slapped him on the back and then tried to wrestle the note from his grip. Pleased with his find, Pat slid it into his pocket. They all returned to the enclosed verandah and continued with the games, the dancing, the singing, and the eating. One of Mary's friends produced a harmonica and belted out a tune while others entertained the guests with their singing. Laddie led the dancing. Light on his feet, he waltzed the ladies around their makeshift dance floor in one corner of the verandah. Sawdust mixed with kerosene had been sprinkled on the timber boards, making the floor slippery so the dancers could glide through their steps. He was now dancing with Elsie.

'Keep in time with me... one... two... three,' Laddie counted as he patiently led her through the steps. 'You're getting pretty good at this, Elsie,' he said. 'All that practice has paid off.'

'Yeah, but you're not a bad teacher Laddie,' was her response.

Although first cousins, Elsie and Mary looked very different.

Unlike Mary, who was curvy and muscular, Elsie was very slender and slight-framed like her three brothers. Her fine straight hair was cut in a bob and tucked behind her ears with a clip to keep it in place.

Taking a break from the activity, Mary sat down at the trestle table and watched her brother. Laddie was handsome, Mary thought. Most of the single girls there tonight would have agreed with her as they vied with each other for a dance with him. Yet he was bringing a bride from the 'old country'. Around her, Teta Ema and Mrs Coates collected the dishes from the table, clearing it to make room for dessert and her birthday cake.

She smiled. 'Thank you, Coatsey. For everything,' she whispered. Mrs Coates nodded at her and bustled on.

Her Uncle Antun looked relaxed as he sat at the head of the table next to her father. Both men sat in silence, watching the festivities. Antun was tall like her father but lean with a narrow face; his rimless glasses perched on the end of his long nose. Unlike her father, he had a full head of hair. His sparkling eyes looked over his glasses and when he caught her eye, he winked. Her aunt and uncle were good people; she felt lucky they lived so close. She would cross the creek dividing the properties and meet her cousins along the dirt track that joined the farms.

Once more, her mind wandered back to her mother who had been very close to Uncle Antun's wife, Ema. Mary recalled her mother telling her how she and her two young sons had travelled with her sister-in-law, Ema, on the ship from Yugoslavia. Their friend, Mrs Vico, a Yugoslav woman who lived on a neighbouring farm, had also made this journey with them. These three women, all new immigrants in a raw country, would trudge along the tracks and through paddocks to visit and support each other. With these thoughts tumbling in her mind, Mary smiled and winked back at her uncle.

The evening progressed smoothly; the games intermingled with the dancing. The night concluded with speeches and the reading of the telegrams from absent guests, followed by toasts: 'To Mary.

Congratulations!' She was then presented with a large wooden key that had been passed from guest to guest, for everyone to sign.

Flushed from all the dancing and the excitement of the night, Mary finally bid her guests farewell. As the last car drove off, she sat down with her brother on the front steps. The party had been a success and worth all the effort. Twinkling above them, the brilliant stars illuminated the cloudless sky and the full moon glowed softly. Intermittently, the haunting cries of the curlews interrupted the tranquil night.

'I can't wait for the next party to be held here,' Mary said.

When Laddie looked at her quizzically, she nudged him with her elbow. 'Your wedding party, silly.'

A wide grin spread across his face. It had been quite a process, this 'procurement' or 'proxy marriage' as it was known in Australia. It seemed like yesterday that he had decided to select a bride from Blato. Mary had wondered why he had done this, but he was not one to discuss feelings. Whatever happened, he just got on with life, never one to explain nor complain.

'There's always someone worse off than me, so why complain?' was his standard response when hardship struck, which it did often.

He had laboured all his life on this farm. Even as a child, he would work before and after school, like the other youngsters in the valley.

'I want to go to high school and university,' he had pleaded with his father. 'I'm smart, Dad. I want to be a doctor.'

'Who will work the farm then? No, you'll stay home and work,' was the brutal response.

And so, his schooling ended after year seven and he continued to work hard, receiving no wages, never having any cash in his pocket.

And here he was bringing a wife to this farm. He had girlfriends but he'd told Mary he couldn't imagine any of them wanting to live in this isolation. Farm work wasn't easy. Mary thought about all the things she did—the cooking and cleaning as well as working beside the men in the paddocks. She hoped Laddie's new bride would be able to help her. All the town girls just want to shop, she thought, chuckling as she imagined them in the paddocks. Her brother was twenty-nine and ready for marriage and a family, hopefully a big family. This large house needs laughter and lots of children to fill its bedrooms. And, yes, he would be a kind father. She was sure of it.

'Do you think she'll be okay here?' he asked. 'It'll be so different from her own home, I reckon. I can't really remember what Blato was like; I was just a kid when we left.' He lit a rollie and puffed on it.

'Yep, I can't even imagine what it'll be like for her. Leaving everyone.'

'She can't speak English. She'll find it hard.'

Throwing her arm around her brother, she pulled him in close. 'Laddie, she'll be all right. She's got the two of us to look after her.'

'Thanks, sis. I just don't want life to be too hard for her, that's all. She's so young and looks so fragile.'

'She lived through that war. I reckon she'll be tougher than you think.'

He nodded and smiled.

Mary grinned back. She and Laddie were a good team—both on and off the tennis courts.

'Hey, are we still playing tennis tomorrow?' he asked. 'Or are you all tuckered out from this party?'

'Of course, we're playing. The McCoists are coming as usual. They told me tonight.'

'Great. Well, it's late, so let's finish the cleaning and get some sleep.'

Cocooned beneath the mosquito net, Mary lay in bed, exhausted, but sleep was impossible. Her mind raced with too many thoughts. She picked at the stitching connecting the flour bags that her sheets were sewn from. Moonlight streamed in through her open window. The curlews kept up their eerie calls to each other as they remained hidden in the forest that edged the creek running behind their property. She was thinking of her party, but also of her brother's new bride, Maria, trying to imagine what she would be like. In the photos she looked gorgeous but she was so young, only nineteen. Mary had heard her brother say that Maria's birthday was the twenty-third of March. In nine days, she would be twenty. She wondered how Maria must be feeling. Will she be celebrating this birthday with her family or will she be by herself on the ship? What a long way to travel. Mary had not travelled further south than Innisfail. This young bride was travelling from the other side of the globe, alone. She had overheard her brother and father arguing about who was to collect her in Sydney.

'It should be me. I'm her husband,' her brother had protested.

'No! You need to stay here and run the farm. End of discussion.'

Laddie shrugged his shoulders in defeat and walked away.

Poor Maria, thought Mary. Imagine being met by her father-in-law instead of her handsome young groom. What an awful start to her life in Australia. I hope she'll like me, were her final thoughts as she eventually drifted off to sleep, a soft breeze finally dispersing the stillness and fluttering the soft curtains that covered her window.

28

Arrival in Sydney

The trip to Australia continued but was not always easy. The Indian Ocean seemed endless, the winds bitter and the seas rough. Storms with scudding rain and crashing waves emptied the decks. Maria and Katica were often seasick and remained in their cabin, clutching buckets. They used the belts from their suitcases to firmly strap their bodies onto their beds to prevent being hurled across the cabin by the turbulent lurching of the ship. The stench of vomit hung in the deserted corridors. Ivan and Marinka checked regularly and brought food to the girls when they could not bear to leave their beds. Sometimes the smell of this food worsened their queasy stomachs. Hiding in their cabins also helped them avoid the handsome Italian men and their marriage proposals.

Maria wrote home. *Today is my birthday but I can't get out of bed. The sea is cruel. It is rough and I'm sick a lot but the food, when I can eat it, is wonderful, especially the bread. My dress is getting tighter so I think I am getting fatter. I hope my husband will recognise me.* She prodded her stomach and frowned.

Six weeks after embarking on this life-changing voyage, Maria and the other passengers were overjoyed to see Australia loom on the horizon.

On 19 April the ship docked at Fremantle in Western Australia, where the passengers were processed through customs, had their booklets stamped and their baggage checked. Some disembarked, looking happy to be off the ship. The journey was not over for Maria. Laboriously the ship navigated the southern coastline, stopping at Melbourne before terminating its voyage in Sydney on the 26 April, 1952.

Throughout the past month she had forged a strong bond with Marinka and Ivan and their children, Tomislav and Anja. When not seasick, she had passed the hours playing games with the children. These past few weeks she had also tried very hard to distract Katica from her broken heart. I hope her husband is good and loving so that she can easily forget Mario, she thought.

Now it was her time to get excited. Often, she would peek at the two photographs Mladen had sent her. There was no doubt about it. She thought him very handsome, and she felt a little guilty when she thought of the husband waiting for Katica.

Will we stay in Sydney for a few days or will we travel straight to Mossman? she wondered. She had heard that it was a long way, thousands of kilometres. Many thoughts ran through her mind: Will he like me? He was nine years older than her. Will he think me young and silly? She hoped not as she rubbed her wedding band against her clothes to make it shine.

It was mid-morning when the MV *Australia* sailed through the heads into the breathtakingly beautiful harbour and past the majestic Sydney Harbour Bridge, to dock at its final destination. Maria joined the passengers swarming on the deck, staring wide-eyed at this new city. Towering buildings stretched into the distance. Trees lined part of the harbour. The sky was crisp and blue, and cloudless. A frosty wind whipped at her coat. She pulled it close around her body. Crowds had gathered below on the quayside to greet the travellers. Maria stood on her tiptoes, looking over the heads of those standing in front of her as she scanned the faces on the wharf. With so many people, would she be able to pick out Mladen? Her journey with her new husband was about to begin. Apprehension and excitement gripped her at the same time, her heart hopping fast and unevenly.

Before long all the passengers had disembarked. Katica found her husband. He was short and, like the photographs, not handsome, but he looked kind. He was excited to greet his new wife and skipped around her like a playful puppy, kissing and hugging her. Maria said her goodbyes to Katica, hugging her close and wishing her well.

'Be strong and make this marriage work,' she whispered.

She hoped with all her heart this young woman would have a good life. As she clasped her little suitcase to her chest, she watched all the young men milling around her. She chewed her bottom lip. Where is Mladen? she wondered. She searched for the face she had memorised from the photographs. Fear crept into her heart and anxious thoughts filled her mind: Surely, he knows I am arriving today? We have written to each other and I have given him the dates. What will I do if he isn't here? I can't speak English. I have no money, only some lira which will be useless in Australia.

Hovering close by, Marinka was startled by the squeal of her cousin as she pushed through the crowds and rushed towards her. Her cousin wrapped her chubby arms around the children, planting noisy kisses on their cheeks.

'*Lipo da si došla!* Welcome to Australia!' Her lustrous black curls bobbed as she spoke excitedly to Marinka, her laugh rippling through the conversation. She kept kissing the children and pinching their cheeks.

Maria stood awkwardly to one side and watched this reunion, trying not to be envious of the family warmth, scanning the crowd, anxious to catch sight of Mladen. Then she noticed a tall, severe looking man studying her from a distance. A black felt hat shadowed his eyes. His face was weathered and wrinkled. In one hand was a photograph. He kept glancing at it and then studying her.

Who is this old man? she wanted to know, and why is he looking at me? She looked away and then back again. There must be a mistake; he was not Mladen. Her imagination played with her

138

mind—maybe Mladen is an old man and he sent a photo of when he was young? Maria had heard terrible stories of that happening. Horrified at the thought, she could not stop herself from staring. Her pulse quickened as she watched him stride towards her.

As he reached for her bag, he abruptly introduced himself, saying that she could call him Jack: *'Ja sam Ivan Gavranich, otac od Mladen Gavranich. Mozes me zvati Jack'.*

Maria could see that he was holding the photograph of her. He was her father-in-law. Her initial relief that this old man was not her new husband was replaced by fear and confusion. Where is my husband? Why is his father collecting me? Why isn't Mladen here? Isn't he excited to finally meet me? This was not how it was supposed to happen. During the last year and especially over the last month on the ship she had imagined the romance of their first meeting. Her handsome husband would see her on the dock and they would fall into each other's arms. He would tell her that she was even more beautiful than her photographs and she would blush with embarrassment but be secretly excited. This was all wrong. Her fear escalated.

Bewildered and wanting to know the whereabouts of her groom, Maria stammered, *'Dje... dje moj muz Mladen?'*

'Doma. Dodji sme no sada.' Turning to stride off while gripping her bag, he informed her that her groom was at home, and commanded that she follow him. Maria froze.

Glancing across, Marinka saw what had happened. Pulling herself from her cousin's smothering hugs, she walked over to her young friend and took her by the shoulders, turning her away from the old man and staring into her eyes.

'Go with him. He is part of your new family.'

'But where will he take me? Why is my husband not here?' Her bottom lip quivered.

'Dodji!' Jack repeated, getting impatient.

'It's fine. It's not unusual for the husbands to send their fathers.'

'But—'

'It could be to stop the new brides from running back onto the ships when they see their husbands for the first time,' Marinka said, smiling. 'But it's all right. At least you know that your husband is good looking.'

'But—'

Marinka stopped Maria from interrupting.

'Now, go with this man, his father. Have courage. You will meet your husband soon enough.'

Hugging Maria for a final time, Marinka pushed her towards Mr Gavranich and nodded as if to say, 'Go on,' like a mother encouraging a tentative child on their first day of school. Maria swallowed hard, her throat dry. She could feel her legs trembling.

'*Kako si?*' she ventured as a way of greeting. Then Jack grabbed her elbow to lead her away.

Maria turned to take one last glimpse at the ship and the young family that had been her solace for the past month.

∞

The next few days were a blur for Maria. Her father-in-law was an intimidating figure of few words. He told her little and she was afraid. She had so many questions, but she asked none. He was the very opposite of her own gentle father. There was no warmth in his eyes, sunk deep behind his black-rimmed spectacles. His voice was gruff. His breath stank of the pipe that he puffed on incessantly. Maria worried that his son would be like him.

She stayed in Sydney with her father-in-law for two days where he paraded her like a trophy to his Yugoslav acquaintances, boasting, 'Look at the beautiful new bride my son has.'

Timidly, Maria smiled, nodded, and said little. Her voice felt suffocated and her heart was tight. She missed her family and the life she had left. At night her pillow absorbed her tears as she wondered whether this decision had been the right one.

Eventually, they boarded the train to Cairns. There would be no comfort of a sleeping carriage, only a hard, upright seat for the trip northwards. They changed trains in Brisbane because the train gauges were different. Maria took her seat next to the window and rested her hand on her forehead to ease the continual throb. She felt empty.

For most of the seemingly endless trip she sat motionless, her eyes glued to the view outside as the train steadily made its way north. Her rosary beads lay hidden in her palm as she whispered prayers over and over again, calming her thoughts. The landscape was a changing display of colours and textures, but she barely noticed it. The train stopped and started. Passengers got on and off. A slow journey. Day merged into night, and back to day, again. It was nothing like her train trip in Europe. The English language surrounded her, isolating her even more. She understood nothing and felt more alone than she could ever have imagined. Her thoughts went to the unknown man, her husband, whom she had chained her life to. And then she thought of her family left behind. Her eyes stung and her heart wept. She glanced across at Jack, leaning back against the worn vinyl, his hat pulled down over his face, dozing. He frightens me, she thought. Despite these fears she refused to dwell on them. She had made her bed. She had married Mladen and there was no going back. This would work. She had to make it work.

Grassy plains and scrubby bushes stretched to the horizon. Silent sombre mountains, pale blue-grey eucalyptus trees. Emus and kangaroos startled by the rumbling train. Towns with timber houses raised from the ground on wooden stumps.

An elderly lady boarded in Rockhampton. She lifted her small bag into the overhead wooden rack while trying to keep her hat balanced on her silver curls. Looking over her shoulder she scowled at Jack for not offering to help. She sat beside Maria, eager to chat.

As she prattled away Maria waited patiently for her to finish before using her standard phrase, 'No English'.

'Oh.' The woman turned away in disappointment and retrieved a book from her bag to while away the hours ahead.

Maria leant her head against the rocking window frame and dozed fitfully.

29

April 1952: Cairns, Far North Queensland

'Wake up, we're close to Cairns.' Jack stood and stretched, leaning forward and looking out the window. 'Mladen should be waiting for you.'

At last, Maria thought. After all this time she would meet her husband. It seemed so long ago since they had started writing to each other, sending photographs. Their wedding day seemed to have been in a previous lifetime. She hurried to the small toilet at the end of the carriage and washed her face, checking her reflection in the grimy mirror. She was nervous, but she was ready.

Returning to her seat, she sat poised on the edge and watched the landscape rolling by, trying to stay calm as her heart started thudding. The countryside now looked different from the dry plains they had rattled past these last days. Here were endless farms of sugar cane, rows of crowded dusty stalks with leafy tops. Reaching skywards the elegant lavender plumes swayed in the breeze. Sunburnt, hatless men drove tractors along the headlands. Some paddocks had horses dragging equipment. Here and there were houses which Maria thought were inexplicably built high above the ground on narrow posts. Houses of timber with grey roofs. Next to them were round tanks elevated on cement stands. Open sheds with corrugated-iron roofs stood nearby. So much space. So spread out. In the distance, a range of mountains claimed the horizon. They were immense compared to the hills of home. She noticed a strangely shaped hill that stood alone. It reminded her of a triangle.

'This is Gordonvale. Not far now,' Jack said.

The train curved around mangroves that clung with twisted roots to the brackish mud, giving off a faint stench, like rotten eggs. It lurched over timber bridges that spanned narrow creeks, until finally, it chugged into Cairns. Whistling its arrival, the engine and its carriages slowed down and shuddered to a halt.

Many people were waiting on the platform, but Maria spotted Mladen immediately. Standing tall, feet apart and holding his hat in one hand, he was unmistakeable. Cleanly shaven, his skin was tanned. He wore long grey trousers and a white shirt with sleeves neatly folded up to the elbows. He was scanning the windows, no doubt searching for his new bride.

Hesitantly, Maria stepped down from the carriage and walked towards him. Pure delight radiated from Malden's face when he caught sight of her.

Dropping his hat, he strode towards her and took both her hands in his, looked deep into her eyes and welcomed her: *'Drago mi je da se smo vidjeli'.*

Maria was startled by his eyes. Not brown. Green. His hands were coarse but gentle. His voice was husky but warm. He then politely, yet tenderly kissed her first on one cheek and then the other. Like a bird in a cage, her heart fluttered. He was much more handsome than his photographs. Lost for words, all she could do was laugh. Relief washed over her.

'What's funny?' he asked.

'I am just so happy to finally see you. You are lovely, and you're not old, and you don't look mean.'

He laughed with her, his eyes crinkling.

Passengers walked past them and around them. Families greeting families. Friends greeting friends. Momentarily the world stopped spinning and they were lost in their own bubble.

Holding her hand firmly he then greeted his father. There was no hug. No handshake. Following a short conversation in English that she didn't understand, Mladen handed his father the car keys. Quizzically, Maria looked at both men. It was then that she noticed that Mladen had a small grey suitcase by his side. Retrieving his hat from the platform, he wedged it on his head, then tucked her suitcase under his arm before grabbing his own, clasped her hand and led her along the platform.

'We're going on our honeymoon. Three days of no work for me.'

'Where? What?'

Everything was happening too quickly. Her eyes moistened. She had just spent three exhausting days on a train. Where am I going now? I just want to go home. Any home will do, she thought. Perhaps sensing her distress, Mladen invited her to sit down next to him on the railway bench and spoke to her in her native tongue.

'It's okay, Maria. Don't worry,' he patted her hand. 'I'm taking you and me on a little holiday. We're going on this great train trip up the mountain to Kuranda. It'll be so much fun.'

She listened carefully, trying to understand the familiar words cloaked in this strange broad Australian accent. His hand rested on hers. It felt comforting.

'And don't be scared of me,' he was quick to reassure her. 'I won't be your husband if you like. I can be your cousin until you like me enough to be your husband.' He smiled mischievously, giving her hand a gentle squeeze. 'But I'll be a cousin that stares at you all the time because you're so beautiful, and I'll hold your hand sometimes too.' He winked.

Maria laughed.

'And call me Laddie. The Australians can't say Mladen, so I'm Laddie.'

She looked at 'Laddie'. What a wonderful man. Within these few minutes, she already could tell that he was everything his father was not. His enthusiasm was infectious, his vitality powerful, his kindness obvious. She laughed again, delighted to be with her husband alone at last. It seemed so long ago that she had waved goodbye to her family.

'It's fine. It's not far and we're staying in a posh hotel.'

Maria nodded. She was excited. She kept sneaking peeks at him when he wasn't looking. She didn't want to stare. He was so relaxed, so confident. And so quick to smile and laugh.

The train arrived. A long line of red and cream carriages were attached to the steam engine. Laddie carried their luggage and found two seats. They sat facing each other near the window. With a piercing toot the train commenced its journey, trundling at a leisurely pace through the township of Cairns.

'Look,' Laddie said, pointing out the window. 'This is Cairns. It's a lot bigger than Mossman. We come down here to do our serious shopping. I've picked this side so we see the view.'

Maria found Cairns intriguing. The high wooden houses on stilts were surrounded by spacious square patches of grass. White picket fences with wrought-iron gates enclosed the yards. Steep timber steps led to the houses' wooden front doors. So much wood. The streets were so wide. Such a contrast to her village. Children running in the streets stopped and waved as the train puffed by. Some, especially those on pushbikes, tried to race the train. Maria and Laddie waved back, encouraging them. It was not long before the train left the outskirts of the town. It sliced through more sugar-cane paddocks in Stratford and Freshwater before climbing the mountain. As they ascended Maria caught sight of the sea stretching to touch the horizon, flawless turquoise edged by a narrow strip of gold. Further out she could see shadows of deep blue.

'That's the reef. Lots of coral and lots of fish,' Laddie explained.

'I love fish. My father would catch us fish.'

'Good. I will catch you fish too. Big fish.' He stretched his arms out.

She did not believe him. The fish will not be that big. He's trying to impress me, she thought.

'Snapper, coral trout and barramundi.'

'What strange names. I will make you *brudet* with them.'

'Yum. Sounds great. Are you a good cook?'

She frowned as all she knew how to cook was *zeje* and a few other hastily learned dishes, but before she could answer, the carriage was engulfed in darkness. The passengers squealed. Laddie squeezed her hand and chuckled.

'Just a tunnel. There are lots of tunnels. I don't know how many, but lots. There's a really long one.'

The train emerged into the light and curved around the mountain, clinging to the steep railway track built precariously high above the forest floor. Trees grew at angles on the mountain side and silver ribbons of waterfalls trickled down between them. Maria leant out the window, amazed at the dense forest floor far below.

'This is beautiful. So... so...' Maria said, searching for the right word.

'Green? Wait until you really see the rainforest. It's thick. Lots of animals too.'

'Not scary ones, I hope.' She had heard stories of the animals in Australia.

'Just a couple,' he said, and smiled.

The trip was not long. When they arrived in Kuranda, Maria saw that the quaint village, at the top of the range, was surrounded by tropical rainforest. The newlyweds, Mr and Mrs Gavranich, checked into the hotel and were shown to their room. Outside the open window was a leafy canopy. The silence was punctuated by the loud chatter of birds. Maria sat nervously on the edge of the bed. She brushed her hand across the yellow chenille bedspread. It felt new. Laddie threw his suitcase on the bed and retrieved a small brown box from it.

'I have something for you.' He looked pleased with himself as he handed it to her.

Curiously, she opened it. It was an engagement ring. The diamond dazzled.

'You should have had this a year ago, before our wedding, but better late than never, I reckon. I didn't want to risk sending this rock in the post.'

He slid it on her finger until it rested snugly against the gold wedding band.

'There. A perfect fit.'

Speechless, Maria sat and stared at the ring. As she twisted her hand to and fro, light streaming through the window danced on the diamond's facets. Laddie discreetly left the room so she could refresh herself and change. She could hear him wandering up and down the corridor outside. When he returned a few minutes later, she was still sitting on the bed looking at the ring. He left again and returned. Same, she sat motionless staring at her ring.

'You keep looking at that ring on your hand. I think you like it more than me.'

Smiling she shook her head and opened her arms to hug her new husband.

30

Here comes the bride

Three days later, Jack drove to Cairns to collect the honeymooners from the train.

'Here, sit between us,' Laddie said to Maria as he patted the seat. Turning to his father he declared, 'Dad, I'll drive home'.

Maria slid across the cracked vinyl seat, staying close to the steering wheel. The ute smelt of sweat and grease. It smelt of men. Laddie turned the ignition. The motor whirred sluggishly. He tried it again. Same.

'Damn it, that starter motor is still playing up. You haven't fixed it yet, Dad?'

'Nope. I thought you were going to do that.'

Getting out, Laddie grabbed a rusted hammer from the back and walked to the front of the vehicle. Lifting the bonnet, he whacked at the greasy engine.

'Okay, Maria, can you try that now?'

'But, Laddie, I can't drive.'

'Ah, okay. Well, we'll have to change that quicksmart.'

Slamming the bonnet shut, he turned the key once more and the engine spluttered to life.

'Good. We're on our way.' He patted Maria's knee and changed the gears.

'We'll drive along the sea most of the way. Good views.'

'Is it very far?'

'No, not too bad. It's all bitumen these days. Makes it a bit quicker.'

The Captain Cook Highway snaked along the coastline connecting Cairns to Mossman. Tropical palm trees lined parts of the road. They leaned towards the bleached sandy beach, heavy with bunches of green coconuts.

'Have you ever tasted fresh coconut?' Laddie asked her. 'No? Okay, I think you'll like it.'

A slight breeze was blowing, and the sea rippled in the sun.

'Beautiful, heh?'

'It's not as blue as the sea at home. It's different.'

'Yep, that's not all that's goin' to be different. Mossman is a hell of a lot different from Blato.'

'But that will be good, Laddie. A lot of bad things happened back home.'

Patting her knee again he nodded and started to whistle. The narrow road weaved, dipped and climbed as it followed the sea, slicing through massive grey boulders and the scrubby bushland. Pale green leaves clung to the branches of the beige paperbacks. The bark of these towering trees was peeling like sunburnt skin. Wild guinea grass engulfed rusty red anthill domes. As they reached a place that Laddie told her was called the Rex Lookout, Maria caught her breath at the spectacular view. Looking at the sea embracing the horizon, she felt comforted as she imagined this same ocean wrapping around the earth and eventually lapping the stony beaches of her home island.

The ute followed the road inland cutting through paddocks of sugar cane. The hills behind were dense with trees and bushes, a tangle of green. So lush. So different from home, she thought.

Laddie tooted the horn and waved to a man working in one of the paddocks.

'That's Anton. Anton Pisot. You'll get to meet him. He's a good bloke.'

The ute rumbled on as Laddie commenced a running commentary.

'That's the road to Port Douglas. Good swimming beaches there.

And see that creek down there?'

Maria peered down as they rattled across the narrow wooden bridge.

'Well, a man was killed by a cassowary down there.'

'A cassowary?' She frowned.

'Yep. That's a bird.'

She rolled her eyes. 'I don't believe you. Killed by a bird?'

After only a few days together she was getting used to his pranks.

'No, fair dinkum. A cassowary is this hell of a big bird, as tall as me, with a horn thing on its head and big clawed feet. It can kill you with its horn or kick you to death.' She could tell he was struggling to find the right Yugoslav words, slotting in Australian slang every so often.

'And you say this is a bird?' She found it hard to understand him, with his sprinkling of slang and English.

'Yeah, a bird. But a bird with no wings. It can't fly.'

'You're tricking me.' She slapped his shoulder.

'No. No, I'm not. Wait and see. Okay, here's our turn off to Cassowary Valley. If we kept going straight, we would end up at town. A couple miles down thataway.'

Maria stared out the window, wide-eyed. There were cane paddocks everywhere.

Laddie sped up as the ute plunged into a steep dip in the road.

'Hey!' Maria squealed as the ute plummeted, leaving her stomach behind. She squealed again as they rose to the other side, only to plummet again like a roller coaster.

'Be careful with the ute, Laddie,' warned his father, who had been silent the whole trip.

'No, Dad, it's okay. This won't hurt it.'

Turning his attention back to Maria, he pointed to the right. 'See that? That's my school. Cassowary State High. State *High*. Get it?'

No, she didn't get it.

'Well, it's the primary school but it's on posts so it's high. Cassowary State *High*.'

He snorted at his own joke. What a strange looking little building for a school, Maria thought.

'And those pine trees next to it. That's the forestry plot. We planted those trees. And look over there. That's where the Vico family lives.'

'You talk too much,' complained Jack.

Ignoring his father, Laddie continued. 'They're Yugoslav too. You'll meet them soon enough. Mrs Vico was one of my mum's good friends. Nice kids. There's Jean, Mick, Alex and George. The boys are younger than me. Actually, I think Mick's about your age. You'll like them.'

She smiled and nodded. She couldn't understand everything he said. His accent was unusual, and it didn't help that he would forget and break into English. Laddie kept looking across at her and grinning. She knew he was excited to be bringing her to his home. As he changed gears, he would give her leg a gentle squeeze and laugh. His high spirits were contagious.

'Keep your eyes on the road, Laddie,' grumbled Jack.

'Yeah, Dad, yeah.'

The ute dipped and crossed a babbling creek and curved to the right. They were in a valley, Cassowary Valley. Encircled by mountains.

'Here's our road.' They turned left and bounced along a dirt track. 'Look. That's home.'

All Maria could see was a small, corrugated iron shed with square windows cut out from the walls, propped open by sturdy sticks.

'That?' she asked, pointing to the primitive building.

'Haha. No. That's the barracks where the cane cutters live. Look straight ahead.'

As they rounded the bend, the farmhouse greeted her. Wide and white. Standing on cement posts on a grassy area of cleared land, the house seemed impressive but also alone and almost vulnerable.

Its only neighbour was an open shed with a rusted roof. It was surrounded by fields of sugar cane. A second part of the house with a steeply pitched roof was set further back.

A young woman came running down the steps.

'Maria, Maria, Maria. Welcome to your new home,' she said in English. Without waiting for a response, she wrapped her arms around Maria and pulled her in for a crushing embrace.

Maria felt the warmth in the woman's muscular arms and hugged her tightly in return. This must be Mary, her new sister. She had the same broad honest face as her brother. Uncomplicated and happy. After only three days in Kuranda, Maria felt she could trust her husband. After just a few minutes she felt exactly the same with his sister.

As Mary gripped her hand and led her into the house, Maria slowly absorbed her new surroundings. She walked up the four red cement steps, through the bifold wooden doors into the lounge room. Under the floral linoleum the floorboards creaked. Through the windows at the other end of the room, all she could see was sugar cane, trees and mountains. These mountains were not like the craggy rocks of home, but a sea of green. Her nose twitched as she smelt fresh scones.

'Are you hungry? Let's eat,' Mary said and led her into the kitchen.

The table was covered with a lacy tablecloth, with China teacups positioned neatly near the tin of coffee. Wrapped in a floral tea towel, the scones were still warm from the stove.

Mary apologised and said she found it hard to keep talking in Yugoslav. She kept forgetting.

'Nah, that's good' mumbled Laddie through a mouthful of scones. 'We'll talk English. She'll learn quickly.'

That night Maria curled into her new bed. Her husband snored softly beside her, his arm wrapped around her. The household slept but the night was awake and noisy with strange sounds.

She lay still and listened. The clamour of crickets was interrupted by a haunting wail, like a child crying. What is that? she wondered. Frogs croaked. Floorboards creaked. Large empty drums near the sheds boomed as they cooled from the heat of the day. Eventually, she slept, the deep sleep of an exhausted woman; a woman who had finally reached her destination.

31

The 'New Australian'

Mary was so happy to have this 'sister' arrive. For many years she had been the only female in the house. Just her with her brother and father. After a few days Mary and Laddie decided that Maria could pitch in and help with the farm chores. The siblings had a roster and took week about feeding the horses.

'I'll teach her,' offered Mary, 'because I know you, Laddie. You won't show her everything.'

Mary desperately wanted Maria to be happy and hoped that if she kept this new sister busy there might be less chance of homesickness.

At three in the morning, she woke Maria and, as they stepped into the backyard, the glow of their hurricane lamps lit a path for them.

'Okay, first we need to get the horse food. We feed them 'chop-chop'. Here.' She handed Maria a rusted kerosene tin filled with cut-up sugar cane tops. 'Now, follow me.'

An eerie sound pierced the stillness of the night, startling Maria.

'What's that noise? I hear it every night.'

'They're just the curlews in the bush. They're birds.'

'What scary sounding birds. They sound like children crying. Australia has some strange birds.'

The two women walked down the back slope, finding the stepping stones to cross the narrow creek, and then up the hill to the stable. They brushed past clumps of long guinea grass, damp with the early morning dew.

155

Mary walked into the stables first, swinging her lamp from side to side and yelling, 'Shoo! Shoo!'

'Arrghhh!' Maria leapt backwards. 'What are they?'

Captured in the glowing arc of the swinging lamp, the brown warty toads scattered, hopping and croaking, their beady black eyes blinking.

'They're just cane toads. Don't be scared.'

'They're so ugly, Mary. You know, I don't think I've ever seen anything so ugly. Ever!'

Maria squealed and jumped from one foot to the other, avoiding the scurrying toads, her lamp weaving erratic patterns of light in the darkness. The horses stirred, stamping their feet and snorting.

'You'll get used to them. You have to shoo them away or they'll eat the horses' food. They're everywhere. Pests. Just don't touch them.'

'Don't worry. I'm not going anywhere near them.'

They fed the six large Clydesdales, then made their way back home.

'Those were really big horses. We only have a donkey at home.'

'Really? Now, tomorrow you can feed the horses by yourself. What do you think?'

Nodding Maria replied, 'Of course, no problem. But I hope I don't step on any of those toads.'

Day by day, Mary taught her more about the routine on the farm. She showed her the grey slab behind the house that covered the expansive underground well, which held the rainwater from the house gutters.

'You can pump out this water for showers, washing and watering the lawn.' Mary pointed to the copper pump on the edge of the slab.

'Our drinking water comes from these tanks.' She showed her the two above-ground water tanks near the house. 'Just be careful and check the water before you drink it,' Mary said. 'You need to scoop out any wrigglers. Don't wanna drink them. Yuck!'

'Wrigglers?'

'Yeah, you know, mozzie wrigglers.'

Mary wasn't sure if her sister-in-law could understand everything she said and hoped she didn't think everything was too strange and unfamiliar. Maria had been in her new home for just over a week. What a busy week. Sometimes Mary thought Maria looked exhausted, and at other times, exhilarated.

'Okay, Maria, it's time to show you the big smoke. Mossman.' Laddie said, when they'd finished lunch on Friday. 'I'm taking the afternoon off.'

While he was showering, Maria changed into her only good dress and walked back into the kitchen.

'Does this look suitable, Mary?'

Mary glanced over and shrugged. 'Yes, sure. We're only going into Mossman.'

Maria nodded, looking a little puzzled.

They walked out to the ute and Maria slid onto the seat in between Mary and Laddie.

'Remember we drove past the school last week.' He pointed to the timber building.

'Laddie, slow down,' Mary squealed as he accelerated to fly down the two dips outside the school.

He ignored her.

'I'm ready this time,' Maria said as she held onto the dashboard.

They plummeted down the steep dip, their bodies lifting off the seat. Laddie laughed at the screaming girls.

'Okay, we turn left here and go to town. See those railway lines?' He nodded in the opposite direction. 'Gotta be careful during the season for cane trains.'

'The Morosinis and Tolentinis live over there.' Mary pointed out the window.

'Are they Italian?'

'Yep, lots of Yugoslavs and Italians in Mossman.'

The road followed the railway track and the cane paddocks. The ute rumbled over an old wooden bridge that spanned a creek.

Laddie paused and idled the engine.

'Okey-dokes, this is one of the places we usually go swimming.'

The creek was shadowed by the overhanging branches of rainforest trees.

'He doesn't only swim here. In winter, during planting time, he comes here at night with bags of sugarcane shoots to soak them in the creek,' Mary explained.

Maria stared at her, confused.

Laddie shook his head. 'Don't you worry. That definitely won't be one of your jobs.'

'Yeah, you're lucky. It's freezing in the middle of the night when he has to do it.' Mary continued pointing back at the bridge. 'Laddie and his mates jump off this bridge. It's pretty deep there but they're crazy. Can you swim, Maria?'

'Sort of—'

'I know you do. Remember that photo you sent me of you in your togs?' Laddie nudged her. 'You're a good looker. Whoa, those long legs of yours.' He wolf-whistled.

'Stop it, Laddie. You're embarrassing her,' Mary said as Maria blushed.

But Maria smiled, and Mary relaxed. She could tell that Maria was enjoying the attention.

'Now, Maria, your husband is a naughty boy. I'll tell you what he did here a few months ago.'

'Mary, what are you gonna tell her?'

'Well,' she continued, 'he and his mates came for a swim one Saturday arvo and they were skinny dipping.'

'Hey, no. Not that story. She'll think I'm crazy,' Laddie protested.

'No, tell me, tell me,' Maria said, turning to face Mary.

'Well, they were skinny-dipping, you know with no clothes on. And while they were all swimming, Laddie rubbed chilli, this really peppery plant that burns, on the inside of his mates' underpants.' Mary paused checking that Maria had understood this conversation.

'Oh, no!' Maria covered her open mouth with both hands.

'Yes! His mate got a pretty hot surprise when he got dressed,' Mary said.

'Laddie, you are so bad.' Laughing, Maria slapped his thigh.

As they approached the outskirts, Mary glanced around, wondering what Maria thought of the town. It was sprawling, crisscrossed by the wide bitumen streets, and most of the buildings were timber and were all fairly new.

Laddie parked the ute in the main street. Front Street. Donning his aviator styled sunglasses, he linked arms with both women, and they strolled along the pavement, nodding and greeting those they passed. Occasionally, they'd stop so Laddie could introduce his new bride. They passed the Exchange Hotel, a grand two-storey timber building with wide verandahs that straddled the corner of Front and Mill streets.

'It's the best hotel in town. Real fancy. They had to rebuild it,' said Laddie.

'Why?'

'The cyclone knocked down the last one.'

'What's a cyclone?' Maria asked.

Mary and Laddie glanced at each other.

'There's a lot about Australia you don't know. We'll tell you about cyclones later. I don't wanna frighten you,' he said.

Maria stood still, admiring the grand building.

'It's beautiful. Look at all this wood.' She touched the windowsill and gazed into the expansive lounge. A silky-oak staircase led up to the next floor.

'When we have cane cutters working for us, we bring them into town on Saturdays to do their shopping,' Mary said. 'A lot of them end up in the bar here.'

They crossed the street and headed to a store on the corner.

'Maria, you'll like this building,' Laddie said. 'It's called Jack and Newell's. They built it out of concrete. No cyclone will knock this one down.'

'What's a cyclone again?' asked Maria.

'Just a bit of rain and wind. Actually, a lot of rain and wind. Not good for the cane.'

As they walked inside, she looked around, smiling. Mary took her down the aisles, showing her the grocery shelves crammed with food, tins with colourful labels advertising their contents, cardboard boxes and packets of food stacked neatly together.

'I have never seen so much variety, so much colour, so much food,' Maria said.

She wandered into the next aisle, and Mary heard her gasp. Joining her, she saw that Maria was staring at the wall of fabric. Arranged side by side was bolt after bolt of cottons and rayons, bold patterns of flowers, polka dots and even crimson cherries.

Two women brushed past them, chatting as they selected their fabrics. Maria stepped closer to feel the texture of the fabric.

'Ah, there you are,' Laddie strode towards them. 'Thought I'd lost you both.'

He pointed to the office on a mezzanine floor at the back of the store.

'We can book things up. They're good to us farmers. They know we don't get a regular pay and have to wait till after the season when the mill pays us.'

As Laddie was talking, the cashiers secured pound notes and coins into a cup, which then whizzed up to the office in a 'flying fox' style apparatus. Young women, hair in neat bobs, some with glasses balanced on nose tips, sat tip-tapping at their typewriters high above the busy ground floor.

'So, you don't pay straight away?' Maria asked.

'Nope. They're good like that to the cane cutters too.'

Laddie and Mary continued to introduce her to the locals wandering in and out. She nodded and smiled. A group gathered around her and were all laughing now. Seeing Maria's confused expression, Mary thought, I need to help her learn English quicksmart. Can't have her not knowing what people are saying.

∞

The following week Maria visited Jack and Newell's for a second time. Mary needed to do a few errands so she scribbled a short shopping list, pushed it into Maria's palm and said, 'Can you get these things for me?'

Nervously Maria entered the store. It was noisy and busy, and Maria watched as other customers walked up to the counters and asked for various items. She realised then that she would have to talk to the efficient-looking women behind the counter. She hid in the corner behind the shelving, chewing on her bottom lip as she studied the employees. The young woman with short blonde curls and glossy red lipstick looked smiley and chatty, so Maria decided she would approach her.

'Hello,' Maria began. 'How are you?'

She had exhausted approximately fifty per cent of her English. The young woman prattled on to her.

Maria had no idea what she was saying and, not wanting to seem stupid, she nodded, saying, 'Yes. Good. Thank you.'

That was the other fifty per cent of her English. Seeing the confused look on the young woman's face, Maria realised that maybe her responses were not making sense, so she quickly handed over the shopping list, which was now crumpled from her sweaty palm.

'No English.' She smiled broadly and shrugged her shoulders.

'Ah.' The young girl smiled back, flattened the shopping list out on the polished wooden counter and read the list, before collecting the items and packing them neatly in a brown paper bag.

Maria watched and wondered: How do I pay for this? Then she remembered what Laddie had told her about the farmers having an account.

As the young woman waited, Maria stammered, 'Ga... Ga... Gavranich. Laddie Gavranich.'

That seemed to do the trick. The sales assistant nodded and opened a ledger book, penned in the amount and spoke again rapidly to Maria. Maria could pick out 'Bye' in the midst of the jumble of unfamiliar words, so decided this was her cue to leave. Clutching her bag to her chest she repeated, 'Goodbye,' and rushed out of the store. She waited outside, her face feeling flushed from the encounter.

When Mary returned, Maria berated her sister-in-law.

'Mary, I had to talk to them in there. I didn't know how.'

'Ooops, sorry.'

Mary checked the items in the paper bag. 'Yep. You did really well. You got everything. You'll get there. Before long you'll be chattering away to them.'

They returned to the farm and Mary recounted the story to Laddie and Jack who were sitting at the kitchen table smoking. It seemed funny now. The story even managed to make Jack smile.

'Brave girl,' Laddie congratulated his wife, pulling her in close and planting a kiss on her lips.

'No, I wasn't brave,' she said, pushing herself out of his grasp. 'Mary made me do it. I felt so stupid, so dumb. You need to teach me English.'

'You'll be right. You'll learn quickly,' he said, as positive as ever. 'Lunchtime. Let's eat.'

When they had finished washing up after lunch, Mary said, 'Okay, today I'll show you how to use the copper.'

In the laundry, Mary pointed to the copper next to the sturdy cement laundry sink and filled it with water pumped from the well.

'You need to heat up the water in this copper first. It has to be boiling.'

Maria watched.

'Okay, now put these clothes in with the Rinso. We do the whites first.'

Maria was busy stirring them with a wooden paddle. She glanced up and screamed.

'Look! Look up there!'

Curled up on one of the wooden beams that supported the corrugated-iron outdoor roof was a slender snake, napping.

'Laddie!' Mary yelled, waking him from his post-lunch siesta on his outdoor bed near the laundry. 'Snake!'

Racing indoors he grabbed the shotgun from the bathroom, stood on the top step, aimed and fired. The women ducked.

'Bugger! I missed.'

He fired again and again and again. The snake dropped to the floor.

'Lucky I got it, 'cos it's not a carpet snake. That one's a brown one. Deadly.'

Maria didn't know whether to be more afraid of the wriggling snake on the floor or the fact that her husband had a gun in the bathroom that he shot snakes with. The snake wriggled, stopped and wriggled a bit more.

'Look at all those holes in the roof,' Maria said, looking up.

'Yeah, Laddie, you have to stop killing snakes that way,' Mary joined in. 'It looks like that strainer we've got in the kitchen.'

'Hmm. Maybe you gotta point there.'

He disappeared off to the shed and reappeared a little while later.

'See? Problem fixed.'

He brandished a long pole with two nails protruding in a V at the end and held a cane knife in the other hand.

'This is what I'll do.'

He flicked the snake onto the grass, pinned its head with the V of nails, and sliced its head off with the cane knife.

'Yes, that's better.' Maria nodded. 'No more holes in the laundry roof.'

Laddie then tossed the still wriggling snake into the air and it landed near Maria. She squealed. From the back yard a low chuckle started that built to the crescendo of a maniacal cackle. A kookaburra perched on the wire clothesline, rocked back and forth with its beak faced upwards.

'That bird. Look over there. It's laughing at me. Rude thing.'

Mary and Laddie laughed.

'It's just a kookaburra.'

'But how does it do that? It's laughing.'

'That's just their noise. They always sound like that. But I think that one *is* laughing at you,' Laddie said.

Maria sniffed and turned back to the dirty washing. Pretending to ignore both her husband and the bird that was still cackling, she winked at Mary.

Life in Australia was very different, she thought. Even the birds laugh at me.

32

A tropical wedding party

Maria had been in Mossman for a month when Laddie announced, 'I wasn't at my own wedding so let's have a wedding party for the both of us'.

The verandah was decorated once more. It was a good area for a party and was often a popular choice for dances for the locals in this little valley. Cassowary Valley, four miles from the township of Mossman, was picturesque in a rustic way. The canefields were intersected with dusty dirt roads, tree-edged creeks and dotted with timber farmhouses, sheds and barracks. Maria was excited as she helped Mary with the party lights and balloons.

When the guests arrived, Maria stood beside Laddie at the doorway as he introduced her.

'She's a beauty. Watch out or I'll run off with her,' teased one of his mates.

Laddie jokingly clenched his fist at him while putting his arm around her waist. Maria didn't understand a word the men were saying but kept smiling and tried to calm the butterflies in her stomach.

After all the guests had arrived, Maria sat at the head of the table beside her new husband. Freshly picked marigolds in a crystal vase provided a burst of orange on the table, which was covered with a starched white tablecloth. The main course was followed by typical Australian offerings—the wedding cake, a single-tier marzipan-iced fruitcake that was placed in front of the bridal couple, surrounded by plates of lamingtons and raspberry slices.

Maria fidgeted and pulled her seat in closer to her husband's. She looked at the guests seated around the long tables that extended the length of the verandah. These were her new family and friends. She glanced across the table at her father-in-law but quickly looked away, avoiding eye contact. He still frightened her. Beside him and to her left were Antun and Ema Anich, her husband's aunt and uncle. Ema's dimples deepened and her kind eyes warmed as she caught Maria's glance, and smiled. Laddie's friends surrounded them. Tennis teammates, cardmates, the farmers who lived in Cassowary Valley, who called themselves 'cane cockies'—all these new names that would become more and more familiar to her. A gentle breeze wafted in through the open casement windows and the wooden louvres that enclosed the verandah. Her hand checked the pins keeping her curls in place.

She leaned into Laddie and whispered, 'I'm lucky there are so many Yugoslavs here'. She pointed to the Padovans, the Anichs, the Vicos, the D'Addonas.'

'Hey, the D'addonas are Italian, Maria.'

'Yes, I know, but I speak more Italian than English so I'm calling them Yugoslav.'

Under the table his hand squeezed her knee. 'You're doing just fine.'

'Yes, darlink,' she responded in English, her tongue struggling to pronounce some of the words. She found 'g' and 'th' at the end of some words particularly difficult.

Laddie topped up his beer glass from the 'tallie' and then stood to speak. He was wearing his best and only grey suit, white shirt and a tie. His face was flushed—with beer and pride. Motioning for Maria to stand next to him, he cleared his throat and then began.

'On behalf of me wife, Maria, and meself—'

Raucous cheers interrupted. He pulled her close, his arm hugging her waist.

'I would like to welcome you all here tonight to our wedding. Now those of youse that know me, know that I'm a man of few words so that's it. I've said 'em. Have fun. Cheers.'

Clinking of glasses and clapping. Maria grabbed her husband's face and cheekily planted a kiss on his lips amidst a roar of laughter. 'Now that's me wife!' A wide grin spread across his face as he pinched her bottom.

∽

With Maria's arrival to manage the household, Jack agreed to let Mary work outside the home in a paid job, as a domestic at the local Mossman Hospital.

'Come here, Maria,' she beckoned after her first fortnight of work. 'Look.'

She unfolded the pound notes, flattened the creases and counted them.

'I've never had money for myself ever before. Never, ever.'

Maria smiled, happy for her. She understood her excitement as she too had never had a paid job, had never received a wage.

'What will you do with it?'

'I don't know. Why don't we all go to the movies?' Mary suggested.

'Why don't you see if that nice boy wants to come with us?'

'Who?'

Mary blushed.

'Mary, you know who——Dick Fapani.' She nudged Mary.

Both women laughed and Mary nodded. 'All right. And this time I'll pay for our tickets. Laddie won't have to ask Dad for money. I heard that *High Noon* is showing at the moment. The boys will love it. Lots of shooting.'

'Fine.'

'And Gary Cooper's pretty good-looking. I reckon we'll like looking at him.'

A trip to the movies was a favourite treat. They all squeezed into the front seat of the ute and rattled into town. The old theatre was in the Photoplay building in Mill Street, near the Post Office Hotel. Standing at the end of the street was the heartbeat of the town, the towering grey sugar mill. It was crushing season and the

167

mill had been alive all day, spewing grey plumes of smoke from its tall chimney and rattling and clunking as it devoured the never-ending line of steel cages filled with stalks of sugar cane, ready for processing. The sweet almost sickening smell of molasses permeated the town well into the evening.

The two couples entered the theatre, blinking as their eyes adjusted to the darkness. They found their favourite seats, high in the back row.

'We need a new picture theatre,' said Laddie, glancing up as they waited for the projector to roll the movie.

'Yep,' said Dick. 'It looks like that roof is about to fall in. I heard the council's talking about building a new one.'

'Shhh. It's starting,' whispered Maria.

As was the custom then, they all stood for 'God Save the Queen'. This was followed by the newsreel and then the feature film. The theatre quietened. Maria opened the box of Jaffas and popped two into her mouth as she watched the screen. She couldn't understand much of what the actors were saying but there was enough action to be able to follow the story. She liked the look of Gary Cooper and Grace Kelly. She glanced across at Mary and Dick, who were holding hands. She smiled and kept popping the Jaffas into her mouth, trying to crunch the sweet treats as quietly as possible. Until one fell to the floor. She stifled her giggles as she listened to it rattle all the way down the sloping floor before it came to rest at the bottom.

'Oops.'

Movie nights became a fun break for Maria from cleaning and cooking, and a window into the exciting world of exotic destinations and glamorous actors. This was not something that would happen in Blato, but going to the movies was a weekly ritual for most of the residents of this small town.

And day by day, week by week, Maria settled into her new home, growing used to the daytime sqwark and trills of the birds in her endless backyard, and the evening orchestra of the croaking cane toads, the *brawk brawk* of the green frogs, accompanied by the haunting cries of the curlew soloists and the hooting owls. These noises replaced the sounds from her childhood of carts rumbling across cobblestones, donkeys braying and the always too loud chatter of the many neighbours that sounded like arguments but was simply friendly bantering. She missed this banter and missed her sisters, so was grateful that, for now, Mary was still part of her household. The two women spent many hours together, talking, cleaning, talking, cooking and talking. They had already given each other the nickname, 'Botch'. Neither was really sure how that happened, but it just happened.

One afternoon they had finished lunch and were in the kitchen cleaning. Laddie was resting out the back before he returned to the paddocks and Jack was resting in his bedroom. Maria wore a flowery apron, secured with a bow around her waist, and a damp tea towel was draped over her shoulder. She stacked the plates in the metal rinsing tub on the sink. Wiping the table, Mary collected the leftover crusts of bread, leant in front of Maria and tossed them out the open window to the cluster of chickens pecking below.

'Mary! What are you doing?'

'What? I'm just chuckin' out the crusts.'

'You're throwing out food?' Maria frowned. 'That's good food. Did you know, Mary, that there are people in Europe starving?'

Staring at the floor, Mary mumbled, 'Sorry'.

Maria nodded and returned to washing the dishes. As she watched the greedy chickens fighting over the scraps, she thought of her own hungry family thousands of kilometres away and wished she could do more. Her heart carried a background ache, a guilt almost, which she tried to bury with her busy life. True to her word before she had left, she sent parcels to her family— dresses, shoes, cash—all folded in pillowslips and carefully packaged. In turn, Laddie would bring the mail home from the post office, Box 112.

'Letter from the old country, honey.'

As he handed her the envelope with the red, white and blue edging and the slanted handwriting, recognisable as her sister Žuva's, Maria would nod, take it and hide in their bedroom, weeping and reading. Often, she would rush to the toilet, the visceral impact of these letters from home too much for her to bear. Sometimes, they would include photographs. All of them would include gratitude. Wiping her eyes, she would return when her reddened face had cleared.

Laddie would ask, 'All good back home?'

Hugging him, she would reply, 'Yes, they got our parcel. They said, "thank you".'

'No problems. It's good you can help.'

My father was right about this country, she thought. There is plenty of food. It's safe. These phrases would bubble to the surface, especially when times were bleak.

33

Social tennis

Laddie was a larrikin, Maria decided, when she found out what the word meant. When not working, he played sport or went fishing. He loved his tennis and cricket, but especially tennis. So much so that when he was much younger, he had built a tennis court beside the farmhouse. He and Mary were both left handers and a formidable doubles partnership. They played competition as Club Gavranich, but Sunday was always social tennis day.

'It's been raining. The tennis court's still wet,' complained Mary, looking at the puddles in dismay.

'No worries. I'll fix it,' Laddie said.

He fetched a tin from the shed and doused the court with kerosene. The pungent oily smell wafted over to the house.

'Watch out,' he said as he tossed a flaming match on to the court.

It worked—the court was dry and ready for tennis.

'Do you want to have a go? We'll teach you.' Laddie would often ask Maria, offering her a sturdy wooden tennis racquet.

'No,' would be her response every time. 'I'm happy to watch. I never played any sport.'

She thought back to her grim childhood splintered by war, as she watched Mary dart around the court returning ball after ball.

'Good shot, Mary,' Maria called out, as Mary smashed a winner over the net.

The McCoists were regulars on Sundays, and played with the brother and sister team.

Midway through the afternoon, Laddie or Mary would yell, 'Okay. Stop everyone. Remember your game count. It's smoko time.'

Sweaty bodies in white would collapse in chairs around the long narrow trestle table that wobbled on the uneven cement near the court. Maria would help lay out smoko. There would be curried egg and lettuce sandwiches, butterfly cupcakes, raspberry slice and Maria's pride and joy—her vanilla sponge cake smothered with mock cream.

'Maria, did you make this marvellous cake?' Ian McCoist asked, cream-covered crumbs falling from his mouth. 'It's the best cake ever!'

She laughed because he said this to her every week.

It had become a tradition in the evening, to follow the day's tennis exertions with card games. Laddie and Mary and the McCoists would gather around the kitchen table, all still in their sweaty tennis whites to play into the night. In the beginning, Maria would pull her chair close and concentrate as the cards were dealt and games were played.

It wasn't long before she was ready to join in, yelling, 'Pontoon' with the rest of them, while slamming her cards on the table and collecting her pennies.

Late into the night their voices would drift through the open windows, disturbing only the nocturnal wildlife. Laddie's father, Jack, would scowl and go to bed, banging his door shut behind him.

34

Despite all odds

'I'm so happy for you, Botch,' Maria said as she spread margarine on the thick slice of Vienna loaf. She took a large bite and chewed with a smile on her face. Years of hunger had forged a strong love affair with bread. She paused, patted her heavily pregnant stomach as if willing there to be more room, before taking another bite. Mary sat across from her at the kitchen table, mending clothes while she sipped from her mug of coffee.

'I can't believe I'm getting married next week,' Mary said, raising her voice to be heard above the constant clatter of the rain drumming on the tin roof above. 'I love this rain, but I hope it stops before my wedding.'

Maria looked at the wall of rain outside the open windows. She had laid a towel on the lino floor beneath the windows to catch the stray drops as they splattered in.

'It's been raining for days,' she said. 'I've never seen anything like it. At least it's not so muggy though.' She wiped the perspiration off her brow and kept chewing. 'This heat is so, so heavy.'

'Welcome to Mossman and your first wet season.'

'Is it like this every year?'

'Yeah, but never as much as this.'

Maria nodded. She liked this 'wet season'. The steady serenade of the rain embraced her, soothing her heart and making her feel safe and cosy in her home. She thought of how her family back in Blato would be hiding from the bitter winter, trapped in their closed stone houses. Hibernating.

'If it keeps raining my bridesmaid will definitely get flooded in. Inez lives way up past Miallo,' Mary observed.

'What will she do?'

'I heard them say they'll have to bring her across on the rail tracks on the trolley. In her long, lacy dress.' Mary sighed as she looked up from her mending and out at the relentless downpour. 'I don't even want to think about it.'

'Well, Mary, what happens if *we* get flooded in? Laddie will have to take you to the church in that little tin boat of his. In *your* long lacy wedding gown.' She grinned.

'Hey, don't get too cheeky. You'll be right beside me holding the umbrella, even if you *are* seven months pregnant.' Mary laughed. 'You had better hope he doesn't rock that boat too much.'

'No. That's a bad idea. Let's pray for this rain to stop.'

Standing to clear the table, Maria grimaced as she arched backwards and rubbed the small of her back.

'I feel as if I am ready for this baby now. Look at me. I'm so big.' She wiped the crumbs from the table. 'I'm excited for you but sad you won't be here when I have this baby.' She massaged the side of her stomach, feeling it kicking. 'I'm a bit scared.'

She moved to the sink and began washing the dishes, pushing away the thought of being on the farm with a newborn baby and so far away from everyone. So isolated. No neighbours nearby to call for help.

'Botch, I'll always be here for you. You know that.'

'Yes, I am so lucky to have you. We have each other,' Maria said. 'So, what do you think about your dad remarrying?' Maria looked over her shoulder at her sister-in-law.

'I don't know,' Mary shrugged. 'Whatever makes him happy. He said he's found someone in Blato and will bring her out next year. You saw her photo. Do you know her?'

'Not really. I know the family.' Maria dropped her voice. 'I don't think it will be easy for her though. A proxy marriage at her age. Leaving everyone.'

174

Mary agreed. 'In more ways than one. Well at least Dad might leave the farm then. It can finally be Laddie's.'

Maria wiped her wet hands on her apron and pondered, as she looked out the window at the rain. Dare she hope to have this home for herself and her own little family?

Maria and Laddie's first baby, Maryanne, arrived in March, 1953, and Maria was overwhelmed at the intensity of her feelings. She especially loved watching how smitten her husband was with this cherubic baby. She truly felt that they were now a family. All she needed was some certainty about what their future held.

'You should ask him now. He's sitting in the kitchen,' Maria said to her husband one day after lunch.

'Yeah, I reckon I need to get this sorted out, once and for all,' said Laddie.

Maria pushed her laundry trolley over the freshly mown backyard to the washing line, a sturdy rope strung between two pickets. The white cloth nappies flapped with the gusts of wind. Glancing back, she saw her husband hesitate. He brushed some dirt off his hands before shoving them into his pockets. Warily he climbed the four wooden steps into the kitchen.

Maria turned and began unpegging the dry nappies, her lips moving as she murmured her prayers and hoped.

Jack sat at the kitchen table filling his pipe with tobacco.

'Dad, I need to talk to you about the farm.'

His father didn't look up, his attention on his pipe.

Laddie sat down at the table opposite him and said again, 'I need to talk to you about the farm'.

'What?' Jack growled, still not looking up.

'Well,' he paused, clearing his throat before continuing, 'you'll be leaving when your wife, Mara, comes. You said you're moving into town.'

'Yes, and?' Jack grunted.

'What happens then? To the farm?'

'What are you talking about? Nothing happens to the farm.' Jack lit the pipe and began puffing.

'You know it's part mine, Dad.'

Jack swivelled his head and glared at Laddie.

'Not on your life! It's mine. It's all mine!' He thumped his fist onto the table, rattling the plates.

'But, but, Dad, I've worked for you for no wages since I was twelve. You pulled me out of school.'

'So?'

'You knew that I wanted to stay at school. You knew that I wanted to be a doctor.'

'Don't... forget...' Jack said slowly, his voice low and his lips drawn back in a snarl, 'that I've given you somewhere to live. A roof over your head. I've fed you *and* your wife *and* your baby. I've paid all their costs.' He scowled. 'Paid for her,' he pointed out to the backyard, 'to come out from the old country. Where the hell do you think that money came from?'

'Yeah, but Dad I'm thirty-one. I'm not a kid. I've had to ask you for money all my life. If I want to take my wife to the movies, I've had to ask for cash.'

'That's fair. I don't see any problem. If you want this farm, you'll have to buy it from me. If you don't, I'll just sell it to whoever wants it.'

Laddie's voice waivered and his shoulders sagged in defeat.

'Well... well, okay. If that's how you want to do it. But will you at least loan me the money for a deposit? So that I can get a loan from the bank to buy it off you?'

'No. That's not my problem.' Jack looked out the window. The conversation was over.

Pushing his chair back, Laddie stood abruptly. Clenching and unclenching his fists he strode off.

As he drove away, Laddie gripped the wheel tightly, cursing under his breath, a cloud of dust and gravel swirling behind the ute.

It skidded, cutting a corner and narrowly missing a hedge, before tearing down the slope beside the house. He followed the dirt track through the farm, thinking of the years he had spent cutting cane, working the land. He was the only son left. He had sacrificed so much. Was it for nothing? He crossed the creek and swerved into his uncle's front yard. Surely, Uncle Antun would know what to do. Even though his uncle and father had fallen out, Antun and his wife, Ema, had been a calming constant in Laddie's sometimes stormy life. Laddie would visit them often and he liked to listen as Antun told his stories in his slow drawl. He respected his uncle.

Antun was stringing beans, sitting on the dark-red cement patio steps when Laddie drove up. Ema was sitting on a chair behind him, crocheting.

He stood as Laddie got out of the ute and walked over to him. 'What's up, Laddie?'

He patted his nephew on the shoulder, gesturing to sit down with him on the top step. Laddie's jagged breathing slowly returned to normal. Antun waited in silence.

Finally, Laddie said, 'The old man won't help me'.

He told his story. There was no hesitation with the response.

'It's okay, Laddie. I'll help you. Go home and tell your wife you can buy the farm.'

The men hugged and then hugged again.

'Thank you. Thank you,' Laddie struggled to keep his voice steady.

His uncle agreed to lend him four hundred pounds to help buy the farm.

Laddie continued to work hard. He and Maria were poor, living on credit and soup-bone broth, but it was their farm now. They were working for themselves and their little family.

After Jack's proxy wife, Mara, arrived from Blato, they moved into a timber cottage next to the Catholic primary school in Mossman. Despite all that transpired, Laddie was a dutiful son and continued to help his father. He and Maria visited often, with Maria carrying baby Maryanne.

Sitting around the table one Sunday, in the little kitchen, Maria thought that Jack's tall frame looked too large for his small wooden chair. His black beret covered his bald head and his square-framed glasses were perched on the nose that dominated his increasingly gaunt face. He clenched his pipe between his thin cracked lips, intermittently puffing smoke out the window beside him. Mara busied herself cooking, her chubby arms chopping and slicing. She had a round, friendly face and had told Maria that she felt lucky to have found a husband in her twilight years, an Australian passport being the icing on the cake.

Maria rocked Maryanne to sleep while Mara brought plates of food to the table. They crunched on oily sardines between thick slices of white crusty bread, then mopped up the remaining olive oil with the bread.

With the baby asleep in her basket, the women cleaned up while the men talked. As often happened, the discussion turned to politics, and then to politics in Yugoslavia.

'Dad, you shouldn't discuss their politics like that. Walls have ears, you know,' Laddie warned.

'I can say what I like,' Jack grunted, gripping the table as his body shook with a series of moist coughs. 'You know they called me a rebel back home. That if I stayed, I would probably have been in politics myself. I would have done a good job.'

Standing up, he spat the phlegm out the window onto the lawn below, missing the concrete path that bordered the house.

'That's old news. We're Australian, Dad. Forget the old country. Forget the politics.'

'Hmph,' Jack snorted.

As the barrage continued, Laddie listened in silence. Maria knew that nothing her husband said would stop his father's rants.

'Come, Mara,' said Maria. 'Let's leave the men. Time to do your hair.'

Maria carried a chair out to the front patio and positioned it to catch the breeze.

'Here you go, sit here.'

She clipped a towel around Mara's shoulders and got the foam rollers and the perming solution ready. Methodically she combed and parted Mara's solution-saturated hair and rolled it neatly around the rod, chatting the whole time. She tried her best to help her step-mother-in-law find her slot in the framework of this town. She knew the feeling of being 'alien', laughing as she told her of all the mishaps that dotted her first few years. Maria remembered them well and loved retelling the stories.

'I remember, Mara, it was my first month in this country and we were invited to a neighbour's farm for a get-together. We were told to bring a plate. I asked Laddie, "What does this mean—bring a plate?" I had no idea.'

'Yes, Maria, did they mean bring an empty plate? Don't these people have enough plates?' said Mara.

Maria kept rolling Mara's hair as she chatted. 'You know Laddie. He was listening to the cricket on the radio and I don't think he even heard me. So I asked him again and he said to just bring a plate.'

'Just a plate? That's strange,' said Mara.

'Well, I thought so too but it wasn't my country, so I went with my best empty plate.' Maria chuckled at the memory.

'And?' Mara asked.

'Oh, Mara, I was so embarrassed. When we got there all the ladies had arrived with plates covered with beautiful chocolate cakes, sponge cakes, raspberry slices, frangipane tarts.' Although laughing now, Maria remembered how she had just wanted to run away and hide. She had wanted so much to impress these women and instead had felt utterly humiliated. She had felt so foreign.

'You poor girl,' Mara said.

'I was so upset and when we got home, I told Laddie that I would never ask his advice again. But he didn't understand. I made sure I double-checked with Mary next time.'

'Men!' Mara said as she held the hand mirror to her face to check on the progress. 'You're nearly finished, Maria.'

'Yes, your hair will look beautiful.

35

Maria's Australian family

Maryanne was a thirteen-month-old toddler with a head full of curls and rosy cheeks. And Maria was pregnant with her second child.

It was 1 April, 1954.

'Now, now.' Laddie waggled his finger at Maria as he was about to leave for work that morning. 'It's April Fool's Day. I know the baby's not due for another two weeks so don't you try and trick me with an April Fool's Day joke. All right?'

Later that morning the contractions began.

'Oh, no,' she cried out.

Maria knew Laddie was working at the paddock behind the Anich farmhouse. Standing in the hallway, she dialled the exchange on the large brown phone attached to the wall. Her fingers were shaking. Her call was put through to Teta Ema.

'Can you please go and find Laddie. He's in the paddock behind your house. I need to go to hospital. The baby's coming.' Her voice trembled.

Laddie was summoned to the phone. He listened to Maria and then laughed.

'Ha, ha! No, you don't, you little tricker,' he said, and hung up. 'She's playing jokes on me,' he said to his aunt as he trod carefully out of her house, trying not to leave a trail of dirt.

By the third phone call he realised this was not a joke, and following a speedy drive to town, Maria gave birth to her daughter, Joyce, thirty minutes later; luckily, in a hospital.

Two more children, John and Debbie, followed and within a few years Maria was a busy mother with four children under the age of eight. She poured her love into her little family, drawing them close and encircling them with threads of devotion and pride. They were the sunshine that warmed her heart, especially when she yearned for the comfort of her Croatian family. With every year, she thought, her roots to this foreign country grew deeper, anchoring her. Her English improved and although she stumbled with some words and pronunciations, she loved to talk and to tell stories, especially to her children.

Throwing a blanket over the kitchen table one evening, she began her ironing. She had starched the clothes that needed starching and was now ironing the sheets, pillowslips and hankies.

'Tell us a story,' begged Maryanne, as she and Joyce sat cross-legged on pillows on the kitchen floor. In their matching pyjamas, they cuddled their matching dolls—dolls that were almost as big as them.

While Maria told a story the sisters listened intently.

'Please, Mum, just one more...'

'Okay,' she said, pulling another sheet from the ironing basket. 'One but a time there was two little childrens. They was walking in a deep, dark forest in a place far, far away from eart' and gotted lost in a land full of giants...'

While her English was still to be perfected, her accent seemed to embrace the girls like a comfortable woollen blanket. Maria looked up from the ironing and smiled at them as they sat in silence, ready to hear what would happen next. Her stories always had a happy ending.

During the season, Laddie worked seven days a week. Then, when the season was over, he and Maria and their young family would spend weekends at the beach house that he had helped to build. The small white fibro home at Newell Beach, north of Mossman, was the scene of fun and frivolity.

'Okay, kids, time to go dragging,' Laddie announced one weekend.

Maria stayed in the kitchen cooking for all the visitors who would arrive over the weekend.

'Dad, I'll carry Debbie,' Maryanne said. She picked up the chubby one-year-old and balanced her on her hip as they crossed the road.

'Ouch. Ouch. Ouch,' they all yelled, bouncing across the sand that was still hot, even though it was nearly dusk. John was swinging an empty bucket in his hand, to collect the bait in.

Laddie followed them, carrying a stick in one hand and draped over his shoulder was the net that was still damp from the morning's drag. The children helped him unravel it on the beach, pulling out the bits of seaweed that were entangled in it. Laddie pushed the stick to stand upright in the sand and walked out to sea, lugging behind him the outstretched net to trap the fish.

'Yell out if you see any shark fins,' he called to the children, laughing.

'Who brought the baby? She's a nuisance. Take her back,' said John, as he held the stick to keep it straight.

He was five, tanned and wiry.

'Mum's too busy to look after her.'

'She'll run away. What'll we do with her?'

The older sisters looked at each other and one said, 'I know. Let's bury her.'

John's eyes glinted with mischief. This sounded like a great plan.

'But only to her tummy so she can't run away.'

'Yeah. Let's do that.'

Laddie could hear the children talking about their plan, but he didn't think they were going to follow through with it.

Looking back to the shore a little while later, he saw that the girls had dug a deep hole in the wet sand and had plopped the unsuspecting toddler into it, filled in the hole before she'd had a chance to escape, and covered her legs. Her face crumpled as she struggled to free herself.

183

'Quick! Give her something to play with. She's gonna scream,' John said.

Laddie kept an eye on the activity on the beach while he kept walking with the net. He wondered if he should go back to check on Debbie, but noticed that the children had collected some shells and scattered them in front of her. This seemed to do the trick and she looked quite happy.

'All right. Good. She's stuck. She can't go anywhere. Let's go and help Dad,' he heard Joyce say.

As John held the stick firm the girls splashed at the water's edge and ran up and down the beach, waving at their father as he scooped the sea in a wide arc and began dragging the net back to shore.

'Is the baby all right?' he yelled when he noticed Maryanne frolicking in the water.

'It's fine.' She pointed. 'See.'

Laddie laughed. 'I hope a dog doesn't run up and pee on her.'

As he dragged the net in, the children collected the little fish that were trapped in it. Some long silver garfish were mixed with the bait and the kids threw them all into the bucket full of sea water.

'We've got lots of bait for tomorrow morning's fishing. Go and collect your sister and don't tell your mother what you did to her,' Laddie said. 'And make sure you dunk her in the sea to get all that sand off her.'

John ran ahead as they made their way back.

'Mum. We're home,' he called. 'What's for dinner?'

A spicy aroma wafted through the small house.

'Is it spaghetti?'

'Go and wash your feet—look at all the sand,' Maria exclaimed in mock reprimand.

Too late. He had raced into the kitchen and wrapped his arms around his mother's legs. She ruffled his dark hair with her spare hand as she stirred the rich meat sauce. Then she dipped a teaspoon in and let him taste it.

'Yum,' was his response.

Looking over his head she watched Joyce carrying Debbie, who was dripping wet.

'What happened to Debbie?'

'Oh, she just ran through a few waves while we were holding her hand. Don't worry, Mum, she was safe,' Joyce reassured her, poker-faced, her eyes glancing towards her sister.

'Right. Well, you all go and shower before dinner.'

Sitting around the table on the front patio, the family chatted and laughed as they devoured the spaghetti. White crusty bread was used to mop up the rich tomato sauce. Laddie burped.

'You're the best cook ever, isn't she, Spud?' He grinned at his son. They called each other 'Spud'.

'Yep, the best cook, Spud,' John agreed.

After dinner Maria relaxed on her plastic saucer-shaped chair, patting her full stomach and ignoring the children arguing in the background about whose turn it was to wash up. She found the sound of the waves crashing onto the beach hypnotic. The coconut trees, silhouetted against the sea, swayed in the gentle night breeze. She could almost taste the salt in the air. Saturday. Away from the farm. Relaxing. Laddie reached over and intertwined his fingers with hers. Their eyes met and Maria knew their thoughts were identical. Newell Beach was idyllic, perfect for a weekend away from the farm.

'Don't forget. We've got church tomorrow morning.' She broke the silence, calling out to the children who were still bickering in the kitchen.

They all groaned. 'Do we have to? Why doesn't Dad go?' piped up Joyce.

'Nah,' he said. 'Instead of praying I just keep my fingers crossed.' He winked at Joyce who smothered her giggle with her hand as her mother frowned at his irreverence.

Racing in from their early morning fishing adventure next morning, the children rushed to dress in their Sunday clothes. Standing in front of the dressing-table mirror, Maria smoothed her dress and checked for any loose threads from her newly sewn outfit. Stepping back so she could see the hem, she twirled slowly to check one more time that it was even. She gave a final spray to her hair, her nose tensing from the pungent smell. Then she secured her hat on her stiffened hair and checked her stockings for any ladders; she prided herself on having good taste, and she liked to look nice, believing that self-pride was not vanity but showed self-respect. A wolf whistle greeted her as she stepped downstairs to the back patio.

'Looking good, Cookie.'

Fish scales were scattered around Laddie's feet.

'Careful, kids, don't step on the fish guts. Not in those nice church shoes.'

Tiptoeing around the fish, the children scrunched up their noses. The girls were in their best clothes, from the hats on their heads to their long white socks and shiny black shoes.

'Pick up Debbie,' Maria said to Maryanne. 'Don't let her walk over near the fish.'

'Yeah, you'll stink out the church,' Laddie laughed, and kept scaling the fish and slicing off their heads.

'I'll fry these up ready for youse for breakfast when you all get back. Say hi to God for me,' he said cheekily.

Maria ignored him as she bundled her brood into the station wagon and drove the few miles south to Mossman. The church was the hub of the little primary school, St Augustine's. It was situated between the convent, where the nuns who taught at the school lived, and the presbytery that stood behind a towering Moreton Bay fig tree.

As the children climbed the steep wooden steps that led into the high-set church, their shiny patent shoes made a tap-tapping noise. After dipping their fingers in the bronzed bowl of holy water, completing the sign of the cross on their bodies, they found a row to fit the five of them. Standing behind, Maria made sure the three older children genuflected in the aisle before taking their place in their pew. Maria knelt next to them. Familiar faces from this little community filled the church, nodding to each other. Looking straight ahead at the altar with its starched white cloth, her eyes drifted to the statues on either side, one of Jesus with his sacred heart and one of Our Blessed Mary. Bowing her head, she closed her eyes and whispered her prayers, oblivious to the movements of the congregation. As the priest delivered the mass, memories of her cousin delivering this same message in her stone church flooded back.

Church was followed by the ritual Sunday lunch which despite being in the tropics was always a roast of chicken, lamb or pork. There would be crispy roast potatoes and pumpkin, smothered in gravy. Dessert never changed: ice cream with tinned fruit salad and tinned cream.

'You have to take a bit of each flavour,' Maria would order.

'But Mum, I hate the pink. Why do we have to get Neapolitan?' was the usual grizzle around the table. Then silence as they shovelled the dessert into their mouths.

Maria watched her family eating and felt grateful, as always, that her children did not know the fear of hunger.

36

Mossman, early 1960s: the diaspora

As time ticked on, Maria felt increasingly settled in her Queens-land home. She formed bonds with many of the local women and joined the CWA (Country Women's Association), enjoying their meetings and functions. Sunday church, which she never missed, was a constant reassurance in her life.

She sat at the kitchen table, writing to her younger sister of the events of the last month. It was hard to keep her handwriting neat on the flimsy paper. The overhead light encircled the table in a warm yellow glow while the rest of the house slumbered in darkness. It was late and everyone else was in bed. Laddie always went to bed early. Ever since his hips had collapsed a few years ago, his sporting days had finished. The doctor called it Perthes Disease and told him he would be in a wheelchair within five years. He was stubborn and defied that prediction, fighting on, working hard and never complaining.

Looking up, Maria put her pen down. She always liked this time of night; it was so peaceful. Gazing out the kitchen window, she could see the outline of the barracks behind a bare paddock. The cane had been cut and the cane cutters had moved on, leaving the barracks empty and almost ghostly in the pale moonlight. She was familiar with the noises of the night now, although the wailing of the curlews still made her feel uneasy.

She sipped from the still-warm cup of coffee and pondered her next paragraph. She had told her sister about the four children and what they were doing, about the little timber school up the road that the older ones were attending. She wrote with apprehension about the boarding school in Herberton they were thinking of sending the girls to and wished she could discuss this decision with her sister.

You would be pleased, Žuva, that a while ago I learnt to drive, she wrote. *Laddie was very patient. At first the car jumped up and down like a kangaroo but now I'm much better.*

She wrote of the Mossman Show that they had all just attended. She had spent hours late into the evenings making new dresses for herself and her girls. They all had hats to match. The show was still a novelty for her. The competitions held in the oval seemed so bizarre—the wood chopping, a broom-throwing contest, a catch-the-greasy-pig race.

My darling sister, there are so many different competitions. For sugarcane, for fancy work, for cooking cakes and jams and everything. I was brave this year and entered my sponge cake and got second, she wrote. She was proud of her sponge cake and her secret ingredient that made it so light and fluffy. *Laddie was interested in looking at new tractors,* she continued. *The girls loved it when we bought them these little plastic dolls on top of sticks.*

Her hand was getting tired but she kept writing, asking questions about all her family back home, about Žuva's three children, knowing that the answers would be months away. Phone calls were rare, non-existent almost. Much too expensive.

Glancing up at the clock on the wall, she realised how late it was. Yawning, she finished off her letter. She wanted to pack it with the bundle of clothes, shoes and cash she had ready to send. She stood up and stretched, rinsing her cup before tiptoeing off to bed. She was looking forward to the next day. It was Sunday and they were visiting their friends in Feluga, near Tully.

She would have to be up early to pack sandwiches and a flask of hot coffee for the long drive south. The highway was narrow with many one-way bridges. It took hours.

'It's always so good to see you, Mara,' Maria said as she stepped out of the car and wrapped her arms around Mara Posinak, a proxy bride like herself from Blato who was now Mara Bacic and also lived on a sugarcane farm. Their farmhouses were alike, both located at the end of a curvy, dipping dirt road surrounded by an expanse of grass and paddocks of sugar cane.

Maria knew that Mara would have spent all morning in the kitchen cutting, chopping, sizzling, preparing a meal for the two families to enjoy. For migrant women, food was the glue that cemented the cultural bonds. And indeed at lunch the table was covered with dishes and plates, complete with bowls of white crusty bread and olive oil. As the families surrounded the table and devoured the feast, voices competed with each other to be heard. They spoke in English at lunch, the two mothers' heavily accented voices contrasting with the broad Aussie accents of their husbands and children.

'Remember us talking back in Blato? Seems like hundreds of years ago,' Maria said as they cleared the table after lunch. 'You asked me if I was married in the church. In front of my cousin, the priest?'

They reverted to the comfort of their native language, a language easy for their tongues and minds.

'Yes, I remember. It was Sunday when we were walking home after Mass,' said Mara as she started washing the dishes in the soap-filled sink. 'You told me to do the same.'

Maria boiled the jug, lining up the cups, spooning coffee and quite a few teaspoons of sugar into each one. Being cane farmers, their husbands liked to 'support the industry'.

'And, did you?'

'No, I was too scared. I wish I had, though. I guess I wasn't brave enough.'

'No, you were always a brave little thing. I remember when you hid in our house during the two-day war.'

'Yes. We were so young. So long ago.' Mara paused, remembering.

190

'And look at us now. My mother told me that when I came to Australia, I would be getting away from all the hard work. Well, that didn't happen!' She threw her sudsy hands in the air and laughed at herself. Mara was still small, a lot shorter than Maria. Her dark curly hair almost touched her shoulders.

'Do you think you'll ever go back?' Maria asked.

These women had such a similar timeline, having lived through the war and left their families and a fragment of their hearts behind.

'I don't know. It's too painful to think about. I just get on with my life,' Mara said as they finally sat at the cleared kitchen table and sipped their coffee. 'You were so lucky that you had your sister-in-law, Mary. Whereas for me, I had no one.'

'I know. Mary has been a rock to me. But look at you, Mara—so capable, five children and raising your nephew; and you worked the farm when Tony was sick.'

Mara reached for a biscuit and nibbled at it. 'I feel this is the lucky country. Think about the opportunities our children will have.'

'Yes, ones we never had,' agreed Maria.

They could hear the squeals of the children playing tiggy in the sprawling yard, leaping across the vegetable garden and weaving in and out beneath the water tanks. They could also hear the deep voices of the men outside, discussing the sugar prices and drinking their coffee. They enjoyed the safe bond of the diaspora.

Maria and her family would also visit the Cetinichs, another family with Blato connections. They lived near Mareeba on the Atherton Tablelands and grew tobacco. Vicki, Sima and Visco's daughter, and Debbie would play for hours in the massive sheds, running, jumping and hiding amongst the large yellow tobacco leaves that were laid out for drying.

'Girls! Lunch!' Sima would call out.

The girls would race in, their hair smelling of the strong but not unpleasant tobacco odour. They would all squeeze around the table as plate after plate of food appeared and all were encouraged to eat.

'*Jedi*,' said Sima.

The conversation between the adults here would always be in Yugoslav—loud and exuberant, with arms waving. Maria and Sima would exchange news from back home.

The children, first-generation Australians, would listen, understanding the foreign language but talking amongst themselves in English. Although entirely comfortable with their heritage, Maria knew that these children saw themselves as being as Australian as their classmates.

She told Sima how she would pack Australian little lunches of Sao biscuits with Vegemite and butter and how Debbie would tell her how she loved squeezing the biscuits together to get 'worms'. Mossman and Mareeba were small towns with blends of nationalities. These children were the lucky ones, she thought. Racism was rarely witnessed now in these communities in the 1960s.

For Maria, however, it was a fine balancing act. Laddie wanted her to be 'an Aussie with Aussie kids' but she also felt she needed to preserve her own identity and language; she did not want her language to fade. She needed it to use it to write to her family and for the infrequent and very expensive telephone calls and maybe, just maybe, if she were ever to see her family again.

37

1974: Goodbye to the canefields

'I still can't believe this is happening,' Maria murmured to Mara, her friend from Feluga, as she clipped her seat belt and pulled it tight across her lap. 'I can't believe that we're going back to Yugoslavia.'

'I never thought this day would come,' said Mara.

Maria placed her hand on her chest to calm her hammering heart. She had never been on an aeroplane before and here she was flying south to catch a flight to Europe. It seemed like a dream. Twenty-two years had passed, and her four children were all almost adults. She peered through the plane window, grateful that she was on the side facing the passenger terminal.

Pushing her face close, she strained to see the distant figures gathered behind the high mesh fence at the Cairns airport. It was easy to spot Laddie, bent over and leaning on the railing. He seemed so much older than his fifty one years, she thought. Although he never complained, over the years she had watched the relentless ache of his arthritic hips take their toll. It had been an ongoing struggle for him to work the farm these past thirteen years, replacing his tennis with a diet of painkillers and building a shed on his beloved tennis court.

On either side stood her two eldest daughters, Maryanne and Joyce. She thought how pretty they were, their mini-dresses accentuating their long legs, Maryanne's long brunette hair contrasting with Joyce's crinkly curls. They were both working, Maryanne as a high school French and English teacher and Joyce in a pharmacy. Maria's heart expanded a little with pride. She recalled well-meaning friends saying that her children would struggle with English as they had migrant parents. How wrong they were. What wonderful children she had.

Laddie had been adamant: 'Just because they're girls, doesn't mean they don't get an education,' he'd say. 'I don't want my girls to have to rely on a man to support them.'

These words echoed in her mind. What a forward thinker her husband was. John, her only son, was in Brisbane at university studying Medicine, and Debbie was in boarding school in Herberton and already talking about university. As the plane taxied to the end of the runway, she lost sight of her family.

Maria gripped Mara's hand as the plane soared high over the mangroves, the mudflats and the town of Cairns. Excited, they leant close and both peered through the window at the scenery below. From the air the city looked like a patchwork quilt, pockets of green, edged by asphalt streets and expanses of grass and densely bushed hills. Maria smiled and thought, I'll be back soon, my little family. Not like the last time I left my family twenty-two years ago.

Her throat tightened as she recalled the scene, picturing the receding outline of her Croatian family, especially her father. She was so young. It seemed like someone else's story, not hers. And her fears had eventuated. She never did see her father again. She thought back to that day eight years ago when Laddie returned from town. He walked up the back steps, gripping the mail from their post office box. As soon as she saw the overseas envelope edged in black, she knew.

'No!' Her hands flew to her throat. 'There's been a death back home. Please not my father.'

With trembling fingers, she tore the envelope open. Sepia photographs fell to the floor. They were images of a body in an open coffin surrounded by flowers. Her father. Her head swam and her legs crumpled. Laddie caught her and lowered her to the kitchen chair. He squatted beside her, his face level with hers. She wrapped her arms around his neck and buried her face, weeping.

'He's gone. He's gone. I'll never see him again.' Her voice was thick with grief.

'I know, darling.' He hugged her tightly, gently patting her back as her body shuddered with sobs. It felt like hours that they clasped each other, united in their sorrow. His heart ached for her, feeling her pain as images of his older brother and mother's death flooded back. His brother's death at twenty-one and his mother's not long after, had been difficult for their little family. As the sobs subsided Laddie released her and collected the scattered photos from the floor.

'He looks pretty peaceful. Like he's asleep,' Laddie said.

Maria blew her nose and brushed away the tears with her embroidered hanky. She stared at the photographs of the funeral procession. Men in sombre suits carried the coffin as the procession wound its way towards the cemetery on the hill. Her dear cousin priest, Don Ivo Protić, led with his stately cross. Her mother and sisters followed, draped in black, heads downcast and clinging to each other. Her brother and brothers-in-law walked in a line behind them, black berets covered their heads, long coats over their suits. The stark trees in the background mirrored the bleakness of the photograph. It was February.

It will be hard to return to Blato when he's not going to be there. So much will have changed, she thought. She was forty-two years old. Almost middle-aged. Her husband had even retired.

Laddie had asked John if he wanted the farm.

'Me? Thanks, but no way.' John spread his hands in front of him and looked at them. 'These hands aren't built for the farm. I'm going to uni, if that's okay with you, Spud.'

Within months Laddie had sold the farm to his neighbours and fishing mates, Graham and Billy Bunn.

Maria and Laddie's Mossman friends had asked, 'Moving to Cairns? But why? Mossman's your home.'

'Our kids are growing up. There's nothing for them in Mossman,' was Maria's explanation.

'The airport's in Cairns, and you know what? I'm sick and tired of driving all the way to Cairns to collect the kids every time they come home,' was Laddie's response.

Change didn't frighten Maria. She was looking forward to this new life.

'The first thing I will do once we sell the farm is to send you back to the old country, Cookie,' Laddie had said.

'Really? You think?' Her heart had skipped a beat. She was excited, but somehow also nervous. She had now lived in Australia longer than in Blato. Were her memories accurate? How would she feel seeing her home and family again? Would they have changed? *She* had certainly changed. Would it be painful to say goodbye to them a second time?

Before she could catch her breath, the farm was sold, their furniture packed, and a house bought in Cairns. In Edge Hill. She walked through this new low-set, red-brick house, marvelling at its modern features—sliding windows, insect screens, security screens, carpet and even ceiling fans. It was so different from the old farmhouse with its louvres, tongue and groove timber walls and wooden verandahs.

When they drove down the dirt road for the last time, Maria turned to look at the receding scene—the old farmhouse, the hedges, the flower beds with low, uneven cement borders, the open sheds built randomly around the large house, the overgrown tennis court, partially hidden by a crooked shed, the original long shed crammed with tools, tractors and jeeps. Its roof was rusting. This was the home she had arrived to twenty-two years ago. Each building told a story. As they turned the corner in the dirt road, she could only see the peaked farmhouse roof, standing out above the sugar cane.

Maria smiled wistfully as they rumbled past the derelict barracks that had housed the seasonal cane cutters—the immigrant workers

196

whom she had welcomed, cooked for and helped. Strong in her memories were scenes of the ferocious cane fires. Laddie and the Yugoslav cane cutters would set fire to cane at the corners of the paddock with their flaming trash torches, ever-watchful of the wind direction and ensuring there were enough firebreaks to prevent the fire leaping to where it wasn't welcome. The flames would roar upward, as bandicoots, snakes and rats scuttled out from the crackling blaze. Maria and the children would help by beating the embers and smouldering grass with heavy sodden sacks. She could still smell the sweet hint of raw sugar on the bags as it mingled with the smell of the fire. A shower of ash drifting from the smoke-darkened sky would complete the image. She was always a little afraid that the sweaty, blackened men would lose control of this magnificent force of nature.

Maria thought back to all the years she had worked hard in the paddocks. The children would laugh at her as she shielded herself from the harsh sun with long-sleeved shirts, trousers and a broad-brimmed hat. It was hot, sweaty work. The men used cane knives with razor-sharp metal blades and worn wooden handles. They'd all spend hours stripping trash from the cane that was required for planting. The trash was prickly, leaving hairy-marys embedded in their palms.

That was all in the past. The cane cutters had left with the arrival of the harvester. For some years now the old cane-cutters' shack had been home to birds, lizards and a solitary set of groper jaws suspended from the ceiling out the back, Laddie's prize catch from one his many fishing trips.

'Don't look back.' Laddie had interrupted her thoughts as he'd patted her knee. 'The only way to look is forward.'

She'd agreed. Taking her sunglasses from her handbag, she put them on and looked straight ahead as they'd turned off the dirt road onto Lower Cassowary Road and left the valley behind them.

Maria stared out as the plane flew high above the dark ocean, leaving the continent of Australia behind. She reclined her seat and leant back, closing her eyes, waiting for the stillness of sleep to calm her busy thoughts.

38

1974: Return to the old country

The plane began its descent. Maria had slept well and felt refreshed, excited. The two women chattered like schoolgirls about who would be meeting them at the airport, would they recognise them, would they cry? Through the plane window Maria could see the familiar craggy grey cliffs, peppered with threads of green. Her chest tightened and she exhaled slowly. As they circled above Split her memories returned to the last time she had passed through this city. It had grown, spread outwards and upwards. Tall white apartment blocks clumsily mingled with the aged, red roofs. The bay was dotted with boats and ferries. And the sea. She had forgotten how blue it was, its brilliance almost artificial as if splashed from an artist's palette.

The plane bumped along the runway and slowed to a halt. Maria checked her image in her little hand mirror and reapplied her lipstick. Mara did the same.

'We're here, Maria!' Mara said as she emerged from the aeroplane. 'Breathe the air. It even smells different.'

Maria followed her, stepping carefully down the stairs in her high heels, steadying herself with the rail as she clung to the pale blue handbag that matched her elegant suit. The wind gusted as she walked across the tarmac and her hand automatically patted her hair, grateful it was stiff with hairspray. Her fellow passengers milled around and she smiled, her ears recalibrating as she listened to them chatter loudly in her native language.

As Maria walked through customs she saw her brother, Ivan, waiting for her. He had been thirteen when she had left. He was now thirty-five, a surveyor in Split. He was tall, well-dressed with a beret covering his brown hair.

He rushed over to her, smothering her with a hug and then he kissed her—one cheek and then the other.

'My brother, we look so much alike!' Maria exclaimed, astonished, as she pulled away and inspected him. 'I never noticed it in the photos you sent me.'

'Yes. Yes. I have your nose.' He touched his button nose. 'Come. We have so much to catch up on. I have so much to tell you.' He wrapped his arm around her shoulders.

They collected her luggage and said their goodbyes to Mara and her family. As Ivan led Maria from the airport she blinked. Somehow the sky seemed brighter and the sun more golden. She had finally returned.

Maria stayed a few days with Ivan in Split. Together they spent hours walking the narrow alleyways and sitting talking in the most popular cafes. The coffee cooled in the small ceramic cups as they chatted.

'Ivan, introduce us to your gorgeous new girlfriend,' an envious friend asked him one evening as he passed a café where Maria and Ivan were sitting.

Ivan laughed, his eyes twinkling with pride.

'This is my sister, visiting from Australia,' he said as he waved at his friend.

'What happened to you after I left?' Maria asked. 'You didn't end up on the farm like our father?'

'Well, I have the pharmacist in Blato to thank.'

'How? What do you mean?'

'Well, he noticed that I was smart and inquisitive. He said to our father that I was a scholar, an intellect and he should let me go.'

'Just like that?' She asked, surprised.

'Yes, our father sent me to Zagreb to high school and then university. And here I am now, a surveyor.'

A waitress interrupted, 'More coffee?'

They nodded without looking up.

'Our father was a good man to let you go, you being the only son.'

'I think he recognised the poet in me. I like to think that somehow, maybe, I was a little like him.' Maria could hear the pride in his voice.

'Yes, Ivan.' She patted his hand. 'You're a gentle man. A good man. I'm grateful for all the support you gave to our parents and still give. I realise they didn't get a pension as they weren't communist, not members of the Party. I...' she faltered, 'I am sad that I missed all those years with you'.

'Do you know, Maria, if I had been older, I think I would not have let you go.'

'Really? But why?'

'Yes, really. You were so young. It could have turned out so badly. Think of that. So far away from your family, from us.'

He explained that over the years he had thought of her often, worried for her, wondering whether she was truly happy or was she just telling them what they wanted to hear.

'No, Ivan.' She shook her head. 'It was my destiny. It was the right choice.'

She dragged her chair across the marble pavement to sit by his side, and together they looked out over the sea to the islands in the distance, sprinkled with pinpricks of light, and nearby, to the gently rocking fishing boats moored to the wharf. Their silence was comfortable. Behind them the white limestone walls of the Diocletian's Palace threw shadowy fingers across the esplanade. Faint sounds of traditional music drifted from the restaurants scattered throughout the Old Town.

39

Blato, Croatia

Maria left the bustling port city of Split to finally return to her island and her home. It felt as if time had paused in Blato. The bleak mountains and the fig trees. The vineyards and the olive trees. The old stone houses. The linden trees still lined the main street, their branches interlinked like a guard of honour above the busy narrow thoroughfare.

Maria's heart warmed to see her sisters once more. The years melted and tears flowed as the three women hugged. Dobrila lived with her husband and their family in the seaside town of Korčula. Žuva had married after Maria left and remained in Blato with her family.

With arms linked, the sisters and various other family members promenaded through the streets and up towards Maria's old house where her mother still lived. The uneven cobbles were difficult with high-heeled sandals. A flood of memories overwhelmed her as she approached her childhood home. She was surprised that she had forgotten how imposing the front door was. Bit by bit the olive-green paint was being consumed by patches of rust. She pushed it open and stepped into the courtyard. The door still creaked. Instinctively, she glanced to the left for the donkey. The space was bare, but she was sure that the musky smell of animals still lingered. Carefully, she climbed the partially crumbled steps to the open balcony. Weeds sprouted beneath the loose roof tiles. Pot plants of flowers and herbs sat on the windowsill near an upturned worn, scrubbing brush.

Her mother shuffled out of the kitchen to greet her—now an old woman, frail and dressed in black. A shawl covered her wispy white hair. Her shrunken eyes were barely visible in dark orbits encircled by the characteristic shadows common to her people, and she had the sunken cheeks of the almost toothless. Most of the elderly women in Blato were widows and looked alike.

'Tell me your name again,' she mumbled through her thin lips as her claw-like hand reached for Maria's. 'That's right. You're my baby, Marija,' she said as she patted Maria's hand. It was only then, as Maria gazed on this shell of a once robust woman that she realised how long she had been away.

As she stepped towards the balcony edge, images of her father engulfed her. She pictured him returning from the farm with the donkey every afternoon. It seemed like yesterday. She wished she could have joined her family in farewelling him. She rested her hands on the cool stone and looked out at her village. Still the same. The messy array of terracotta roofs spilling down the hill below and climbing the opposite slope. On the top of the hill, surrounded by trees, was the church, small in size but a significant beacon to the people. In the far distance, across the Adriatic Sea, she could see the cliffs of the mainland.

'Photos, ladies,' suggested Jakica, Žuva's sixteen-year-old daughter, as she lined the women up, with the township as the perfect backdrop. 'Smile.' She clicked away at the various combinations of siblings with their elderly mother. They wrapped their arms around each other, encircling their diminutive mother.

Maria threw her head back as she laughed, soaking up the closeness of her family.

'You look just like a movie star, Aunty Maria,' her niece said.

'No, sweetheart, I am no different from your mother.'

But Maria was not being completely honest. She *did* feel different. How could she not? She was no longer a girl from Blato. Her world had expanded, and she felt a guilty bond to her new country as she struggled to keep the English words from sneaking into her conversations.

They took her from house to house, from cousin to cousin, from feast to feast, where she was treated like royalty and encouraged to eat.

'*Jedi*.'

Maria together with sisters, nieces, nephews, cousins and cousins of cousins would gather around tables covered with food. The table would not be complete without a carafe of red or white wine.

'Here. Drink.' The host would announce. 'This is from my grapes. What do you think? Good?'

A pause.

'Excellent.' Maria would say every time.

And the wines were excellent. The grapes were exceptional, and the wines were sublime. Thick aromatic Turkish coffee would accompany the sweets—the curved, sweet pastry *kroštule*, and the fried doughnut-like *pušurate*. Swirls of laughter followed rivers of tears followed swirls of laughter—for Maria it was an emotional rollercoaster.

'Tell me, sister, what is life like in Australia?' asked Žuva.

The two women sat on the balcony of Žuva's two-storey stone house. Their metal crochet hooks were weaving in and out of the ivory-coloured cotton thread as the doilies took shape. Žuva's husband was at work and her mother-in-law wandered in and out from the nearby kitchen. She was a bird-like woman, dressed in black and constantly muttering and wringing her hands.

As their hooks looped and double-looped almost automatically, requiring little attention, they looked down the main street, beyond the vegetable patch that was directly below the balcony. Žuva's house was on the western end of the main street. Cars drove along slowly, pulling aside to allow trucks and other wider vehicles to pass in the narrow street. Women carrying shopping bags strolled past, waving cheery hellos to the two sisters.

'You know, Žuva, I call Australia the lucky country,' Maria began. 'There is so much freedom. There are jobs if you want to work hard. And lots of different people.'

'What are they like?' Žuva had lived in this village her entire life.

'Lots of people are like us, from the old country. But there's Italians, English, Aboriginal, Greek. There are so many different people and so many different religions.'

'Not just Catholic?'

'No, not just Catholic.'

'Being Catholic can be hard for the young people here,' Žuva whispered.

'How?' Maria's teenage years lived under the newly formed Communist Party now seemed buried beneath layers of Australian democracy. Maybe she took for granted her freedom to attend Sunday Mass in her beloved church.

'Because young people will do better if they join the Party and not go to church. It's not so hard for us older ones.' Žuva knotted the thread and then cut it. She held up the small doily, admiring it before starting on the next. 'You know our father went to church every day, sometimes twice.'

The conversation stalled as they both thought of their father, the only sound being the background muttering from Žuva's mother-in-law.

'He was a good man,' they both said at the same time.

'And Mladen? What is he like?' asked Žuva.

Maria's eyes smiled. 'He is a good husband.'

Žuva was inquisitive about this man she had never met.

'Tell me what you thought when you saw him the first time. When you got off the ship. What did he say to you?'

'Nothing. His father came to Sydney to get me.'

Žuva stopped her crocheting and stared.

'His father? You never told me that. Why?'

'I'm not sure, but I think his father wouldn't let him leave the farm. It was awful.' She shuddered. 'I was so scared.'

'Well, we won't talk about him then. Tell me about when you met Laddie.'

Maria told her so many stories. The sisters had missed out on many years together and many stories, stories that couldn't be told in letters. She told Žuva how she felt when she saw Laddie at the train station in Cairns, how she felt when he whisked her away to Kuranda for their honeymoon.

'Do you know what he told me?'

Žuva shook her head and leant in closer, eager to hear.

'He said that if I felt that I could not live with him, if I could not love him, he would annul the marriage and let me come home.'

'But, Maria, you knew you couldn't come home.'

'I knew that. I knew I couldn't come back. I don't think he knew that, though. So he worked very hard to make me happy.' She laughed. 'But, you know, he wasn't hard to love. Love grows. That's what I always tell my children. Love grows.'

Maria could tell that Žuva enjoyed listening to these stories. In turn, she told Maria of life in Blato, about her children, about their cousins and their friends.

'You heard what happened to Katica, from Smokvica?'

'No?' Maria felt uneasy as she remembered the young bride from the boat. Although they had not kept in contact, she had occasionally wondered what path her life had taken.

'Her marriage didn't work out. She... um... she took her own life.' Žuva lowered her eyes.

The colour drained from Maria's face and her crocheting dropped to the ground.

'No!' Both hands covered her open mouth.

'Well, she couldn't come home.'

'But to have taken her own life?'

Žuva shrugged. 'She wasn't the only one. There were others. Not all the marriages worked out.'

Maria thought back to herself and Katica as young girls on the boat. That's what they were—young girls. She sighed and closed her eyes, making the sign of the cross while silently thanking her Lord for her own husband and how she had grown to love him. She felt she was one of the lucky ones.

Maria told Žuva of life on a farm in Cassowary Valley. She told of her nervousness each time nature called her to the fetid outhouse, the small timber building perched at the edge of the back yard.

'I didn't know what I would find there. Sometimes a cane toad, sometimes spiders, sometimes beetles and even snakes. Sometimes all of them.'

Žuva shivered with repulsion.

'I used the potty under my bed when I could.'

Žuva listened to the endless stories while rushing in the kitchen to prepare Turkish coffee on the gas stove. She dared not take her eyes off it as it was quick to boil. Without interrupting her sister's monologue, she brought the long-handled copper pot out to the balcony and poured the dark liquid into the small porcelain cups. Maria reached for her cup, but quickly reminded herself to let it stand to allow the sludge to settle to the bottom. It was different from the instant coffee back home.

'Keep telling me about all these people you live with,' said Žuva.

Maria continued, describing the characters in Mossman. She spoke fondly of the women she had met, her neighbours and her friends.

'Laddie's sister, Mary, is kind, so kind. Right from the start she has been a sister to me.'

'That was so good for you.'

'Yes, there's not a bad bone in that woman's body. You would love her. But she and Laddie are cheeky. They played so many tricks on me when I arrived.'

'Like what?'

'Well, Laddie would send me into shops to ask for things and tell me rude words to say. I would have no idea until I noticed the shopkeeper look at me strangely and laugh.'

'No!'

'Yes, and I remember one time I found these little round balls in a winter coat pocket and I asked Mary what they were and she told me they were lollies so I put them in my mouth.'

'What were they?'

'Mothballs. Ewww. So horrible.' Maria glanced down at her watch and began to pack away her crocheting. 'Look at the time. We should go in and cook.'

'No, that can wait.' She rushed inside and brought out a plate of *pušurate* and beckoned for her sister to eat the sweet dough balls.

'Did you make friends easily?' Žuva asked.

'Well, Mary was my best friend, my sister. But you know me. I love people. There was a lady who came to one of the farms a few years after me. Her name was Joan.'

'Was she Yugoslav too?'

'No, but we got on well. We both liked to look pretty and we both loved sewing and fashion. She would laugh with me at the way I spoke.'

'What was wrong with the way you spoke?'

'Nothing, I thought. But in English I can't say some sounds so the words come out sounding funny. Like "eart" and "tutpix".'

Maria looked at Žuva and could see that her sister had no idea what she meant.

'But we named each other after movie stars, Elizabeth Taylor and Sophia Loren.'

Žuva nodded. 'I have heard of these movie stars. And who were you?'

'Well, I wanted to be Elizabeth, but she told me that I had to be Sophia as I looked more like Sophia. So I would ring her and say, "Hello, Elizabeth, are you busy scrubbing that bathroom?" And she would say, "Yes, Sophia, are you scrubbing that long verandah? Where are your servants?" We knew the ladies on the phone exchange would be listening to us and thinking we were crazy farmers' wives.'

'It would be hard being on the farm so far away from everyone.'

Maria agreed and told her how isolated she would feel as the sugar cane grew and hid the house on the farm next door. She explained how she would stand on a chair and look through the narrow kitchen window to see the neighbour's roof above the sugar cane so she did not feel so alone.

'Tell me more about Laddie. Do you fight?'

Maria smiled and raised her eyebrows. 'He says this and that and this. I just say, "Yes, dear, fine dear," and then I go ahead and do what I want. So, no, we don't ever fight.'

'It sounds like Australian husbands are different from the men here.'

'No, it's not that. I think I am just blessed.'

Time ticked steadily on as she recounted all the little stories of her children growing up so far away from her family. Žuva crocheted as she listened.

'So they all speak Yugoslav?' she said.

'Laddie's father insisted. So yes, all except Debbie.'

'One morning when the children were little, I was "playing ladies" and had guests for morning tea. The women sat around the kitchen table. I had baked cakes, slices, scones. I went to a lot of trouble. I had set the table with my best tablecloth, the fancywork one. And I had my best cups and saucers. Joyce was only little, and she walked around one of the women staring at her.

'*Ona je gruba i prida i zada.*'

'What did your little girl say?' my friend asked me.

'She said that you have a beautiful dress,' I lied.

Žuva slapped her hand on her thigh and laughed. 'She said that she is as ugly from the front as she is from the back!'

Maria nodded. 'Yes. Lucky my friend couldn't speak Yugoslav. Lucky Joyce couldn't speak English.'

'So when did they learn English?'

'When it was time for Maryanne to start school, we realised we had to make sure she and the other children could speak English.'

Putting her crochet hook down, Maria stretched. 'Žuva, we are very naughty. We've been sitting here for hours. We need to get lunch ready. Your husband will be home soon.'

Žuva agreed and stood up. They packed away their crocheting, and Maria followed her sister inside.

40

Walls have ears

It was late in the evening; moonlight shimmered through the gauze curtains. Maria sat beside Žuva in her sister's tiny kitchen. The house was quiet, everyone else was asleep. The kitchen smelt of the coffee they had brewed on the gas burner in the corner. Bodies almost touching, the women sipped their syrupy coffee as they went through the pile of glossy photographs, each framed with white edges. Moving the yellow Kodak envelope aside, Maria selected several photographs. She had packed so many.

'This is Laddie when he bought his new boat. He loves fishing.' Maria pointed to an impressive white boat with a red stripe along its hull. 'Oh, that's a photo of Debbie with us in front of the boat on her new pushbike. And that's a photo of when she fell off. Joycie must have taken that one. I think she's crying. Naughty Joyce for taking a photo of her sister crying.'

Žuva giggled at the ridiculous photo.

'Sssh, don't wake anyone,' Maria said as she continued. 'Oh, and this is when Laddie and his friends caught a groper.'

'That's a big fish. It's bigger than them,' Žuva exclaimed as she looked at the photo of the impaled fish, upright and towering over the group of shirtless tanned men.

The two sisters basked in this intimacy as they reminisced over all the old photos that Žuva had, photos that Maria had sent from Australia of her children growing up. Each one with its own story. Žuva had her own album ready.

'Maria, look at this one. My wedding photo.'

211

'Beautiful,' whispered Maria as she held the photograph close, examining every detail.

'You know that I wore your dress at my wedding?' Žuva passed her a bowl of grapes and reached for a bunch herself.

Maria picked at the grapes, chewing noisily. 'Yes, you told me. I left it here for you, remember? Look how stunning you are!' She wrapped an arm around her sister, pulling her in for a hug followed by a kiss on the cheek.

'Guess how many of the young girls in this town wore your wedding dress?' Žuva said.

'Others wore my dress?'

'Yes. Twenty-four!'

'Really? Twenty-four?' She studied the delicate dress in the photograph. 'This dress?'

'Well, yes. There was no material here to make a dress. You know that. Some made them out of the parachutes left from the war. But yours was beautiful! Lucky we're all, well, all the same size. Sort of. It didn't look as good on some,' she said, 'but it was a wedding dress. No one complained.'

A tap at the half-opened door startled them. Goran, a good friend of the family, stood just outside, shifting from foot to foot. They hadn't heard him climb the steps that led from the courtyard to the balcony outside the kitchen.

'Sorry to come so late, Žuva, but Maria I, I have come. I need to talk to you.' His eyes darted towards the window.

Žuva beckoned him. 'Come in, Goran. Come in.'

He closed the door behind him, strode over to the open window and glanced outside. The street was dark and empty. He pulled the window shut and then dragged a chair close to the two women. He pushed the photos to one side, resting his arms on the table.

'Coffee, Goran?' offered Žuva. 'We have plenty. We just made some. You want some grapes? *Jedi.*'

He shook his head. 'No, thank you, no.' He turned towards Maria. 'I am very worried for you. There is talk.'

Maria frowned, puzzled.

'It's not good what I was told today, not good at all.' His leg jiggled, rattling the small table.

'I don't understand,' Maria said.

'Things are different here compared to Australia. You know that? Communism—it's different. It's strict.'

'I know that, but I still don't know what you're talking about. I've done nothing wrong. I am just here visiting family. On a holiday.'

Her hands clasped tightly together under the tablecloth.

'There is talk about your father-in-law. He is known here in Blato. He was a rebel and has said things back in Australia. Things about here. We hear these things.'

'Has he?' Maria had no idea what her father-in-law did. 'So?'

'The Party. They know you're in the country. They know where you are, here in Blato.'

'So?' she repeated.

'Maria.' Goran leaned in and whispered slowly and deliberately as if she were a child. 'You have dual nationality. You're travelling with your Australian passport, but the Party still recognises your Yugoslav passport. You know they can keep you here.'

'What?' Her spine stiffened.

'They can do whatever they—'

'What does she need to do?' interrupted Žuva, her voice shrill with panic.

Lowering his voice further Goran said, 'Listen carefully. Tomorrow you need to go to the Party office here in Blato. You tell them that you have heard of what your father-in-law has done. But tell them that you are a good Yugoslav citizen.'

'Tomorrow?'

'Yes, and don't talk about this to anyone. No one. I have a good friend who works in the Party office. That's the only reason I know this. I trust him.' He looked from Maria to Žuva.

The women stood and kissed him on both cheeks as he left.

'Thank you,' said Maria.

213

His steps faded as he walked into the darkness.

'This is not Australia, you know,' Žuva whispered.

'I'm finding that out.'

She did not mention this episode to anyone, but did exactly as she had been advised. She was concerned. What did her father-in-law's opinions have to do with her?

Although Maria's holiday continued, an uneasiness grumbled in the pit of her stomach. Was it the discussion with Goran and the uncertainty that may await her at the airport that disturbed her? She felt as if she were peering through frosted glass. She thought of this as her home, but really it was no longer her home. Her family was here but her family was in Australia. She missed her husband and children. She knew she was Croatian, but she felt Australian.

∞

It was Sunday evening and Maria's final day in Blato. Neatly stacked piles of clothes and souvenirs surrounded her open suitcase. As she packed, her sister sat on the edge of the bed chatting.

'You look tired,' Žuva said as she handed items to her.

Maria *was* tired. It had been a busy day, which had begun with Mass in the All Saints Church. She had attended Mass as often as possible during her stay. It was a comfort to watch her cousin conduct the service from behind the marble altar in this familiar old building. Today it was followed by a family lunch and lots of farewells.

She packed her folded clothes into her suitcase and checked the gifts again. White traditional peasant blouses with embroidered flowers decorating the round necklines, gathered with red drawstrings and puffed sleeves. One for each of her girls. She had also bought miniature dolls in traditional costume, gold earrings, angels on golden chains, ornamental plates, wine glasses. Yes, she had enough gifts. There was plenty of room in her suitcase as she had left most of her dresses behind for Žuva. She zipped her large blue case closed, lifted it off the bed and stood it upright near the door ready for departure.

'Do you think this is your last time here? Will you come back to us?' Žuva mustered the courage to ask as she clasped her sister one more time. Maria could tell that she was afraid to hear the answer; Žuva knew she was spread between two worlds that were too far apart.

'That's in God's hands,' Maria answered. She too wondered whether she would see her Croatian family again.

41

A new life in Cairns

When Maria returned to Cairns that nagging feeling deep in her heart had settled. She had seen her family and her home again. The brush, ever so slight, with the communist regime had frightened her, and it took her a little while before she shared the story with Laddie.

'What?' He was gobsmacked. 'You know they could have kept you—you're still a Yugoslav citizen.'

She nodded.

'We should make sure the kids know this. Especially John. They could make him do the compulsory year military service if he ever goes over.'

She nodded again. She felt grateful for the freedom of Australia and also the freedom her husband gave her.

She quickly settled into a new life in Cairns where she enjoyed the proximity of neighbours, just being able to step outside her door and yell, 'Yoo hoo' to Margaret and Bev, who lived on either side of her. Being able to chat over a wire-mesh fence was a novelty after the years of isolation on the farm. It was never hard for Maria to make friends. Before long she was helping out at the local Catholic church, Mother of Good Counsel, welcoming new parishioners at the door as she once was welcomed, assisting with religious education for the children and mothering any of the young parishioners who were in need. She shared her love of her faith, teaching Religious Education to the Year One students at the local state schools. Like her father, she went to Mass daily, sometimes twice, especially at Easter.

However, Laddie and Maria's ties to Mossman remained strong, with friends and relatives visiting often. When Laddie's father died, his wife returned to live out her sunset years with her own relatives in Blato, her Australian pension making her life very comfortable.

Time marched on. Their children married, grandchildren arrived. With the birth of each grandchild, Maria's heart expanded a little. She babysat and helped as much as was needed and spent many hours on the back patio sewing on her old Singer sewing machine. The front of her dress was often full of pins as she perfected her creations, from wedding dresses to baby clothes. Her life was full—as well as taking a job cleaning at a motel, her phone was always ringing with calls from friends and family.

'I can't understand it when people say they're bored,' she would often say.

She enjoyed seeing her husband retired. Even though he was only in his fifties, his body carried the aches and pains of someone much older. Despite this, he managed to pick up a racquet and return to his beloved tennis. His hips prevented him running but with his skill at placement it didn't matter. He hadn't lost his touch.

'Come over here, Cookie,' Laddie said that evening, patting the white wrought-iron chair beside him on the patio. 'I'll pour you a dinkie dink.' He was still in his tennis whites from his day playing fixtures at the Esplanade courts.

'Just a little one, sweetie.' Maria put aside her crocheting and pulled her seat closer beside him and sipped at the glass of sweet sherry diluted with water. They sat, content in their silence, waving at neighbours and watching the sun set. The mouth-watering smell of spaghetti sauce simmering on the stove wafted out.

Their eyes met over the glasses as they clinked them and said, '*Živjeli*'.

42

Maria's last trip

The honey-coloured glass feature wall behind the lounge suite shimmered as it reflected the soft glow from the ceiling light. Although it was only mid-afternoon, the brown carpet and heavy curtains made the room feel dark. Debbie perched on the edge of the lounge and watched as her baby son, David, crawled towards his three-year-old sister, Stephanie, who was playing with Lego. Debbie cleared her throat.

'Mum.'

'Yes, love?'

Maria paused and looked up from the dress pattern spread on her lap. She was in her usual place, her recliner chair in the corner near the front door, her thin legs stretched out from beneath the white dress with purple flowers that seemed two sizes too big for her now.

Maria put her hand up to check on the coarse brown wig. It felt so itchy and fake; nothing like her own hair. She used to be so fussy with her hairstyle. She was so meticulous with colouring it that Laddie had no idea she had been regularly dying it.

'So, you've been grey for years?' he had asked, astonished.

Maria would joke that her heated rollers, teasing comb and hairspray were her best friends.

Today her tongue was so swollen she couldn't close her mouth properly. It had been nearly a year since a diagnosis of bone cancer had explained the gnawing pain that had kept her awake at night.

218

She had endured her radiation and chemo like always, with a smile and a kind word to those who looked after her.

'Mum, we want to send you back to Croatia,' Debbie said.

'You do?'

Maria was sixty-three and it had been eight years since she had lost her Laddie. She gazed out through the sliding door at the patio, as if expecting to see him sitting there cradling his 'dinky dink' and patting his faithful dog, Nicki. She could never verbalise the ache his sudden death left.

That afternoon eight years ago in September 1987, when she had arrived home from her cleaning job and seen his yellow-and-black Mini Moke still in the garage. That day when he should have been at tennis with his Thursday afternoon group. Etched in her memory was the moment she had found him, cold and unmoving, on the bathroom floor amongst the scattered glass. How heavy her heart was as she buried him in Mossman and returned alone to this house. How, without him, the darkness would close in on her at night. She had busied herself with her children, grandchildren, church and friends. But she missed him so deeply, the man who had enticed her to this foreign country.

Now she looked back to her daughter who repeated the words, adding, 'I think it would be nice to see your family again, Mum'.

'Back to Croatia? It's been so long,' Maria mused. 'Twenty, no twenty-one years.'

'Yes. Too long. Would you like to go? And see your sisters and brother?'

'Hmm. I hadn't thought about it. You think?'

'Well,' Debbie started, 'I've been talking to the rest of the family and they think it's a good idea'.

Debbie stood and picked David up as he tried to dismantle Stephanie's tower of Lego. She ignored his protests and his flailing arms.

'So, you've been planning this, you cheeky girl.' Maria waggled her finger.

'No. Well, yes, I guess so. We just thought it would be nice.' She bounced the eight-month-old on her lap, trying to distract him.

'So you think I'm going to die soon?' She chuckled her throaty laugh. 'Is that why you're sending me? Take out insurance in case you need to bring me back in a box. I need to be buried here remember. Up in Mossman. Next to my darlink.' Maria grinned.

'Mum!'

'Sorry, love. Just joking.'

'Well? It's safe to go now, isn't it?' Debbie asked. 'The war's over.'

'I haven't seen much on the telly lately, but the family back home say all is good.'

For the past five years Croatia had been at war. It was called The Homeland War.

Maria recalled when President Tito died in 1980. Debbie was at university and had rung her to ask for prayers before one of her exams. Maria would smile to herself, wondering if Debbie thought she had a private line to God.

'Speak to me, darlink,' was her usual response. She'd listened as Debbie told of her woes while she had promised to say the usual number of rosaries required for an exam pass.

'Did you hear?' Maria had said, 'Tito is dead'.

Her children had grown up hearing about Yugoslavia, communism, President Tito, ethnic divisions. As a child, Debbie had told her parents she wanted a Yugoslavian pen pal but her father had said, 'No! You might end up with a Serbian pen pal, so no! Too much politics!' Little Debbie did not understand. She only understood that Yugoslavian politics was messy.

'So, Tito is dead. What will happen next, do you think?' Debbie said.

'Love, he was the one who kept Yugoslavia together all these years. Trouble is coming. I think there will be a war.'

Tito had been the leader of this communist country since World War II and had generally been regarded as a dictator who trod the challenging path of neutrality during the Cold War years that followed. He refused to allow his country to come under the Soviet thumb, and thus Yugoslavia was able to receive much-needed economic aid from the West. He had somehow managed to suppress nationalism and the tensions between the different ethnic groups.

After Tito's death and the subsequent years of increasing nationalism, economic hardship and frustration with the government, Maria felt nervous for her family. Yugoslavia eventually imploded. She remembered 1991, when Croatia and Slovenia declared their independence, wanting to control their own economy and be rid of the ruling hand of Belgrade and Serbia. She had watched the ABC News with trepidation, sad that she couldn't pat her Laddie on the hand and say, 'What do you think? Will my family be all right?'

When the Slovenian war was over in a mere ten days, she was hopeful that it would be the same for Croatia.

It was not. Ethnic tensions bubbled and an all-out war erupted between the Croatians and the Yugoslav-backed rebels in 1991. The outside world didn't really understand what was happening in the Balkans, and it seemed to Maria that no one really noticed. Not until October 1991 when Dubrovnik was bombed. Maria recalled sitting with Debbie and watching the TV news in dismay as grenades showered the city cowering beneath a smoke-blackened sky. Under siege from the ships in the harbour, the skies above and the hills behind, shells rained on the ancient walled town.

'I... I... just can't believe this is happening, Mum,' Debbie had stammered. 'This city is precious. What do they call it? The Pearl of the Adriatic?' She shook her head. 'And it's being bombed?'

In her twenties, backpacking through Europe, Debbie had visited this magnificent historic city. She had written home to her parents that she was amazed by the marble streets and awestruck as she climbed the ramparts of the fortress surrounding the Old Town, Stari Grad, a UNESCO World Heritage site.

Stunned, the mother and daughter continued to watch the news. Foreign journalists in khaki flak jackets described the carnage while camera crews captured shaky images of mortars exploding in bursts of flames, leaving piles of rubble and the elderly sitting frightened and mute in underground shelters beneath the mediaeval city. These citizens had seen war before, and the journalists reported that many had fled to this historic city, mistakenly believing they would be safe. In the background, the unnerving wail of air-raid sirens pierced the eerie stillness of a once busy city.

'I knew it. This is why I am over here, lovey.' Maria had exhaled and tut-tutted. 'You know, all your cousins have probably been called to war,' she said. 'All the young men right up to about fifty. I pray they stay safe.' She automatically made the sign of the cross. 'I'll ring my sisters and brother again. Just to check.'

And they had watched on in disbelief as the genocide and atrocities continued.

'There has always been so much hatred,' Maria told her daughter. 'I don't think anyone will ever understand the history of my country.'

∞

As Debbie sat with her mother thinking about a return trip to Croatia, she remembered her mother's reaction in 1983 when she had announced, 'Okay, family, I'm going overseas. Backpacking through Europe. And I really, really want to visit your family, Mum.'

'Well, that's lovely, darlink,' Maria said, supportive as always. 'But if you visit my family in your little short shorts and a backpack, looking like a hippy...' Her voice trailed off, edged with concern.

'But, Mum,' Debbie said. 'I'll be coming from the Greek Islands. In summer.'

'There'll be talk. I don't want you looking like a hobo.'

Debbie pondered this. The notion of not bringing shame to the family was deeply ingrained in her mother's being.

'Okay. What if I buy a backpack that I can convert to a suitcase?

And I'll pack a few sets of dressy clothes and even some high heels. Will that do?'

'That would be good, sweetie,' her mother answered, giving her a hug.

Debbie wondered how she could squeeze these non-essentials in with her sleeping bag, sleeping sheet, sandshoes, socks, thongs, medical kit, traveller's cheques, toiletry bag, camera, endless rolls of film, towel, diary, undies, togs and her three changes of clothes. But she did. And in her fancy clothes she had wobbled off the ferry in Korčula in the heat of August, negotiating the uneven cobbled street in her black high heels while leaning precariously to one side carrying a very heavy suitcase that fifteen minutes ago had been a backpack.

'Will anyone speak English?' she had asked her mother before leaving.

'Yes, of course. All your cousins learn it at school,' had been the reply.

Little did Debbie realise that they had forgotten or not used their English, and as a result her Croatian improved dramatically through necessity and immersion. Her mother's family had showered her with warmth and love. She mainly stayed with her Teta Žuva. Her cousin Jakica had dressed her in the traditional Blato costume— the white long-sleeved blouse was covered by a full length, dark brown dress with a golden waistband. Several strands of gold and red beads adorned the bodice while her head was encircled by a red and black band. The image had been completed with golden dangling earrings.

Day after day, Debbie met more and more family members. She was hugged and kissed and ate and ate—food was the heart of this culture. Family and friends gave her the local food to try— octopus, stuffed capsicums, fried sardines, fish soup. Some dishes were familiar from her mother's cooking, some different.

'Are you related to everyone here?' her travelling companion, Lyn, had asked her as they visited house after house.

'Well, I have more relatives here than back home.'

Debbie was fascinated by the traditional Kumpanija sword dance held in the town piazza. She was mesmerised by the blue of the Adriatic Sea, and enjoyed swimming with her newly met cousins and listening to their music as they played their guitars and sang in their bands. She explored the house her mother grew up in, where photos of herself and her siblings still hung on the walls.

Knowing that both her parents and centuries of ancestors had lived in this village both captivated and absorbed her. She couldn't explain it, but she had felt her heritage embedded here, in the stones, the olive trees, the old churches and the sea. How hard it must have been for my mother to abandon all of this, Debbie thought—her family, her extended family, her friends, her culture, her language, all that was familiar.

For the first time, she had grasped the enormity of her mother's decision, made at such a young age. How brave she was. Debbie desperately wanted her mother to return to this country one final time.

'Yes. It seems like the war is over. So, what do you think, Mum? We'll buy your ticket, so don't worry.'

'Going back to the old country? That's very generous. I'll think about it.'

'Mum?'

'Well, you're right, I guess it's now or never.'

43

Family reunion

The plane touched down in Split. It was the 2 August 1995. Those cliffs again, Maria thought as she peered out through the window. The tarmac shimmered under the blaze of the Mediterranean sun. She stepped carefully off the plane, feeling a bit unsteady on her feet. The last thing her brittle bones needed was a fall. A small vinyl handbag was slung over her frail shoulders. Sunglasses shielded her sensitive eyes and, as she traversed the tarmac, she held onto her straw hat. Deciding to dress for comfort on the long flight, she had travelled in a pantsuit, an unusual choice for Maria with her love of pretty dresses. Long black pants and a black jacket covered her pale pink shirt, which matched her pink lipstick. She always made an effort to look pretty.

As she passed by the sliding door to the waiting crowd, her welcoming party engulfed her, hugging, crying and chattering. Her brother had changed little in the last two decades. Towering over her, he was still slim. His brown hair had thinned. More creases lined his tanned face, but his smile was still broad and his teeth white. He wore jeans with a smart collared short-sleeved shirt. He took off his aviator sunglasses and his eyes sparkled as he introduced Maria to his wife, Vida. Taller than Maria, Vida was an elegant woman. As a widow she had brought a young son to the marriage, Nikica, who was now in his late twenties.

Maria tilted her head back as she looked up to his face.

'So, this is Nikica. You are a very, very tall and handsome young man.'

Nikica had a shock of unruly brown hair. His gold-framed glasses slid down his nose as he leant forward to cautiously hug her.

'He is a surveying engineer,' Ivan pronounced proudly. 'And here is your namesake, Marija.' He gently pushed the shy thirteen-year-old towards her aunt.

In one of his letters, Ivan had written to her that young Marija had grown up captivated by stories of Maria's life. She had been named after her aunt and he later explained to Maria that his daughter had felt an instant connection to her—this woman from Australia who now gazed at her warmly.

'I have brought a special present for you from Australia,' Maria told the young Marija. 'Wait till we get to your home. I think you'll like it.'

The five of them squeezed into Nikica's car. It was one hundred and sixty-five kilometres to Metković, the small town where her brother now lived with his family. They bypassed Split and followed the narrow road that curved around limestone cliffs and through small villages. Evidence of the recent war was everywhere. Buildings riddled with bullet holes. Signs warning of minefields. Nikica wound the windows down.

'Sorry, Teta Maria. Sorry that it's so hot,' Nikica said as he looked over his right shoulder at his aunt.

Maria had slipped off her jacket.

'It's okay, love. I'm okay.' She leant forward and patted his shoulder. 'I'm comfortable. And you're a good driver. I feel very safe.'

Before long they were driving alongside the Neretva River. The road's edge was dotted with stalls displaying a colourful array of fruit and vegetables—green watermelons sliced to show their rich red flesh, boxes of bright red peppers, bunches of hanging garlic, and jars of preserved fruits.

Ivan stretched his arm across Nikica and pointed.

'Look at this river, my sister. This is the inspiration for so many of my poems. This mystical river.'

226

'It's beautiful. I have never seen this part of the country,' Maria said.

Although a surveyor, in his heart her brother was a poet and had written many poems. Haiku poems. He talked passionately about his poetry as they drove.

'You'll have to show me. I would love to read them.'

Before long they reached Metković, a town split by this ribbon of blue. The hills of Bosnia Herzegovina were a few kilometres to the east.

'We live on the fourth floor of this apartment,' Vida told Maria, as they parked near a tall grey building.

She had noticed that many buildings in this town were drab and cheerless, a leftover from the communist years. Sited so close to the border with Bosnia Herzegovina, there was a mixture of religions. Above the town on the hilltop stood the two churches, the Serbian Orthodox and the Roman Catholic, ironically, side by side. Behind each church, surrounded by stone fences, was a cemetery for its worshippers. Ivan pointed towards the white building. Below the cross that adorned the apex of its roof, the war scars in the façade were visible, even from a distance.

'See, dear sister, there is my church. I go every morning. You can come with me.'

'Yes, I'd love that but I'm not sure how far I can walk now. Is it steep?'

'It is, but we can try and see how you go.'

'I would like that a lot.' Maria smiled. Nothing would please her more than sharing her faith with her brother.

Vida hurried the family along towards the entrance.

'Come, Nikica will bring your bag.'

She looped her arm through Maria's as she led her over the uneven footpath and up the steps.

'There is a lift in this building. The first one in town.' She sounded proud of this. 'Only four can travel in it. Nikica can take the stairs.'

Ivan and Vida's apartment was warm and alive with photographs and books.

Maria was quick to give the young teenager her gift. Like her brother, Marija was tall. Her dark hair was cropped short, with a fringe pushed back from her forehead. It was the middle of the summer holidays and her skin was tanned.

They sat beside each other on the lounge, the two Marijas, as the young girl tentatively unwrapped the gift. She peeled back the tape, careful not to rip the bright paper covered with images of balloons.

'I will use this paper again, this lovely Australian wrapping paper.'

'It's only cheap paper, don't worry,' Maria said.

'No, it's pretty. I like it.'

She inhaled sharply as she saw what lay within the wrapping.

'Oh, my goodness!'

'So, you like it?'

'It is the most amazing present. Ever. Thank you, Teta Maria. You are too generous.'

Holding the large box of brightly coloured makeup tightly, she turned and kissed her aunt.

'Thank you.'

'I thought, what would a young lady who is thirteen like? Yes, makeup. Perfect.'

Maria watched fondly as the young girl stared, awestruck, at this simple gift, picking up the eye shadows in various hues and opening the jars of sparkling lip glosses. She ran off to show her mother.

Maria was tired now. She leant back into the softness of the lounge chair and closed her eyes.

She could hear the clatter and chatter as Vida bustled in the kitchen, preparing their lunch. The smell of freshly brewed coffee filtered through the small room. Her brother sat down beside her. They chatted quietly, of family, of God and of politics.

'This war has been difficult, you know,' he said. 'Before the war everyone was the same. But when the war started, people began asking, "Who are you?" It was not good.'

Maria nodded. She knew too well the tremors of distrust that had always rumbled beneath the surface, a constant warning of the earthquake that could break apart a country, communities, families.

'Opening up old wounds,' she said. 'So sad. So much suffering.'

'Yes. So many stories of neighbours turning on neighbours.' His shoulders sagged a little more.

Vida called them into the kitchen for lunch where they gathered around the table laden with food.

'*Jedi.*'

Marija smiled her widest smile and tapped her front teeth.

'Look at us,' she said to her brother, 'still with our own teeth. Remember scrubbing them with charcoal?'

'Well, it must have worked,' Ivan said, as he returned the smile and tapped his teeth.

With lunch over and the plates cleared, he left the room, returning with his poetry. Together they sat, side by side, as he read to her, and once again she listened, as she had when he was a young boy.

44

Fleeing war, again

The ringing of the phone splintered the morning stillness of the little apartment. Ivan stooped as he cradled it to his ear, murmuring and nodding. His eyes narrowed and his lips pressed tightly together.

'What is it, brother?' Maria asked as she sat on the narrow balcony overlooking the town. It was Friday morning and she had been watching with interest the hustle and bustle of the street far below. This scene was so different from the ambience of her own patio in her leafy suburb back home. Cars rumbling and honking as cyclists wove in between them, the large shop windows reflecting the glare of the rising sun. With both hands holding the cup, she sipped her morning coffee as she waited for his response.

Ivan glanced across at her.

'Yes. Yes. I understand.' He listened. 'I will tell her. Thank you, Jakica.'

'What is it?' Maria said again, sensing the news was not good.

He joined her on the balcony and rested his hand on her shoulder, giving it a gentle squeeze. 'That was our niece, Jakica. On the island.'

He hesitated, then continued, 'They have been listening to the radio. More fighting has started this morning. Early this morning.'

'Where?'

'North of here but it's not good. Who knows what will happen?'

'Okay, so what will we do?' Maria asked calmly.

'Jakica says to bring you straight away to the island. It will be safer there.'

'When?'

'Today. I will call Nikica. He will drive us.'

'I don't want to bother him. Is this really necessary?'

'Maria, nothing is certain. My dearest friend was driving in the street with his children, not far from here. The planes were above and they shot at the car. All killed. Even his little children.' His face was pained as he stepped back into the lounge room to retrieve a photograph to show her. 'This was my best friend. Gone. Just like that.'

Maria held her breath, staring at the photo.

'Yes, Ivan, you're right. It is a war.'

'We need to go,' he said. 'Now! It is best to keep away from Dubrovnik. It's not safe there.'

With a sense of urgency but not panic, Maria packed her few belongings into her suitcase. She fumbled with the two belts that encircled and secured it. The arthritic nodules made her fingers stiff. Wistfully she recalled the belts encircling her original suitcase when she left her home all those years ago.

As soon as Nikica arrived they all got into the car but had not travelled far when Nikica pulled over to the side of the narrow road, to allow two tanks to rumble by. Green shrubs covered these bulky vehicles, each proudly displaying a Croatian flag with its checkerboard of red and white. Young boys, barely men, sat perched high amongst the older men, all in their khaki uniforms. They waved at those waiting patiently in the cars by the roadside. They were men of all ages, of all occupations. Fathers, brothers, nephews, cousins. Not soldiers. Some wore green helmets, some red felt berets, some waved rifles, some had ammunition draped like sashes across their chests. Despite the yells and cheers, their eyes were grim. They were entering the unknown, a battle. The ground shook as they rolled past, leaving swirls of dust.

'I don't believe what I'm seeing, Ivan,' Maria whispered.

'Yes, there have been ugly things happening here.'

'This is not good.' Maria sighed as she watched the tanks disappear in the distance.

231

She shuddered. Maria had left as a teenager because this country was ravaged by war. History was repeating itself. It was at war again. How could this be?

Nikica sped along the narrow road leading to the coast. It was hot. Rivulets of sweat trickled down his back.

'Are you all right, Teta Maria?' He glanced around and noticed the beads of perspiration on her top lip.

'I'm good. This breeze is nice.'

He explained that the quickest way was via the mainland town of Ploče, twenty-five kilometres from Metković. The car ferry would take them to Trpanj on the Pelješac Peninsula. He didn't want to risk staying on the mainland roads too long. The ferry was infrequent, he said, but he breathed a sigh of relief as they neared the town and saw the line of cars on the wharf. The approaching ferry was still in the distance. They had made it.

It was an hour's trip, so the passengers climbed the narrow metal staircase to the lounge above.

'Do you want something from the bar to eat or drink?' asked Ivan, attentive as ever.

'No, I am happy to sit here and chat to Marija.'

The two Marijas sat side by side watching the mainland disappear.

'Tell me about school. I'll bet you're clever like your brother.'

And Maria listened as the teenager talked about her life, her school and her friends. She liked listening to the young. She loved their energy. She could see the goodness and the potential in this shy young girl.

'You know, Marija. You remind me of myself.'

'Really?'

'Mmm... You do.'

'No.' She lowered her eyes self-consciously and then looked up at her aunt. 'You think so?'

'Yes, I do.'

'You know, Teta Maria, I was sent to live on the island four years ago, when the war started,' said young Marija, her trust increasing.

'No, I didn't know that, love.'

'My parents thought I would be safer. I lived in Korčula with Teta Dobrila and went to school there.'

'It's good that they sent you there. It would have been hard though. You were only young.'

Young Marija nodded and turned away. Maria thought of herself and the hardships that war imposes on children. She clasped Marija's hand and intertwined their fingers. They kept chatting.

The ferry passed the statue of the Virgin Mary, perched high on the rocky outcrop of the wharf as they entered the bay of the little town of Trpanj on the Pelješac Peninsula. A pretty town. They disembarked to drive over the hill to Orebić, past shrubs, clumps of trees and carefully tended vineyards. There was one more ferry to catch, a fifteen-minute trip to the island of Korčula.

'You will see the difference in Korčula from the last time you were here,' Ivan said as they stood on the deck and watched the town approaching.

The town of Korčula was like a miniature Dubrovnik, a historic fortified town encircled by stone mediaeval walls.

'How?'

'The tourists have gone. The war has scared them off.'

'I can understand why. It would be hard for the locals.'

Waiting for her were her family.

As she hugged both her sisters, she said, 'See, we thought that I would not be back, but here I am again'. Smiling at her extended family she exclaimed, 'Look how you've all grown since the last time'.

Many of her nieces and nephews were now in their twenties and thirties, married with children of their own. Tall, lean children with olive skin and handsome faces were surrounded by energetic toddlers. They bundled her off, following the road that ran along the spine of the island, connecting all the small towns, until they reached her hometown of Blato. Once again Maria felt a surge of emotion as they drove down the main street, narrow and flanked by trees. It was all still the same. She couldn't quite put her finger on it, but it even smelt the same. She would stay with her sister Žuva. They had both lost their husbands since her last visit over two decades ago. And this time Maria was unwell, her illness loitering in her life like an unwelcome relative who comes to visit but settles in and refuses to leave.

'You will probably live for two years after your diagnosis. That is the average,' was the cold calculation delivered to her by the medical specialists.

I will show them, she had thought. No one tells me when my time is up. I'm strong and I'm a fighter.

Here she was, back in Blato. As usual she had packed her pretty dresses, knowing there would be hordes of friends and family to visit. On her first morning at Žuva's home, she dressed in her blue and mauve floral suit, buttoned down the front with ivory gold-edged buttons. Her mauve skirt matched the sash on her fashionable straw hat. Her gold clip-on earrings complemented the outfit and around her neck were her two gold chains, one with a cross and the other an angel. Before leaving the bedroom, she studied her reflection in the dressing-table mirror. Her wig looked flat and unnatural, so she had teased the top a little to give it a bit of body, then combed the fringe that curled halfway down her forehead. She pursed her lips and applied her lipstick. Her makeup was subtle but added a glow to her increasingly drawn features. Her skin was still smooth and unlined by the wrinkles of time. She pinched her cheeks and then brushed on a little more blush. Just because she was unwell didn't mean she was a prisoner to this illness.

At lunchtime the family gathered around the table on the balcony, eager to talk. Maria noticed that the tablecloth was decorated with images of Australian animals and plants, a souvenir she'd given Žuva during her last visit all those years ago. Glasses were filled from bottles of sparkling water; no one drank the tap water. Žuva's daughter Jakica, now a woman in her mid-thirties with two children of her own, pulled a seat close to her aunt. Jakica was attractive with light brown curls, almost hiding her gold hoop earrings. Her bright red lipstick matched her floral red blouse.

'We're alike, Teta Maria, you and me. We both like to look nice,' Jakica said.

'Yes, it's important to look nice, darling. I think you're right. We're very much alike.'

Maria's two sisters gathered close. Although six years older, Dobrila looked strong, especially compared to her frail sister. Her short grey hair was brushed off her broad forehead, accentuating the mole above her eyebrows, and her skin was weathered like Žuva's. These women worked hard and scaled steep cobbled streets as part of their daily life. Žuva was younger than Maria yet her resemblance was so strong; they could have been twins. They chatted and laughed, reminiscing about the eight months Žuva had spent with her in Australia ten years ago. They had visited their old home earlier that day. It had been vacant since their mother passed away some years before. They took photos on the balcony once more, two decades later.

Maria had felt the fear that hovered once again in the village.

'You know, Teta Maria, we have a boat at Vela Luka, ready to evacuate the women and children to Italy,' Jakica said. 'I have a suitcase packed. I have had it there since the beginning of the war.'

'How will you know when to go?'

'A siren. We'll know. The fighting was very close to us at times. Near Ston, over on the Peninsula.' She pointed eastwards.

Maria understood. The war in Bosnia Herzegovina was now raging and NATO had commenced air strikes. She could see the fighter jets roaring over the island to the war zone.

'Where are they coming from?' She asked her niece.

'From bases in Italy.'

Maria felt like that young girl again, standing in the street and watching the planes roar overhead, counting the bombs on their wings as they passed. She remembered waiting for them to return, minus their bombs. Over fifty years had passed and wearily she felt that not much had changed, with the ongoing bloodshed and hatred.

Over the next few weeks, Maria spoke regularly to her family back in Australia.

'Mum, I don't think it looks good over there. I think we should bring you home early,' Debbie said.

'It looks like the war is over in Croatia but still going on in Bosnia Herzegovina,' Maria said.

Maria's children convinced her to leave earlier. The date of her flight was changed so she could return to the safety of Australia.

Those few weeks spent in her homeland had been nourishing for her soul. This was where she was born and where she had spent her childhood. Her brother and sisters were here, and her nieces and nephews. Her roots were here. But she had grown. She had built her life in a country far away from this village. Even though she looked Croatian and spoke English with a thick accent, she felt Australian. Australia had given her a husband, a good husband, and her children and grandchildren were there. This family she was so proud of. Even though she and her husband had little education, together they had provided the opportunities for their children that had been denied to them— their children's careers included a teacher, a paediatrician and a physiotherapist. Australia was truly a land of opportunity, opportunity that she had grasped with both hands all those years ago as a young woman, not knowing where her future would lead her.

As she whiled away the hours on the long flight home, she thought of the tearful farewells with her Croatian family. She knew that she would not see them again. Although this was difficult, she felt at peace with the finality. Her mind drifted to the family she was returning to, and her heart warmed. She had so much to go back to. Her life was anchored in Australia. Although her husband was gone, she kept his memory alive.

With Laddie she had built a nest. It was strengthened with twigs of hardship and softened with feathers of love. And she dozed, her head resting against the plane window, dreaming of this family and country she was returning to. Her country.

237

Postscript:
Newell Beach, Mossman, 6 March 2016

It was hot and humid. The family clustered around the table on the cement patio at the back of the small white fibro home. Cousins, cousins of cousins, second and third cousins, aunts, uncles. As usual, the table was covered with food. The hot chooks, bread rolls, salads, potato bakes, and vegie slices had been cleared and the bowls of *kroštule* and *pušurate* were being brought out while the jug was being boiled. The old culture intermingled with the new. The scene was busy with chattering, eating, laughing, mingling, chairs dragged from one group to another.

Beside me was the matriarch of the Gavranich family, Mary Fapani. My father's sister. My aunty. Today was her birthday. She was eighty-five. I studied this woman closely. Snow-white hair framed a weather-beaten face etched with laugh lines. Although I didn't see her regularly, my Aunty Mary was a constant in the ebb and flow of my life, a quiet anchor. She was always present at those important events—weddings, farewells, funerals. Regular with phone calls, just checking in on me as she did with my siblings. I shifted my gaze to the cane fields bordering the back fence, partly hidden by the rusted shed and trees. Mary had lived in this house for many years. My earliest memories came from this house when it was our beach house. I remember running around the side of the house, clasping my new Christmas doll to my chest. Her name was Paula and I was three.

Today was a day for memories. I had decided to fulfil my lifelong dream and write my mother's story. With both my parents long passed on, I turned to Aunty Mary. I had already spent many hours in Croatia on sun-kissed patios under grapevines capturing stories of my mother's childhood from the fading memories of her siblings. Now I needed to fill in the gaps of the story, her early years in Australia. I had driven up with my sister, Joyce, and my twenty-four year-old daughter, Stephanie.

'Come on, let's talk about Mum,' Aunty Mary said, beckoning us with her hand. Like bees to honey, the chairs were pulled closer and the family swarmed. I placed the dictophone close enough to catch her stories, and switched it on.

'What was your impression of Mum when she arrived?' I asked.

'A very, very brave woman,' said Mary.

'Did she have any English?'

'No. None. But even though many couldn't understand her, your mother was not hard to love. Everyone took to her. We were like sisters. She was happy, outgoing.' Mary looked out at the canefields and paused, as if choosing her words carefully. 'Well, she had to... to survive.'

Across from her sat Elsie Anich, Mary and Laddie's first cousin. Elsie was a slight-framed woman with salt and pepper hair and a soft voice. 'I was thirteen when she arrived. She lived in the farm behind ours.'

'And what were your memories?' I asked, pushing the dictophone closer to the quietly spoken woman.

Elsie pushed her glasses up from the tip of her nose.

'I remember Maria as a good sewer. When it was Mossman showtime, she would stay up all night making pretty dresses for you girls on that pedal Singer sewing machine.'

'Yes,' piped in Mary as she turned to her cousin, 'she taught herself to sew. She would practise on hessian bags.' She pointed to the dress she was wearing. 'Look at this dress. Can you believe that Maria made it for me over twenty-five years ago. And it's still good.'

I remember the hours my mother spent at the sewing machine on the verandah of our farmhouse. We would tiptoe around, wary of the pins that had dropped in the cracks between the timber floorboards, in case any had landed upright. She would sew late into the night after we had gone to sleep.

'Oh, I remember one time when Uncle Antun Anich gave us a silk parachute to use. We sewed sheets from it. Much better than the old sheets we had made from empty flour bags,' Mary said.

'Parachute?' quizzed one of the younger listeners.

'Yes, the war came to us too,' Mary said, leaning forward. 'Maria seemed surprised as well. She knew what the parachute was as soon as she saw it. She had seen them when she was a child during the war, but she didn't realise that the Japanese were attacking us. Darwin was bombed and they even dropped a bomb up past town somewhere.'

'But Dad didn't go to war, did he,' Joyce said, rather than asked.

'No, he was in the Reserve. He stayed in Australia as he had to work the farm. He would go into town on weekends and train with his gun. I liked it because he would bring back chocolate. Probably from all the American soldiers stationed up the hill.'

'Anyway, Maria was a wonderful sewer,' continued Elsie.

'She used to say that sewing for her was as easy as peeling potatoes. And just think of all the wedding dresses she made,' Joyce said, 'for us girls and all the others as well'.

'And all the bridesmaids,' added Ann-Marie, Aunty Mary's daughter. 'Time for a coffee top up,' she announced, standing and collecting the empty cups. 'Who wants one?'

'I will,' said one.

'Me too,' said another.

'I'll help,' offered Joyce, as she pushed her chair back and brushed the sugar from the crumbly *kroštule* off her lap.

I kept my position next to my aunty, absorbing her stories. Talking about my mother kept her alive.

'We spent a lot of time together,' Mary said. 'And you kids too.'

We all nodded, thinking back to the years spent at this house, first when it was our family beach house and then the Fapani family home. We had spent hours on the beach that was dotted with the swaying coconut palms.

Joyce returned, balancing fresh cups of coffee, and the reminiscing and laughing continued.

'I remember when you kids were little and spoke mainly Yugoslav and mine spoke only English,' said Mary. 'One day your brother was telling Ann-Marie a story in half-English and half-Yugoslav. Ann-Marie had asked, "What is a *skaline*—a boy or a girl?".'

John, who was actually telling a story about stairs, had no idea what she had asked. 'Boy,' was his answer.

Ann-Marie laughed. 'Yes, we played lots together.'

'Do you remember when we got our first TV?' said Joyce.

'Yes!' I said. I remembered vividly that day as my mother watched on in dismay as sawdust flew through the air into her spotless kitchen. The television took pride of place in the lounge room between the old upright piano and the glass china cabinet that was decorated with doilies and framed photographs. Dad wanted to watch this new novelty while he ate his meals in the kitchen, but a wall blocked his view. Mum quickly retrieved her precious statue of Jesus from the corner ledge as Dad proceeded to cut an enormous rectangular hole in the wall dividing the lounge and the kitchen.

'Mum tried to make it look like that huge hole in the wall was meant to be by decorating it with doilies and little knick-knacks,' said Joyce.

'Ours was the first TV in Cassowary Valley, so all the neighbours would come at night to watch it. The kids in their pyjamas.'

And the chatting continued. The funny stories and the sad ones.

'The war had such a big impact on her, you know,' Aunty Mary observed.

'I know,' Joyce replied. 'She could never watch war movies.'

'I remember as a kid playing a war game with John and we were yelling and saluting each other with "Heil Hitler". Mum was furious at us and told us to never ever do that again,' said Debbie. 'I was young and didn't understand.'

'But she didn't live in the past. She was always so busy. Always helping people. Her phone was never cold.'

'Yeah, she called it her best friend.'

'And she was so very very proud of all you kids,' said Aunty Mary. 'Don't you ever, ever forget that.'

There was a lump in my throat; I struggled to control my tears. I did know how much she loved us and all thirteen grandchildren. And in return we all did what we could to help her, to keep her with us that little bit longer. Maryanne was so knowledgeable about natural products and worked hard assisting her with what she should eat during her illness; Joyce with her strong faith prayed with her, prayed for a miracle; John with his medical knowledge was supportive.

My brother was the only boy and adored by all of us. I remember my mother being particularly proud that he had five children. And me... well... I was the youngest and the traveller. I knew she despaired with me ever settling down but when I eventually did, she was alone. Without Dad to help, I deliberately chose to live close by. I somehow think that I benefited more from this arrangement. She was a constant in my life, adoring my children and showering them with love. Yes, at sixty-four she had left us too early.

The hours flew by and it was time to go. I switched off the dictophone, placing it in my handbag.

'Did you have that on the whole time?' asked Aunty Mary. 'I forgot it was there.'

'I've recorded it all and I've got plenty of stories about Mum,' I said, hugging my aunt one more time. 'Thanks, everyone.'

'Well, don't take too long,' said Aunty Mary. 'I'm not getting any younger.'

'I'll do my best.'

The drive back to Cairns was quiet, as if we were all digesting the memories. We passed the cemetery where both our parents were buried. I silently thanked my aunt for visiting them and occasionally placing flowers in front of their simple plaques.

My mind drifted back to a day twenty years ago. With colours so vivid it was etched in my memory as if it were just yesterday. It was the school holidays, September 1996. I had three young children, the eldest at preschool. Mum had been fighting her cancer for two years and we had all learned to live with the constant blood tests and the anxiety as we waited for results, hoping and praying they would be favourable. Mum, as usual, never complained. I lived around the corner from her, and we saw or spoke to each other daily. This wasn't because she was unwell. This was because she was my mother, and this is what we did.

This particular day she rang saying, 'I don't feel well, sweet girl. Can you come down?'

There was an urgency in her tone. When I slid open the wide security door into her lounge room, I saw her on the recliner with a wheat pack clasped to her chest. My older two children ran to hug her and as she leaned forward to plant kisses on their cheeks, she grimaced. Groaning, she fell backwards, her breathing laboured.

'Is Nanna okay?' two-year-old David had asked me.

I rang the GP and on his advice contacted an ambulance to take her straight to the Calvary Private Hospital.

'No... no. It's okay. I probably just need some strong painkillers. I don't need to go to hospital,' she had protested weakly.

As I packed her overnight bag, I methodically ticked off the next steps. Okay, I thought, I've rung the ambulance, now I need to call all the siblings to let them know what's happening.

It was the 23 September, 1996, and we were gathered around her bed. Half-sitting, half-lying, propped by white pillows, Mum didn't look comfortable. She had been in hospital a few days now. Her face was gaunt, cheeks sagging. Her pain was increasing. It was dark outside. She was in a bay with four beds.

'The doctor said that I have broken some ribs and probably some other bones,' she whispered in between her shallow breaths. 'He wants me to have more radiation.'

'That's okay. It will help your pain,' offered Maryanne, my eldest sister.

'Did you know Botch came to see me today?' Mum smiled weakly as she spoke of her sister-in-law.

'We rang her to say you were in hospital. Let's try and make you more comfortable,' I said as I caught the attention of a busy nurse.

The nurse was impatient and not gentle as she tried to reposition my mother.

'Careful, you are...' I started before I noticed Mum shaking her head, not wanting me to complain or criticise.

'It's okay, love. I'm all right. Let's not bother the nurses. They're busy.'

She let go of the hospital triangle above her bed, her arms flopping to her side, and rested her head back onto the pillow, her newly grown hair fine and grey. Her eyelids closed and she drifted in and out of a restless sleep. Her skin looked pasty, almost grey.

'We should go,' said Joyce, 'and let her rest. We'll come tomorrow.'

I remember leaning forward and kissing my mother's cheek, inhaling her scent. Her eyes remained closed. I stopped and looked back one last time before I left. She looked even paler under the stark fluorescent lights.

Impatient ringing of the telephone pierced the silence of our home. It was three in the morning. I answered and held my breath as I listened to the words on the other end of the phone. I cannot really remember what the doctor said to me. Only fragments remain.

'Had a turn a few hours ago... Taken to intensive care... Sorry, there was nothing we could do.'

As my husband Michael stirred and mumbled, 'Who was that?' I paused, trying to find my voice.

'Mum just died,' I said flatly. What do I do now? I wondered.

I rang my sisters, who lived in Cairns, and my brother in Brisbane to tell them. As I sat motionless in bed I wasn't sure what to do next. What do you do when you hear that your mother has died? Then I knew what I had to do.

'I need to go in to see her,' I said to my husband. 'I feel my sisters should come in too.'

I rang them back.

'I think it's important that we go in to see her. We just have to, I think.'

Michelle, our youngest child, was only four months old, so I took her with me in case she needed to be fed. Driving along Sheridan Street in the early hours of the morning, I felt eerily calm. There was no traffic on this Tuesday morning, the tall streetlights cast an artificial glow on the street. I twisted the radio knob to find a station. A mournful voice crooned, filling the car. The lyrics of 'Unchained Melody' seemed to breathe air into my suffocating heart. Tears trickled down my cheeks. My sleeping baby didn't stir.

The three of us sisters huddled in the small waiting room, wordlessly weeping, hugging, as we waited to see our mother.

She was the only person in this small intensive care unit. A soft yellow light cast a pale glow over her inert form, leaving the corners of the room in shadows, hiding the metal trolleys laden with equipment.

We approached her tentatively. She looked asleep. The gauntness had left her face and it was unlined. Her hair was brushed and her arms were resting by her side. We sat beside her for what seemed like hours but was probably only minutes, breathing in her presence. Joyce touched her hand. It was still warm and soft. Her fingernails neat and curved.

'She looks at peace,' said Maryanne.

'Yeah. Do you know what she told me when she was diagnosed?' I turned but focused on an empty space between my sisters, not wanting to make eye contact. Not wanting to see my pain reflected in their eyes. Without waiting for a response, I continued, 'She told me that when she died, as painful as it would be for us, we would feel relief'. My lips curled at the edges in a half smile.

'You know what? As usual, she was right. I actually do feel relieved. Her suffering is over. I can now stop worrying about her.'

Together we all sobbed.

Although years ago, it seemed like yesterday.

On the drive back to Cairns after Aunty Mary's party, my mind was on replay and I thought back to that day in September when we buried her. It had been hot. Was it because it was September in Cairns, or was it because there was standing room only in the small church? Family and friends squeezed shoulder to shoulder to allow more mourners into each pew. I looked around at a sea of faces, all grieving. The mahogany coffin facing the altar was simple in its finality. Draped on top was a set of topaz rosary beads. The glass beads glinted, catching the sunlight as it filtered through the windows.

Mum's friend Anne delivered the eulogy, telling a tale of a woman, a new migrant in this country, a brave young woman. She told of the hardships that our mother had endured silently and how they served to strengthen her. She told of her optimism and compassion. How loved this woman was and her capacity to love. How this migrant had made Australia her home and her people.

The altar was crowded with priests, not one but seven, as if assisting the occupant of the coffin on her final journey. If there was one thing we were all sure of, it was that she had never feared death. She loved her God and believed He would take her soul on a long journey, one more time, to join her husband. This time her husband awaited her, not in Australia but in Heaven. She truly believed this. She needed no help on this journey. This was my mother, Maria Gavranich. She was already a saint to so many on this earth.

Debra Gavranich
Cairns, Australia, 2021

Memories from Maria's grandchildren

From Charmaine Chalmers (1ˢᵗ grandchild)

I remember:

- Wriggling into her lap in the armchair next to Gin-gin's recliner and having a warm bossomy cuddle against her cotton dress.

- Sitting with cousins on a checked blanket in the lounge room at night while she invented stories of flying Mini Mokes.

- Family dinners with the table laid with spaghetti and *zeje* on a rusty-red tablecloth with cream thread and the filigree metal table brought in from the patio for the kids.

- Watching *Sale of the Century* together after dinner on a Thursday night.

- Measuring tape around her neck, pins held in the side of her mouth, peering through the bottom of glasses at her sewing.

- Playing mahjong and giggling about the winds and pong-toilet humour that never grew old.

- Her pronunciation of 'lillie' for little.

- Delicious shortbread biscuits.

- Her love of bread and its aroma.

From Michael Gregory (2ⁿᵈ grandchild)

'Little Nanna', as my brother (Adam), sister (Melissa) and I used to affectionately call her, was the most warm and loving grandparent a child could ever wish for, growing up. Although I was only 18 years old when Nanna lost her battle with illness, I was old enough to realise that she was an incredibly special and inspirational woman (daughter, sister, wife, mother, grandmother and friend), one of a kind, who made an overwhelmingly positive contribution to many people's lives including my own. I am sure, like many family and friends, Nanna is regularly in my thoughts and prayers and I love sharing with my wife (Helen) and children (Charlotte and Ethan) some of the memories and reflections here that I cherish most from the wonderful times I was blessed to spend with Nanna:

▷ Warm and wholehearted hugs and affection.

▷ Comforting back rubs when I was a young child, tired and looking to snuggle into the familiar lounge in the Gavranich family room.

▷ An energetic, warm and sensitive tone of voice and personality that radiated an enduring love of life, family and friends and a person who would do anything for those she loved along with anyone else if it meant improving their physical and spiritual wellbeing.

▷ Sharing the occasional laugh with Nanna about the way she pronounced certain words in English, including her love of the word 'darling'.

▷ The plentiful savoury treats in Nanna's fridge such as olives, different cheeses and salami.

▷ Hearing true stories about growing up through World War Two which always had my brother (Adam), sister (Melissa) and I captivated and eager to hear more about a place and life experience that was far removed from the freedoms and comforts we were growing up with in Bayview Heights, Cairns. Stories of eating grass and anything else that was edible, and having to collect these sources of food under the threat of watchful enemy soldiers' eyes always stayed with me.

▷ An amazing home cook, who especially loved preparing food that was reminiscent of her childhood and memories with family in the former Yugoslavia (now Croatia), Mossman and then Cairns. Nanna's spaghetti, *Blitva* (but what Nanna and Grandad referred to as *zeje*) and *pušurates* were my favourites.

▷ Late-night sleepovers involving Adam, Melissa and I that always involved a midnight snack, usually *pušurates*, and during the month of July watching Wimbledon and cheering on Goran Ivanisevic and Monica Seles who were Yugoslavia's top tennis players.

▷ Her commitment and love of attending activities that her grandchildren were involved in; for me, I especially remember Nanna attending some of my tennis matches, high school presentation evenings and musical theatre events such as rock eisteddfods and high school musicals.

▷ A passion for sharing her memories and knowledge of the history of the Nadilo, Gavranich and associated families and the Croatian culture. Nanna's passion for sharing her own memories and the information she brought with her from Croatia over many lengthy chats with us (including lots of back-and-forward questions and answers from Adam, Melissa and I) inspired Adam and I to want to do more research about this side of our family heritage, and our planning for the holiday we had in Croatia in 2002 where we spent a lovely time meeting up with great aunts and uncles, second cousins and various other Nadilo family members in Metkovic, Blato and Zagreb.

▷ Despite battling her illness, I feel very blessed and treasure the memories of Nanna attending my year 12 high school graduation in 1995, and I especially cherished a photo of the two of us at my graduation after Nanna lost her battle with illness during my first year at Griffith University in Brisbane. This photo was on my desk in my small, single bedroom at Griffith University (the usual room for a student living on campus), and it always felt like Nanna was with me (which I knew she was, in a spiritual sense, watching over and guiding me).

▷ One of only a few people in my life while she was still with us, other than my Mum and Dad, whom I could share and talk openly with about prayer and my faith and its importance to me in living my life.

From Melissa Gregory (5th grandchild)

Maria Gavranich, better known to us, her grandchildren, as 'Little Nanna', was an amazing woman who lived her life with gratitude and grace, and was unapologetically herself. Her heart was huge and compassion inspiring. I was 13 years old when she passed, and some of my fondest memories were times spent at her place over the school holidays. We'd sit down and watch one of her favourite soap operas, and laugh as she would unknowingly and so innocently mispronounce the character's names. Upon reflection now, I think it almost certainly became intentional, but she knew it made me laugh, and so it continued.

The nights would always end with Nanna cooking a Croatian specialty—*pušurates*, likened to a deep-fried doughnut ball, dusted in cinnamon sugar. It was an absolute must when I stayed over. I think, what I enjoyed the most, even more than eating the treat, was watching and waiting in anticipation, to see what shape each dollop of batter would turn into as it hit the hot oil.

Little Nanna was always there supporting me in every performance and eisteddfod I took part in, and I can tell you, there were more than a few. Even now, when my memory of specific details fail me, her constant presence in my life is felt and remembered. I'm truly blessed to have been gifted a Nanna in Maria.

Katherine Gavranich (6th grandchild)

I was 9 years old when my Nanna passed away and to say I was heartbroken was an understatement. I can still to this day remember where I was and what happened, at Brownie Camp with my friend and didn't get picked up by my parents and had an extra sleepover. When I was asked if I wanted to contribute memories or stories about my Nanna from when I was little, I realised that a lot of my memories are from photos and remembering back. Though looking back on photos, it was clear that she had a great love of family and spending quality time with those who she loved. One memory that I do remember was all the time spent lying on the carpet in front of the bronze coloured glass wall watching *Cinderella* and sitting up at the table eating meals together; funnily enough I can remember the smell of her house.

While we spent a lot of time up in Cairns, I remember all the times that she spent down in Brisbane, unaware of her illness and her struggles. She was a lady who was taken away from us much too soon, though never failed to smile and share her love.

Elizabeth Gavranich (7ᵗʰ grandchild)

I was very young when my Nanna passed. All I have are some vague recollections of her presence sporadically throughout my early years—the smell of her house, the kind sternness in her voice coaxing me to eat up all my meat. Other things are not so much memories, but photographs and stories that others have told me—the matching dresses she used to make us, and the song she used to sing us whilst sitting on her lap. From everything I have heard and the respect with which others around me hold for her, I am sad to have not had the chance to know my Nanna. Even not knowing her all that well, I still feel a deep sense of loss at not having her in my life. I hope this book will give me a connection to the wonderful lady that was, is, and will always be Maria, my beloved Nanna.

Maria's recipes

Brudet (Dalmatian Fish Stew)

Marinate fish in olive oil, chopped garlic and lemon juice for a few hours.

Sauté half a chopped brown onion and garlic in olive oil.

Add two tablespoons tomato paste, one quarter of a cup white wine vinegar, salt and pepper.

Season fish with salt and pepper and place the fish in the pan and mix well.

Add enough fish stock or water to cover the fish.

Bring to boil.

Do not stir but shake the pan to avoid breaking the fish.

Lower heat to medium and cook until fish is cooked (20-30 minutes).

Serve with white rice.

Zeje

Put water on to boil.

Cut one bunch of silverbeet into 3 parts and cut white ends into 8 cm strips.

Cut 2 potatoes into 4-5 cm portions.

Cut any other green vegetables you want to use (such as beans) into pieces.

Place white ends of silverbeet into boiling water and cook for 10 minutes.

Add rest of silverbeet and potatoes for about 20 minutes.

Add other green vegetables (if using)—zucchinis or beans are good.

Once all vegetables are cooked, drain the water and mash the vegetables.

Add finely chopped garlic, olive oil and salt (until tastes great).

Pušurate (Croatian doughnuts)

Beat one egg lightly, then add the following:

- Pinch of salt
- Half teaspoon sugar
- Handful of sultanas
- Two and a half cups SR flour
- One and a quarter cups water

Mix altogether to the consistency of a thick pikelet mixture and let stand for half an hour.

Heat the oil. Scoop thumb-sized piece of dough and shape into a small ball.

Drop balls of mixture into hot oil and fry until all sides of the ball are golden.

Remove from oil and rest on paper towel to drain excess oil.

Roll in caster sugar while still hot.

Good to eat hot or cold!

Kroštule (sweet pastry)

2 cups plain flour

2 tablespoons gin

2 eggs

Pinch salt/pinch sugar

1 level teaspoon butter

Beat eggs, salt, butter. Add liquid then all the flour. Knead well and divide into 3 portions.

Roll each portion out to very thin pastry (the thinner the crispier).

Cut into strips (approx. 15 cm long and 4 cm wide).

Make a small cut along the length of the middle and thread one end through the slit so that you end up with a twisted ribbon.

Heat oil to medium high. Fry each piece for about 15 seconds.

When they change colour turn on other side and fry for a few more seconds, then take out and drain on paper towel.

Sprinkle with sugar.

Acknowledgements

I have many people to thank.

Michael (my wonderful husband) and his incredible passion for my project. He patiently sat for many hours in the 'listening chair' in our office as I would read aloud each chapter that I wrote. I would turn around to ask, 'How was that?' to see the tears streaming down his face. This reassured me that my words had touched his heart.

Our amazing and much-loved children. Stephanie always reassured me with the words, 'I love it! I love it!' David kept me supplied with endless cups of coffee and neck rubs during the many hours I spent at the computer. A special mention for Michelle (the writer in our family) as she patiently proofread my many versions, added to my words and polished my paragraphs with her constructive comments. Thank you!

My siblings (Maryanne, Joyce and John) for giving me permission to write about our mother and encouraging me every step of the way.

Janine Nicklin for the beautiful artwork on the cover and the endless hours involved with me on this amazing journey.

Bron Postlethwaite for offering to write a song for my book. What a 'novel' idea. Thank you.

My mentor Mary Serenc (née Srhoj), for her energy and useful critical appraisal.

Both editors—Melanie Myers and Bernadette Foley for their useful appraisal and advice on my manuscript.

My publisher Catherine Lewis from Wild Dingo Press for taking a chance on me and believing in this story. Her limitless energy and attention to detail have been instrumental in the successful completion of this book.

My extended family and friends both in Australia and Croatia for spending hours talking to me about the 'olden days' which provided many of the stories that you will read about in this book.

Information obtained from the following books:

Nikola Bačić, dr.med., Blatsko zdravstvo kroz vjekove (Blato healthcare throughout the centuries), Split, 2004; Maclean, F., *Eastern Approaches*, London, Cape Publishers, 1949.